Ayr United — The Compendium

Also by Duncan Carmichael:

Official History of Ayr United Football Club Volume 1, *Contour Press, 1990.*
Official History of Ayr United Football Club Volume 2, *Contour Press, 1992.*
Images of Sport Ayr United FC, *Tempus, 2001.*
Ayr United Classics, *Tempus, 2002.*
100 Ayr United Greats, *Tempus, 2004.*
Walking Down the Somerset Road, *Fort Publishing, 2006.*
Ayr United Miscellany, *Amberley, 2011.*
Ayr United At War, *Mansion Field, 2014.*
Ayr United On This Day, *Kennedy & Boyd, 2016.*
Ayr United FC Managers, *Kennedy & Boyd, 2017.*
Nine Titles – Ayr United triumphs, *Kennedy & Boyd, 2018.*

Ayr United
- The Compendium

Duncan Carmichael

Kennedy & Boyd

Kennedy & Boyd,
an imprint of
Zeticula Ltd,
Unit 13,
196 Rose Street,
Edinburgh,
EH2 4AT,
Scotland.

http://www.kennedyandboyd.co.uk
admin@kennedyandboyd.co.uk

First published in 2019
Copyright © Duncan Carmichael 2019
Cover design © Zeticula Ltd 2019

Every effort has been made to trace copyright holders of images. Any omissions will be corrected in future editions.

Paperback ISBN 978-1-84921-179-6
Hardback ISBN 978-1-84921-190-1
All rights reserved. No part of this publication may be reproduced, stored in a retrieval system, or transmitted in any form or by any means, electronic, mechanical, photocopying, recording or otherwise, without the prior permission of the publishers.

To the memory of
Helen Nelson
and
Hugh Nelson

Acknowledgements

During the writing of this book Hugh Nelson passed away. Until succumbing to terminal illness he continued to attend Somerset Park. He will be remembered for doing a power of work to develop the Black & White Shop which was located at the back of the north terrace. The shop was opened in 1971 and survived until 1993 when the fight against theft and vandalism became insurmountable. After the funeral service on 29th March, 2019, mourners were invited to tea in the Ally MacLeod Suite, appropriately located on the same site as the former Black & White Shop.

In paying respect to Hugh's memory I am grateful for his gesture in turning up at my house one night in 2018 with a large haul of old Ayr United photographs. That haul was supplemented after his passing and many of the images within this book belonged to his private collection.

Hugh was pre-deceased by wife Helen in 2004. In 1976 she became the secretary to manager Alex Stuart. By the time of her departure from the role in 1995 she had also worked for Ally MacLeod, Willie McLean, George Caldwell, Ally MacLeod again, George Burley and Simon Stainrod.

Many of the historic images woven within the text originated with the *Ayrshire Post* and the *Ayr Advertiser*. Grateful thanks are extended to each.

Thanks are also extended to the *Daily Record* for their kind permission to use the splendid photo of Willie Furphy in action at Rugby Park.

Calum Campbell and Willie Craig provided insightful information on media operations within the club. I thank you both for your kind and informative co-operation.

The Supporters' Club committee 1956/57. Left to right: W.G. Boyle, W. McVey, W. Hood, J. McKenna, W. Cumming, Jack Stirrat, M. Faber, Willie Burt, J. Vance, R. Kay, and R. Cumming. Not all of the committee members were present when the photo was taken.

Contents

Acknowledgements	vii
Illustrations	xi
Introduction	xv
Abandonments	1
Age	13
Appearances	21
Attendances	22
Biggest wins	30
Broadcast media	50
Captains	56
Championships	57
Christmas Day Football	73
Clergy	78
Coincidental happenings	79
Colours	88
Corner–kicks	91
Corruption	94
Debuts	101
Defeats	105
Discipline (Loss of!)	115
Draws	126
Family connections	144
Farmers	151
Film	154
First Kick	159
Floodlights	160
Foreign players	164
Foreign tours	171
Foreign teams at Somerset Park	176
Foreign teams - Other matches against	178
Foreign travel 1928/29 – The season of English rejection	179
Goals	188

Last day escapes	206
League - all time record	216
League - opening games	218
League Cup	224
League competitions: Texaco Cup / Anglo-Scottish Cup	226
League competitions: Centenary Cup/ B & Q Cup / League Challenge Cup/ Alba Challenge Cup / Ramsdens Cup /Petrofac Training Cup / Irn Bru Cup	227
Managers	229
Maternity	232
Nicknames and soubriquets	234
Penalty kicks	238
Points	242
Postponements	243
Quotations	247
Scottish Cup	255
Scottish Internationalists	285
Sequences	290
Shutouts	294
Special titles	296
Substitutes	298
Tallest players	299
Testimonials	300
Trainers / Physiotherapists	322
Transfer fees	324
Turnover	325
Weddings	326
Index	327

Illustrations

The Supporters' Club committee 1956/57	viii
Railway accident in Glasgow	1
Evening Times, 29th November, 1952	2
Centre pages of the programme for the abandoned match at Airdrie on 23rd February, 1957	4-5
Willie Paton, Sam McMillan and John Gallacher	6
Ayr United versus Kilmarnock on 4th January, 1982	8
David Craig	10
Stewart Kean	12
Henry Smith – the third oldest to have made a competitive appearance.	14
Michael Renwick	15
Darren Henderson – the oldest scorer	17
Jacky McGugan – the third youngest captain	19
Kilmarnock versus Ayr United in the Scottish Cup	23
Ayr United versus Alloa on 17th March, 1984	25
Gerry Christie and Steve McLelland	27
George Watson in the thick of it at Rugby Park	29
Clyde versus Ayr United at Firhill on 2nd September, 1989	32
Willie Furphy at Rugby Park on 31st August, 1991	33
Stevie Evans	35
Scottish Cup quarter-final day on 11th March, 2000	36
Bob Hepburn gives you his greetings	38
Bobby Yorke	41
Jim Flynn	42
In January 1929, the club had a Scottish Cup tie at Berwick	43
Eddie Annand	46
Pat McGinlay	47
The broadcasting studio on the drawing board	52
David Kennedy	55

In February 1929 Tottenham Hotspur made a confidential enquiry regarding the availability of Jimmy Smith	58
In November 1928 Stoke City asked Ayr United to name a price for Jimmy Smith	60
This letter dated 25th April, 1929, confirms Joe Riley's loan deal from Celtic	61
29th March, 1958 – the programme cover for an historic game for Peter Price	62
Alex Glen (left) and Jim McGhee (right) – team mates in the 1958/59 title winning side	64
Ayr United versus Raith Rovers on 25th March, 1989	66
Tommy Walker	67
Catering workers at the club in 1956	70
John Traynor	71
On the same date six years earlier it was the same result at the same venue in the same competition	80
Ayr United FC 1924/25	85
Fally Rodger when at Northampton Town	98
Ayr United FC on 15th August, 1964	103
A letter from Stoke City enquiring about the availability of Billy Brae in May 1929	106
Ayr United FC on 27th April, 1966	109
Ally Graham	112
Malky Shotton	113
Barry Prenderville	116
Jim Hughes	117
Ludovic Roy	120
Joe Love, Ross Scott and Davy Wells	121
Referee's report from 1929	123
Ross Scott	124
Jim McCann	125
Dave Curlett on the treatment table	132
2nd September, 1961. Programme cover	133
Eric Morris	135
Gerry Collins	136
Willie Bradley, Ian Hamilton and Ramsay Burn	138
Des Herron	139
John McNiven	140
Norrie Anderson	141

John Milton	142
The programme cover for the marathon Scottish Cup replay at Palmerston Park on 18th February, 1976	143
Letter from Bob Shankly	145
George McIntyre	146
Derek Whiteford	149
Alex McAnespie.	150
Mark Campbell	152
Ian Cashmore senior	153
STV schedule on 15th November, 1958	155
Carrick Street Oval	160
Jim Gilmour	161
Brian Kristensen	166
Colin Miller	169
Johnny Hubbard	170
Letter from Canadian F.A.	174
Letter from United States F.A. Inc.	175
Rejection letter from Burnley F. & A.C..	180
Rejection letter from Leeds United A.F.C.	181
Rejection letter from Newcastle United	182
Workington programme cover and centre pages	183-185
Letter from the Supporters' Club	186
A more cheerful letter	187
Neil Tarrant	189
Alex Bone – scorer of the 5,000th league goal.	192
Ayr United versus Berwick Rangers on 22nd August, 1964	196
Hugh Sproat	204
From the *Glasgow Herald* on the Monday	208
Craig Buchanan	209
Jimmy Brown	211
Lawrie McGee	213
Hugh Sproat in opposition to Ayr United	215
Ian Cashmore senior looks on	217
Ayr United versus East Stirling on 17th October, 1981	219
David Reid	221
Stewart Rennie	223
Presentation for reaching the League Cup semi-final in 1980	225
Davy McCulloch	226
Alex Stuart	228

Ayr United versus St.Mirren in a Scottish Cup tie	231
Mark Shanks	233
Mark Duthie	235
Brian Ahern	236
John Duncan	245
Tommy Sloan	246
Neil McBain on 15th January, 1963	248-249
Campbell Money	252
Ally Fraser – two Scottish Cup goals for Ayr United	254
Jim Dick	256
Paul Agnew – the man in possession	258
Kenny Wilson	260
Peter Weir	261
Roddy Grant	262
Andy Lyons	264
David Winnie	265
Gary Teale	266
Paul Shepherd	268
Marvyn Wilson	270
Ayr United versus Hibs in the Scottish Cup	271
Paul Lovering	273
Derek Frye	280
Willie Furphy	283
Jimmy Hogg played for Scotland on 4th March, 1922	286
Jim Nisbet played for Scotland in the continental tour	287
Wilf Armory	289
David Purdie	309
Clydebank versus Ayr United at Kilbowie Park	312
Gordon Cramond	313
David Smyth	316
John Sludden	317
Nigel Howard	319

Introduction

"There are lies, damned lies and statistics." This pearl of wisdom is attributed to Mark Twain. Herein we may have the first lie. There are counter claims about the origin of this quote. This leads neatly to the concept of argument. In the world of football the concept of argument is woven into the fabric of the game and we can view this as a positive.

After all the game cannot die for as long as it is discussed. Statistics have the power to either solve an argument or fuel it further but the intended premise of this book is to authoritatively provide solutions to Ayr United-related arguments. Why? Who? Where? When? How many? For every question there is an answer and those answers are about to be revealed. You will even be told which Ayr United player had "nary a blemish on his escutcheon."

In a beautiful world the forthcoming pages would be brimful of triumphant information generated by glorious success. Yet for every 'all time best' there is an 'all time worst'. The glorious is punctuated with the inglorious. Even the most spellbinding statistics can lose their allure when presented in list form. That is why narrative has been used to bring life to what otherwise could be interpreted as raw information.

Up until 1975 references to the First Division and Second Division are precisely as suggested. From that year onwards the leagues thus labelled ceased to be the first and second tiers. Some statistics have merited an entry in more than one section.

The information within these pages was valid as at the close of season 2018/19. (then adding) Inevitably a new record was created as this book went to print. On 13th July, 2019, a 7-0 win at Berwick constituted not only a club record away win in the League Cup but also in any away competitive match. This a compelling example of why it is worthwhile getting along to watch Ayr United. You just never know when fresh records are going to be set.

Abandonments

11th November, 1911. The first of the ten Ayr United matches to be abandoned took place on this date. Closer scrutiny reveals the date to be 11/11/11. The kick-off time was scheduled for 2.45 pm and, to be truly pedantic, the numbers in the time add up to eleven. The alliteration of the number one will be extended by letting you know that the premature halt took place with the score at 1-1, the Ayr marksman being Charlie Phillips. Owing to a railway accident the Vale of Leven team arrived late at Somerset Park so this Second Division fixture did not get underway until 3.45 pm. Predictably, in the 72nd minute, the cause of abandonment was bad light. Four weeks later Ayr United won 4-0 in the rescheduled fixture to maintain a 100% league record. The rail accident creating the chain of events was tragic. It happened near Parkhead Station in Glasgow's east end. This was not on the route taken by the Alexandria-based Vale of Leven but the resultant chaos impacted on the overall rail network within Glasgow. Four railway workers were carrying out maintenance work on the line in dense fog and, unable to see the train's approach, they were mown down and killed.

> **RAILWAY ACCIDENT IN GLASGOW.**
>
> **FOUR SURFACEMEN KILLED.**
>
> **RUN DOWN IN THE FOG.**
>
> A terrible accident occurred on the North British Railway near Parkhead Station, Glasgow, on Saturday morning, four surfacemen being run down by a passenger train and instantly killed, while two were injured. The sad affair was due to the dense fog which enveloped the city at the time.
>
> The names of the men are:—
>
> KILLED.
>
> Bernard Hearghty (21), single, 18 Ravel Row, Parkhead, Glasgow.
> Thomas Carleton (37), married, 61 East Nelson Street, Glasgow.
> James Burke (37), married, 5 Reid Street, Shettleston.
> John Grimes (23), single, 697 Duke Street, Glasgow.

18th December, 1937. This date saw the nickname of The Honest Men open to challenge. Even by the standards of 1937 it was highly questionable whether this First Division fixture should have begun. The Dens Park pitch was described as being as hard as iron from the start. At half-time the Dundee ground staff scattered several cartloads of sand over the pitch. In the 71st minute Lawrie, the Dundee right-half, went down with cramp. Referee McCulloch laboured under the mistaken belief that the player had broken his leg due to the conditions. Being 3-1 down, the Ayr United team reinforced that belief by smartly trooping off the field. The ruse worked. Match abandoned! Spectators voiced their disapproval while the home team displayed a reluctance to accept the decision. The fixture eventually got rescheduled for Monday, 11th April, 1938. Justice was regrettably served with a 5-1 home win.

Evening Times, 29th November, 1952

29th November, 1952. When Ayr United turned up for a 'B' Division fixture against Albion Rovers a postponement could have been justified not only because the pitch was bone hard but also because Cliftonhill Park was shrouded in fog. Referee Barclay's decision to proceed was prompted by a glint of sun in the sky above Coatbridge. In the 12th minute Mike McKenna scored although it was to no avail. Nine minutes later this particular Ayr United goal and the 1-0 lead was rendered void. By then the fog had already descended to such a degree that further play was out of the question. When this pea-souper was at its thickest Mike McKenna was the only player visible from the press bench. The police had then to be pressed into action to disperse a crowd shouting for their money back. With so little action there was justification for feeling short changed but by way of atonement the rescheduling brought splendid value for money. On the Saturday afternoon of 24th January, 1953, the result was Albion Rovers 5 Ayr United 6. Later in the afternoon of the November abandonment (5.25 pm to be precise) your writer was born!

23rd February, 1957. Abandonment number four took place about two miles from abandonment number three. The location was Airdrie's Broomfield Park. When Willie Paton put Ayr United ahead after ninety seconds this was a significant development in the quest to avoid relegation from the First Division. Compounding the significance was the fact that he had scored in the face of driving snow. Jimmy Welsh equalised on fourteen minutes then Airdrie came straight back down the field and got a penalty when Alex Paterson handled the ball. Ian McMillan put them ahead from the spot. Just after the half-hour mark veteran full-back Willie Kilmarnock made it 3-1 with a speculative attempt from forty yards. Within a minute Guy Lennox trimmed it back to 3-2 but the same player was left mortified when he shot over the bar from two yards just four minutes from half-time. For half-time read full-time. Brushing and sawdusting failed to defy the weather and referee Gerrard called the game off amidst a whiteout. On 30th October, 1897, the olden-day Ayr FC were involved in an abandoned match at Broomfield Park. Back then the issue was bad light and the match was terminated with ten minutes left and the home team winning 5-1. Justice was served when Airdrie won 4-1 in the rescheduled match back in those Victorian times. Unfortunately history repeated itself on the evening of 27th March, 1957 when Airdrie also won 4-1 in the rescheduled match.

13th December, 1958. In glorious pursuit of the Second Division title the only likely impediment on this day was Mother Nature. Two minutes before the advertised kick-off time the gates at Forfar Athletic's Station Park remained shut. The players and officials, still unchanged, stood around in the centre circle where the visibility did not exceed twenty yards. Mother Nature relented and the mist vanished but she was merely playing a trick. Play got underway twenty minutes late then the return of the fog compelled

Tel. Coatbridge 1273

West of Scotland Excavations Ltd.

PUBLIC WORKS CONTRACTORS
EXCAVATORS & TRACTORS FOR HIRE

KIRKWOOD STREET COATBRIDGE

DRESS WEAR "HIRE SERVICE"

Be Correct "At All Times" consult

DANSKIN'S
The Men's and Boys' Outfitters,
32 GRAHAM STREET, AIRDRIE
PHONE 3290

The Golden Dollar Fish Restaurant
ANGIE'S FOR QUALITY
Fish Fresh Daily From Aberdeen

14-16 East High Street,
AIRDRIE

Follow your team, " Buy " a car at

DOUGLAS MOTORS
130 ST. GEORGE'S ROAD,
GLASGOW, C.3
Telephone: Doug. 9078

All types of second-hand cars in stock. H.P. arranged. Spot insurance. Part exchange welcomed.

Mechanical, Agricultural, Structural, General Jobbing, Welding, Arc and Oxy-Acetylene, General Smith Work, Playing Field Accessories Made To Order

MALCOLM SPEIRS, Engineer
9-11 PARK PL., CHAPELHALL, by Airdrie
Telephone No. Airdrie 3491 (House Exten.)

Telephone Nos. 2255 and 2256

JAMES HENDERSON & SON
ENGINEERS
Iron and Machinery Merchants
AIRDRIE

Discuss the Match at

Eastercroft Hotel
(Opposite Hillend Loch)

FOR THE BEST IN FOOD AND WINE

CAL. 205   Prop. Mr R. Beattie

MAITLANDS (IRON

AIRDR

MACHINE TOOL CASTINGS

Kilmarnock (
Price (4)   Q
Rankin (7)   McMillan (8)

Referee:
D. GERRARD,
Aberdeen

For Print & Comm
Wm
17½ C

McMillan (11)   Whittle (10)
Haugh (6)   B
Thomson (3)

AYR

GOOD QUALITY GREY IRON

7,000 BARNARDO CHILDREN DEPEND ON YOUR SUPPORT—Please Send a Gift of ANY AMOUNT to Barnado House, Stepney Causeway, London, E.1.

This space has been donated by
A. & J. LAING, HAULAGE CONTRACTORS,
203 EASTFIELD ROAD, CALDERCRUIX, by AIRDRIE

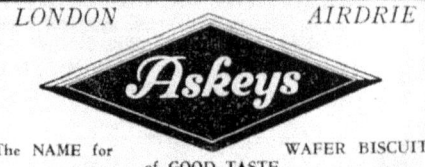

LONDON   AIRDRIE
Askeys
The NAME for   WAFER BISCUITS
of GOOD TASTE

Printed by Baird & Hamilton, 46-50 Graham Street, Airdrie.

CARS **AUSTIN** TRUCKS
WE SELL THEM
WE SERVICE THEM

Colston Garage Co.
CARLISLE ROAD
AIRDRIE
Phone 2004

If you love animals and hate cruelty

remember the

R.S.P.C.A.

and please send a donation to:

The Chief Secretary, R.S.P.C.A., 105 Jermyn Street, London, S.W.1.

(DERS) LTD. AIRDRIE

ONIANS

lker
Shanks (3)
y (5)   Quinn (6)
I (9)   Welsh (10)   Duncan (11)

Linesmen:
W. L. Fyfe, Edinburgh
(Orange flag)
E. Harkin, Glasgow
(Red flag)

ice (9)   Paton (8)   Murray (7)
(5)   Traynor (4)
Paterson (2)
vers

NITED

GENERAL ENGINEERING CASTINGS

STINGS UP TO 7 TONS WEIGHT

Contractors to H.M. Government
JAMES RAEBURN & SONS LTD.
Public Works Contractors

Excavators, Bulldozers, etc., for Hire. Specialities — Mineral Boring Excavations, Shaft Sinking
Telephones:—
Airdrie—Office 2614-5; Works 3706

PLEASE HELP
CANCER RESEARCH

by sending a gift to Sir Charles Lidbury, Hon. Treas. (Dept. AFC), British Empire Cancer Campaign, 11 Grosvenor Crescent, London, S.W.1., or to your local committee. This space generously donated by John McCarron, 10 William St., Lurgan.

Please Help
SPASTICS

by sending a gift to

NATIONAL SPASTICS SOCIETY
28 FITZROY SQUARE
LONDON, W.1.

Telephone: AIRDRIE 3208
ISOBEL B. LOW
Fruiterer, Florist, Confectioner and Tobacconist
61 HIGH STREET, AIRDRIE
Fresh Vegetables Daily —— Accounts Weekly

DENIS KANE
Coal Merchants and Contractors
For Quality, Value and Service
31 MAIN ST., PLAINS, AIRDRIE
Phone Caldercruix 286

Phone: CALDERCRUIX 282
ALEXANDER DONALD
" FORD FORGE," by AIRDRIE
Manufacturers of Spades, Shovels and Clothes Poles. All types of Electric Welding Repairs, and Gates and Railings made to order.
Railway Address: Plains Station, B.R.

Telephone Airdrie 3388
CALDERVALE FORGE CO. LTD.
Spade and Shovel Manufacturers
AIRDRIE
N. Bairdwatson, Springwells Ave., Airdrie. Tel. 3714.

Centre pages of the programme for the abandoned match at Airdrie on 23rd February, 1957.

Left to right: Willie Paton, Sam McMillan and John Gallacher. Gallacher, signed in 1960, was the only one of the trio who did not play in the curtailed match in 1958.

an abandonment. The scoreless action had lasted for twenty-five minutes. Peter Price was a spectator on account of having had teeth extracted the day before. Coincidentally Bobby Stevenson was home on leave from National Service so he was an ideal replacement. It must have been highly frustrating for him to return to the Army having played for such a little time.

16th March, 1968. The playing surface at Dumbarton's Boghead Park never had a reputation for being lush although on an average day it was seldom much worse than the average pitch. Unfortunately this was far from an average day. Conditions of almost continuous driving rain solicited a view in the *Ayr Advertiser* that: "Football skill was subservient to strength and luck." Being uncomfortably adrift in the promotion chase this Second Division match had limited importance. Ally MacLeod had pledged to field a trialist in every match until the end of the season and he did so in this one even although the pledge was not maintained. By the 74th minute the pitch and overhead conditions had deteriorated sufficiently to enforce an abandonment. The abbreviated action had been scoreless. On the Monday evening of 29th April the action was restaged in a 1-1 draw. It marked Sam McMillan's 508th and final appearance even allowing for deduction of the discontinued fixtures in 1958 and here in 1968.

29th August, 1979. On a typically nice summer's night Hearts came to Ayr for the first leg of a second round tie in the League Cup. Ian McAllister sent a header beyond Thompson Allan in the 18th minute and the match continued satisfactorily with Ayr United as the dominant team and confidence running high that another goal was inevitable. Then, in the 57th minute, the floodlights went out. Being late summer the place was not plunged into total darkness yet there was clearly insufficient natural light to allow continuance. Two switches had burned out so the lights were beyond immediate repair. Then came the dreaded public address announcement followed by a 'we want our money back' deputation outside the ground. Chairman Myles Callaghan met them at the main door and attempted to soothe their concerns. The second leg was scheduled for the Saturday only for that to become the date for the replayed first leg. It was a 2-2 draw. This preceded Ayr United going through

Ayr United versus Kilmarnock on 4th January, 1982. A visual clue as to why it was abandoned at half-time.

3-2 on aggregate on the Monday. There was an historical precedent for an abandonment in Ayr due to failed lights. This dated to 1878 – yes **18**78. Another section will cover that particular mishap.

4ᵗʰ January, 1982. Two days earlier our First Division fixture (second tier) was postponed because Somerset Park was flooded then immediately rearranged for the Monday afternoon. There was a similar pattern when the nearby race meeting was postponed from the Saturday to the Monday but this counter attraction was removed when the races got called off again. Blizzards contributed to travelling difficulties which in turn contributed to an attendance of 3,878 which was somewhat modest for a New Year derby. When the game got underway the action was blinding – literally! Brian Gallagher scored for Kilmarnock in six minutes and Eric Morris made it 1-1 twenty minutes later. It became reminiscent of the snowscape misadventure at Airdrie in 1957 and history repeated itself when referee Kenny Hope called a halt at half-time. Continuous snowstorms had blighted play and the attempts to clear the lines were futile quite apart from the treacherous conditions underfoot. Kenny Hope came back to Ayr to officiate the re-match, a 1-1 draw, on the evening of 17ᵗʰ March.

15ᵗʰ January, 1994. In days of old there were more instances of fog than we are likely to encounter in the modern age. For this we can be grateful for clean air legislation. That is why it was something of an irritating novelty for an Ayr United match to be abandoned through this phenomenon in the closing years of the twentieth century. A crowd of 2,773 assembled at St.Mirren Park, more colloquially known as Love Street. The quest for First Division points was rendered all the more desperate by the fact that restructuring required a minimum of a sixth-place finish to avoid the drop. In the 13ᵗʰ minute Sam McGivern headed home a corner-kick from Hugh Burns and pulled a hamstring in the process. The joy of scoring was immediately tempered by getting replaced by Colin McGlashan. In the 28ᵗʰ minute Ricky Gillies scored for St. Mirren, a development barely visible from some vantage points. Visibility had been alright at the start but the fog had thickened sufficiently for David Syme to call an abandonment without a recentre. In order to pre-empt dissenting fans, vouchers were made

David Craig

available for free admission on the rescheduled date of Tuesday, 25th January. St.Mirren won 3-1 and, at the time of writing, it is the only league defeat ever suffered by Ayr United on Burns Day.

27th April, 2002. The abandonment on this day was rendered different from previous abandonments because the score was allowed to stand. Ayr United versus Airdrie comprised third versus second in the First Division and 2,775 spectators, by their mere presence, did not consider that the match would be dogged by end-of-season drudgery. How true! Scenes of unprecedented drama quickly unfolded. In the 21st minute a Scott Chaplain corner-kick was played on by David Craig and Marc Smyth. It then fell for Stewart Kean who hooked it home for 1-0. This happened at the railway end and it was the cue for a crowd of Airdrie supporters to emerge from behind that goal to make their way onto the field where they wandered around aimlessly. Referee Bobby Orr took the decision to instruct the players to go inside. The police succeeded in ushering the supporters off the field but, on their way back, some of them hauled down the crossbar. A check of the damage revealed that it could not be immediately repaired so Mr Orr complied with the police advice to abandon the match. Rescheduling it was out of the question because, within days, Airdrieonians went out of business. That summer the club was reincarnated as Airdrie United. The Airdrie manager who gained a runners-up spot in testing circumstances for the club was future Ayr United boss Ian McCall.

Abandonments summary

Ground conditions	4
Fog	3
Bad light	1
Floodlight failure	1
Crowd disorder	1
Total	**10**

Stewart Kean

Age

Oldest players to make an appearance

The oldest player to have made a competitive appearance for Ayr United is Alan Main, who was 42 years 259 days when he played in goal versus Dumbarton at Somerset Park on 21st August, 2010, then proceeded to make three appearances (all league). The third of those appearances was against Alloa Athletic at Recreation Park on 11th September, 2010, when he was aged 42 years 280 days.

The second oldest player to have made a competitive appearance for the club is Alex 'Sanny' Aitken. He was aged 42 years 136 days when playing at outside-right in a league fixture at Dundee's Dens Park on 21st August, 1915. This was an emergency situation created by Switcher McLaughlan missing the train at Kilwinning. Aitken had formerly played for the olden day Ayr FC in the years straddling either side of the twentieth century. Here in 1915 he was the Ayr United trainer.

The third oldest is Henry Smith who was aged 41 years 250 days when he played in goal for Ayr United on 15th November, 1997. This too was in a league fixture versus Dundee at Dens Park.

Youngest players to make an appearance

Sam McMillan is the youngest player to have taken part in a competitive match for the club. He was aged 15 years 212 days when playing versus Queen's Park at Hampden Park on 14th March, 1953. At that time he was registered to Ballochmyle Thistle and when manager Archie Anderson made the approach young McMillan believed that he was being offered the opportunity to play in a trial match. Then came the dawning realisation that he was being fielded as a trialist in a 'B' Division fixture. His inclusion at outside-left

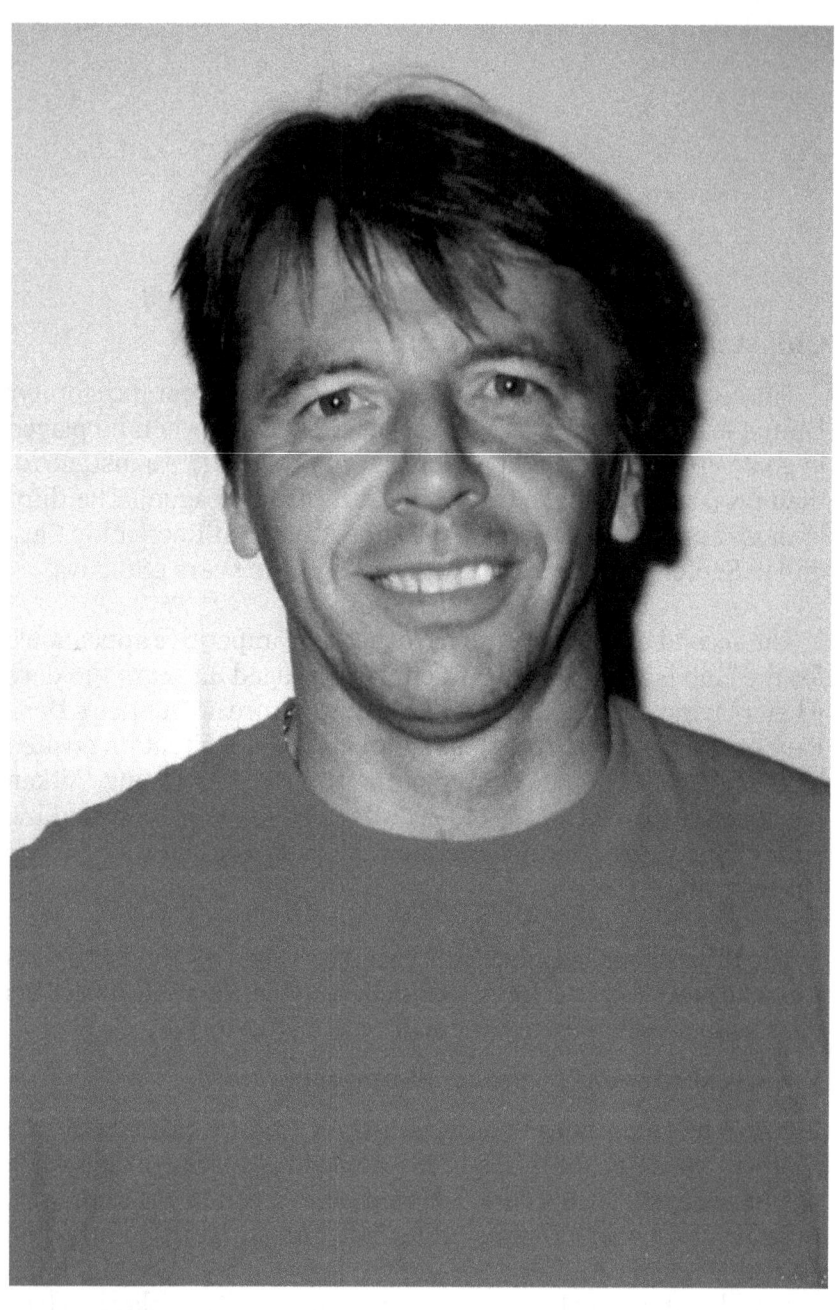

Henry Smith – the third oldest to have made a competitive appearance.

Michael Renwick

was caused by Mike McKenna not having recovered from an injury suffered against Dundee United a week earlier.

The second youngest player to have made a competitive appearance for the club is Mark Shankland who was aged 15 years 300 days when he went on as a substitute against Brechin City at Glebe Park on 7th May, 2011. It was the season's final league fixture with an attendance of 577 but when the teams met there in the First Division play-off final second leg fifteen days later the crowd was 2,404. Young Shankland went on in the 68th minute to replace one of the two David Crawfords in the squad. By an interesting quirk this meant that Ayr United's two youngest players were residents of Mauchline.

When Michael Renwick made his debut on 5th August, 2000, it could have been argued that he was aged just six. This was a First Division fixture at home to Ross County. He was born on 29th February, 1976 and only had birthdays in leap years but we can safely dismiss this for record purposes!

When Finn Ecrepont went on as a late substitute in a league fixture against Dundee United at Tannadice Park on 30th November, 2018, he was the first player born in the 21st Century to make a competitive appearance for Ayr United. He was born on 30th July, 2002.

Oldest players to score

Darren Henderson is the oldest scorer of a competitive goal for the club. He was aged 38 years 88 days when he scored in a third round Scottish Cup tie at home to Stranraer on 8th January, 2005.

The second oldest scorer is Mark Roberts who was aged 37 years 320 days when he scored in a League One fixture at Stenhousemuir's Ochilview Park on 14th September, 2013.

The third oldest scorer is John Hughes who was aged 37 years 205 days when he scored in a First Division fixture away to St. Mirren on 2nd April, 2002.

Darren Henderson – the oldest scorer although not in this game. He is seen here being outnumbered against Morton.

The oldest senior debut

When goalkeeper Eric Phillips went on as a substitute at home to Inverness Caledonian Thistle in a Scottish Cup replay on 16th January, 2006, he was making his senior debut (excepting reserve football) at the age of 36 years and 17 days. He remains the oldest player to combine an Ayr United debut with a senior debut.

Youngest players to score

The youngest player to score a competitive goal for Ayr United is Alan Forrest. He was aged 16 years 321 days when he scored against Queen's Park at Hampden in a Ramsdens Cup tie on 27th July, 2013. On 10th August, 2013, at the age of 16 years 335 days, he scored at Arbroath's Gayfield Park to become the club's youngest scorer of a league goal.

The second youngest scorer is Mark Shankland who was aged 17 years 17 days when he scored against East Stirling in a Ramsdens Cup tie at Ochilview Park on 28th July, 2012.

The third youngest scorer is Stewart Kean who was aged 17 years 56 days when he scored in a First Division fixture at Livingston's Almondvale Stadium on 29th April, 2000.

The fourth youngest scorer is Stephen Reynolds who was aged 17 years 184 days when he scored in a First Division fixture at Dundee's Dens Park on 12th December, 2009.

Jimmy Scott, then aged fifteen, scored in a friendly at home to Derry City on 26th April, 1950, but this cannot be considered for record purposes.

The youngest squad

On 28th December, 2002, Ayr United beat Arbroath 4-0 in a First Division fixture at Somerset Park. Three of the Ayr scorers were teenagers (the other scorer was Mark Campbell). They were Stewart Kean (19 years 299 days), Mark McColl (two days after his 18th birthday) and Andrew Ferguson (17 years 279 days). Ferguson was not in the starting line-up (84th minute sub for McColl). Boyd Mullen (five days short of his 17th birthday) went on in the 85th

Jacky McGugan – the third youngest captain.

minute for Scott Chaplain (19 years 80 days). The starting line-up also included Willie Lyle (18 years 258 days) and Marc Smyth who had only just ceased to be a teenager (it was the day after his 20th birthday).

The oldest manager

The oldest Ayr United manager is Neil McBain. When he quit the second of his managerial stints at Ayr on 31st October, 1963, he was aged 67 years 350 days. In contrast he was aged 18 years 196 days when he joined the club as a player on 30th May, 1914.

The youngest manager

The youngest Ayr United manager is Archie Buchanan. He began the job on 28th January, 1926, which happened to be the date of his twenty-sixth birthday. The vacancy had been created by the Scottish Football Association's sine die suspension imposed on Jimmy Hay a day earlier. Mr Buchanan's duties were predominantly clerical.

The youngest captains

The youngest captain is Willie McStay who was aged nineteen when he attained the captaincy in August 1913 (born 21st April, 1894).

The second youngest captain is Nicky Devlin who was aged twenty-one when he was named as captain in the summer of 2015 (born 17th October, 1993).

The third youngest captain is Jacky McGugan. He made his Ayr United debut as captain on 24th February, 1962, aged 22 years 257 days.

Appearances

John 'Spud' Murphy holds the club record for the greatest number of appearances and along with that comes his record for the longest Ayr United career span. His debut was in a League Cup tie at home to Morton on 10th August, 1963, and his final appearance was in a Premier League match at home to Clydebank on 25th February, 1978. He was released at the end of 1977/78 to complete a playing career in which he played for no other senior club. By that time he had amassed 459 league appearances (plus two substitute listings), 33 in the Scottish Cup, 91 in the League Cup and 14 in the Texaco/Anglo Scottish Cup. The grand total amounted to 597 competitive starts. He scored eight league goals plus two in the League Cup, the overall total of ten being good for a left-back.

Sam McMillan is the player with the second greatest number of appearances. As previously mentioned his debut came as a 15-year-old trialist on 14th March, 1953, but he did not become a signed Ayr United player until the summer of 1955 when he was acquired from Irvine Meadow. His final game was in a 1-1 draw at Dumbarton's Boghead Park in a Second Division fixture on 29th April, 1968. Including the match as a trialist in 1953 he had amassed 404 league appearances (plus one substitute listing), 25 in the Scottish Cup (plus one substitute listing) and 79 in the League Cup. The grand total of competitive starts was 510 but for record purposes this figure must be trimmed back to 508 on account of two abandoned matches in which he was involved. In common with John Murphy he played for no other senior club and he scored more goals for the club than everyone apart from Peter Price.

Attendances

The largest attendances

The largest crowd at any match involving Ayr United is 51,158. This was the attendance at Hampden for our Scottish Cup semi-final against Rangers on 4th April, 1973.

The second highest attendance was also at Hampden and also for a match against Rangers. For our League Cup final on 17th March, 2002, the crowd was 50,076.

On 7th December, 2013, the Rangers versus Ayr United match had a crowd of 45,227. This was a league match in the third tier and it is the highest crowd at an Ayr United league match outside the top tier. It was the second largest attendance in Britain on that day, beaten only by Manchester United versus Newcastle United.

Somerset Park's largest attendance is 25,225. This happened when Rangers visited for a First Division fixture on 13th September, 1969.

Somerset Park's second largest attendance is 24,617. This was for a Scottish Cup second round tie against Celtic on 3rd February, 1934.

Somerset Park's third largest attendance is 24,100. The date was 18th February, 1956, and it was a Scottish Cup sixth round tie against Celtic.

Somerset Park's fourth largest attendance is 23,785. This was for a Scottish Cup quarter-final replay against Kilmarnock on 23rd March, 1938.

Kilmarnock versus Ayr United in the Scottish Cup on 2nd February, 1957. The goalkeeper is Ayr's Willie Travers.

Somerset Park's largest Sunday attendance is 9,346. This was for a Scottish Cup 5th round tie against Rangers on 11th February, 2018.

Somerset Park's largest attendance for a non-Ayr United game is 10,038. This was for a Scottish Cup 5th round third replay between Muirkirk Juniors and Cambuslang Rangers on 5th March, 1949. It was a remarkable crowd considering the weather was so bad.

The largest Ayrshire derby attendances

Kilmarnock versus Ayr United at Rugby Park on 19th March, 1938. The crowd for this Scottish Cup quarter-final was 27,442.

Ayr United versus Kilmarnock at Hampden on 28th January, 2012. The crowd for this League Cup semi-final was 25,057.

Ayr United versus Kilmarnock on 23rd March, 1938. The Somerset Park crowd was 23,785 (on a Wednesday afternoon!).

Kilmarnock versus Ayr United at Rugby Park on 2nd February, 1957. The crowd for this Scottish Cup fifth round tie was 22,192.

The lowest attendances

The lowest attendance at a competitive match involving Ayr United is 197. This was for a First Division fixture against Clydebank at Boghead Park on 27th April, 1999. Originally scheduled for 9th January, it was the victim of ten postponements in the interim period. Even allowing for Clydebank having decamped to Dumbarton this paltry crowd figure should realistically have been exceeded since the Ayr United team was on course for finishing respectably third behind Hibs and Falkirk. Clydebank's problems were illustrated by having to field Steve Morrison in goal. He was a thirty-eight-year-old coach who had not been a goalkeeper during his playing career. The result was 2-1 for Clydebank.

Five of the best contenders in the 'lowest attendances' section relate to Central Park, Cowdenbeath. The visit of Ayr United did little to enthral the locals as evidenced by these crowd figures (all league) which will now be relayed to you in ascending order (but not ascending by very much!). 213 at Cowdenbeath 0 Ayr United 1 on 17th April, 1993; 260 at Cowdenbeath 3 Ayr United 1 on 18th October,

Ayr United versus Alloa on 17th March, 1984. It attracted the lowest attendance for a competitive home match since 1965.

1986; 284 at Cowdenbeath 2 Ayr United 2 on 8th December, 1992; 297 at Cowdenbeath 2 Ayr United 0 on 5th January, 2008, and 344 at Cowdenbeath 3 Ayr United 1 on 21st April, 2007.

The lowest attendance at a competitive 'home' match is 227 for a Ramsdens Challenge Cup tie against Raith Rovers on the evening of 9th August, 2011. You may have noticed a clue in the punctuation that all was not as it seems. Pending the installation of a new floodlighting system at Somerset Park the tie was played at Cappielow Park, Greenock. Roddy Paterson, Jamie McKernon and Ross Robertson scored in a 3-0 win.

On the evening of 1st May, 1991, an Ayrshire Cup semi-final between Ayr United and Girvan Amateurs attracted 106 people to Somerset Park. In more ways than one this did not fall under the category of a competitive match. It was an 8-1 home win. The tie was played in opposition to live television screening of a San Marino versus Scotland World Cup tie.

On the evening of 7th July, 2010, 245 spectators witnessed Stranraer winning 2-1 at Somerset Park. It being a friendly this had no bearing for record purposes. This match was played in opposition to live screening of a World Cup semi-final.

East Stirling 0 Ayr United 4 (League Cup) had an attendance of 295 at Ochilview Park on 2nd August, 2014.

Brechin City 0 Ayr United 1 had an attendance of 308 at Glebe Park on 29th November, 2016. This is a record low for a Scottish Cup tie involving Ayr United.

Meadowbank Thistle 0 Ayr United 1 (First Division) had an attendance of 310 at Tynecastle Park on 18th April, 1992. This fixture was switched from The Commonwealth Stadium due to an athletics meeting.

East Stirling 1 Ayr United 5 (Irn Bru Cup) had an attendance of 318 at Ochilview Park on 16th August, 2017.

Gerry Christie (left) and Steve McLelland (right) at Girvan's Hamilton Park on 22nd July, 1978.

Meadowbank Thistle 1 Ayr United 0 (First Division) had an attendance of 339 at The Commonwealth Stadium on 19th December, 1992.

Girvan Amateurs 1 Ayr United 12 (twelve) was reported to be witnessed by "about fifty people" at Hamilton Park on 22nd July, 1978, but being a friendly this cannot be truly included for record purposes.

Up to the summer of 2019, the lowest crowd for a competitive match at Somerset Park since 1965 is 556 for an Alba Challenge Cup visit from Cowdenbeath on 10th August, 2010.

Ayr United 1 Brechin City 2 (Second Division) on 5th March, 2013, drew an attendance of 631. This was the first sub-700 league attendance at Somerset Park since 17th March, 1984, when 673 turned up for a 3-1 First Division win over Alloa Athletic. That, in turn, was the lowest home attendance for a competitive match at the ground since 1965. The Alloa match just referred to was played in opposition to the televised Scotland versus France rugby international in which Scotland clinched the Grand Slam.

Ayr United 2 Stenhousemuir 3 (League One) drew an attendance of 646 on 13th December, 2014, and there was another sub-700 league attendance at Somerset Park that season. That happened on 3rd March, 2015, when 693 watched a 3-3 draw against Peterhead. This was virtually one year to the night (4th March, 2014) since 656 people watched Ayr United lose 3-2 at home to Forfar Athletic in League One.

Ayr United 2 Dunfermline Athletic 4 (League One) on 14th December, 2013, had a reported attendance of 643. Owing to a computer difficulty that figure was understated. The true attendance could only be guessed at but might reasonably have been approximated at close to 1,000.

During the club's bad years in the early to mid-sixties, official attendances for Somerset Park were concealed. Estimates persistently stated "500".

George Watson in the thick of it at Rugby Park. He is watched by Ian McAllister (left) and Ross Scott (far right).

Biggest wins

Biggest league win

5th January, 1946: 'B' Division: Ayr United 10 Stenhousemuir 1.

Team: Brown, Kirkland, Kelly, Henderson, Smith, Calder, McGuigan, Malcolm, Morrison, Gillan and 'Newman'.

Stenhousemuir: 'Newman', Marshall, Geddes, Anderson, Syme, Beveridge, Arbuckle, Creighton, Whyte, Smith and Duncan.

Goals: Malky Morrison 1-0; George Gillan 2-0; Peter Smith (penalty) 3-0; Malky Morrison 4-0, 5-0 and 6-0; Beveridge 6-1; Malky Morrison 7-1; Peter Smith (penalty) 8-1; Malky Morrison 9-1; Tommy McGuigan 10-1.

The form of the Ayr forwards was devastating, most especially that of Malky Morrison with a personal haul of six. Having scored four in the away fixture he therefore had a total of ten in the two league fixtures played against them that season. Stenhousemuir played a man short for sixty minutes due to an injury to centre-half Syme and the visitors were further disadvantaged by their young trialist goalkeeper who was highly nervous and devoid of confidence.

Biggest away league win (four-way tie)

13th October, 1945: 'B' Division: Stenhousemuir 0 Ayr United 6.

Team: Corbett, Craik, Kirkland, Henderson, McNeil, Smith, Melvin, Malcolm, Morrison, Leitch and Harper.

Stenhousemuir: 'Newman', Horrower, Clarkson, Creighton, Dougal, Campbell, Wilkie, Buchan, 'Junior', Smith and Ormond.

Goals: Malky Morrison 0-1 and 0-2; Peter Smith 0-3; Malky Morrison 0-4 and 0-5; Bert Harper 0-6.

With three away wins on consecutive Saturdays, Ayr United now sat in second place. This was the highest number of away goals scored in the Scottish and English leagues on this day. The 1,400 crowd was considered to be a poor attendance. Future Scotland manager Willie Ormond was in the home team and so too was Willie Buchan who, in 1937, had been transferred from Celtic to Blackpool for £10,000. It was considered that Ayr United were lucky to have a 1-0 half-time lead.

19th October, 1957: Second Division: Berwick Rangers 0 Ayr United 6.

Team: Travers, Thomson, Telfer, Paton, Boden, Haugh, McIntyre, McMillan, Whittle, Fulton and Bradley.

Berwick Rangers: McLennan, Brown, Paterson, Hogg, Harvey, Alexander, Campbell, Bartle, 'Newman', Crombie and Prior.

Goals: Willie Paton 0-1; Jimmy Whittle 0-2; Alastair McIntyre 0-3; Sam McMillan 0-4; Alastair McIntyre 0-5 and 0-6.

The attendance of 953 was poor at this phase of history. A significant omission in the home team was goalkeeper Jock Wallace but, even in face of the result, the *Ayrshire Post* contained lavish praise for his replacement: "Only Roy McLennan, stepping into the senior team in place of Jock Wallace, now with Airdrie, earned any bouquets." In 1967 Wallace was destined to become a Berwick Rangers legend for his goalkeeping heroics when Rangers were knocked out of the Scottish Cup. The *Ayrshire Post* columns had a neat summary of the rout: "At no time did Ayr United turn on the heat. They contented themselves with exhibition football."

3rd October, 1987: Second Division: Stenhousemuir 0 Ayr United 6.

Team: Watson, McIntyre, Hughes, Furphy, McAllister McCracken 77), Evans, Templeton, Scott (Wilson 77), Walker, Sludden and Cowell.

Clyde versus Ayr United at Firhill on 2nd September, 1989. Tommy Walker (hand in the air) has scored. Tommy Bryce is joining the celebration.

Willie Furphy at Rugby Park on 31st August, 1991.

Photo used by permission of The Daily Record

Stenhousemuir: Robertson, Cairney, Gillen, Walker, Beaton, Erwin, Quinn, McCafferty, Condie, Thomson and Jamieson; substitutes – McIntosh and Buchanan.

Goals: John Sludden 0-1; Jim Cowell 0-2; John Sludden 0-3; Jim Cowell 0-4; Tommy Walker 0-5; Henry Templeton (penalty) 0-6.

The state to which Stenhousemuir had become beleaguered was illustrated in the closing minutes when a defender, in a seeming attempt at putting the ball out for a corner-kick, sent a scorching drive against his own post. With luck the tall score could have been improved upon. There were so many close scrapes around the Stenhousemuir goal. The result left Ayr United on top of the Second Division with eight wins, two draws and no defeats. Thirty-three goals had been scored for the loss of five.

2nd January, 2001 : First Division: Morton 0 Ayr United 6.

Team: Rovde, Renwick, Sharp, McGinlay (Reynolds 50), Hughes, Duffy (Campbell 74), Teale, Wilson, Hurst, Grady and Robertson (Scally 66); unused substitutes – Nelson and Bradford.

Morton: Carlin, Naylor, Davies, Robb, 'Trialist' (McGregor, half-time), Stuart MacDonald, Aitken, Curran, Matheson, 'Trialist' and Paul McDonald; unused substitutes – Tweedie, Broadfield, Redmond and Maxwell.

Goals: Glynn Hurst 0-1, 0-2, 0-3 and 0-4; James Grady 0-5; Glynn Hurst 0-6.

Glynn Hurst became the first Ayr United player to score five in a competitive match since Peter Price in an 8-1 league win at home to East Stirling on 26th November, 1955. Hursty managed to net four before half-time. The trialist central defender he was in direct opposition to got substituted at half-time in a clear act of mercy. In his post match comments Morton manager Allan Evans said: "It was men against boys and Ayr could have scored more than six."

Stevie Evans

Scottish Cup quarter-final day on 11th March, 2000. Glynn Hurst troubles the Partick Thistle defence.

Biggest league win in the top tier (two-way tie)

25th March, 1916: First Division: Ayr United 6 Third Lanark 0.

Team: Kerr, Bell, McStay, Hay, Cringan, McLaughlan, McKenzie, "Smith", Richardson, Jackson and Gray.

Third Lanark: Brownlie, Ferguson, Orr, Brown, McPake, Anderson, Goldie, Weir, McLean, King and Crichton.

Goals: Jimmy Richardson 1-0; John Jackson 2-0 and 3-0; Jimmy Richardson 4-0; "Smith" 5-0 and 6-0.

The punctuation on the name "Smith" indicates a concealed identity but his feat in scoring twice indicates that he was an experienced player stationed in the area awaiting a move to the theatre of war. It was a fantastic result considering that Jimmy Brownlie was in goal for Third Lanark. He had played sixteen times for Scotland and would still have been the country's first choice goalkeeper had it not been for the intervention of war.

8th April, 1933: First Division: Ayr United 6 Dundee 0.

Team: Hepburn, Fleming, Ure, Taylor, Currie, McCall, Robertson, Smith, Merrie, Brae and Rodger.

Dundee: Marsh, Morgan, O'Connor, Symon, McCarthy, Smith, Munro, Guthrie, Robertson, Blyth and Troup.

Goals: Mattha Smith 1-0; Tommy Robertson 2-0, 3-0, 4-0 and 5-0; Alex Merrie 6-0.

Scouts from Newcastle United and Arsenal watched this match and they must have been impressed by Tommy Robertson's four-goal haul. The Dundee executive must also have been impressed by the form of The Patna Flyer. On 18th July, 1934, they signed him from Ayr United. Scot Symon may have had a torrid time in this match but in 1935 he was transferred to Portsmouth. In the summer of 1938 Ayr United tried to sign him. He did come back to Scotland but he opted for Rangers where he eventually became the manager.

Bob Hepburn gives you his greetings.

Biggest away league win in the top tier (three-way tie)

31st January, 1914: First Division: Hibs 0 Ayr United 5.

Team: Lyall, W.Gray, McStay, Baxter, Dainty, McLaughlan, A.H. Goodwin, G.S. Ramsay, Phillips, Cassidy and Alec Gray.

Hibs: Allan, Birrell, Templeton, Kerr, Girdwood, Lamb, Wilson, Reid, Hendren, Wood and Smith.

Goals: G.S. Ramsay 0-1, 0-2 and 0-3; Charlie Phillips 0-4; G.S. Ramsay 0-5.

G.S. Ramsay had made a scoring debut for Ayr United on 1st November, 1913, after signing from Rangers. Before Rangers he had been with Queen's Park. At Queen's Park he had been compelled to have amateur status but he chose to retain it. In consequence he would have received no payment for scoring four goals at Easter Road.

9th October, 1915: First Division: Hearts 0 Ayr United 5.

Team: Kerr, Bell, McStay, Getgood, Nevin, McLaughlan, Middleton, Crosbie, Richardson, Semple and McKenzie.

Hearts: Boyd, Frew, John Wilson, Mercer, Martin, Nellies, Sinclair, Miller, D. Graham, Harry Graham and Willie Wilson.

Goals: Johnny Crosbie 0-1; John Semple 0-2; Jimmy Richardson 0-3, 0-4 and 0-5.

Jimmy Richardson's second half hat-trick was a personal triumph. Both clubs were suffering from the loss of players due to military service yet in any context this was a great result. When Hearts came to Ayr for the return league engagement on 8th January, 1916, Jimmy Richardson again scored a hat-trick (in a 3-1 win). Hearts were second in the league at the time of that January fixture.

17th August, 1921: First Division: Queen's Park 1 Ayr United 6.

Team: Nisbet, Smith, McCloy, Hogg, McBain, Gibson, McDougall, Cunningham, Quinn, Slade and Low.

Queen's Park: J. Newton, T. Sneddon, G. Currie, T. Pirie, R. Gillespie, W. Calderwood, E. Scott, J. Gossman, A. Fyfe, J.M. McAlpine and H. Condie.

Goals: John Quinn 0-1 and 0-2; Andy Fyfe 1-2; Donald Slade 1-3; Robert McDougall 1-4; Donald Slade 1-5; Harry Cunningham 1-6.

This was Ayr United's first ever league win at Hampden. The opening exchanges indicated that it was going to be a tight match. It was a false indication. John Quinn scored after ten minutes and the complexion of the game changed. It was only 2-1 at half-time but within eight minutes of the resumption it was 4-1 and the momentum was not stalled.

Biggest Scottish Cup win
17th January, 1931: First round: Ayr United 11 Clackmannan 2.

Team: Hepburn, Willis, Fleming, Yorke, McLeod, McCall, Morgan, Tolland, McGillivray, Brae and Ferguson.

Clackmannan: Shepherd, Jenkins, Ferguson, Robertson, Hunter, Young, Forsyth, Reid, Gordon, Wright and Conacher.

Goals: Danny Tolland 1-0; Pearson Ferguson 2-0; Danny Tolland 3-0; Pearson Ferguson 4-0; Reid 4-1; Charlie McGillivray 5-1; Bob Hepburn (penalty) 6-1; Charlie McGillivray 7-1 and 8-1; Wright 8-2; Billy Brae 9-2; Danny Tolland 10-2; Charlie McGillivray 11-2.

Nationally this result did not have the impact it deserved due to it being an afternoon of tall scoring in the Scottish Cup. There was Partick Thistle 16 Royal Albert 0, Dundee United 14 Nithsdale Wanderers 0, Dundee 10 Fraserburgh 0 and Hearts 9 Stenhousemuir 1. Five clubs scored seven and six clubs scored six. Clackmannan were 8-1 down at half-time. The sixth Ayr goal was a novelty. It was a penalty converted by goalkeeper Bob Hepburn who exercised his right as captain to appoint himself the taker. Charlie McGillivray scored four. The only other Ayr United player to score four in a Scottish Cup tie was Bobby Stevenson versus Berwick Rangers on 4th February, 1956.

Bobby Yorke – he played in the 11-2 destruction of Clackmannan on 17th January, 1931. When the photo was taken he was an Aldershot player.

Jim Flynn – he played in the 7-1 cup rout at Stranraer on 16th February, 1974. Unfortunately he had by then switched allegiance.

TELEPHONE:
No. 2824 DOUGLAS.

TELEGRAPHIC ADDRESS:
ELLIS, BRITISH RAILWAY, GLASGOW."

DISTRICT SUPERINTENDENT,
WESTERN DIVISION,
SOUTHERN SCOTTISH AREA.
JNO. ELLIS.

Letters to be addressed to :—

DISTRICT SUPERINTENDENT,
WESTERN DIVISION,
SOUTHERN SCOTTISH AREA,
LONDON & NORTH EASTERN RAILWAY,
GLASGOW. C. 2.

X.29/19-1.

9th January, 1929.

Mr. Archibald Buchanan,
    Secretary,
        Ayr United F.C.,
            Somerset Park,
                AYR.

Dear Sir,

Ayr United F.C., Ayr to Berwick, Saturday, 19th January.

With reference to your call in company with Mr. Moffat regarding the Ayr United Football Club's First Round Scottish Cup Tie at Berwick on Saturday, 19th current, your suggestion to stop the 10-5a.m. Glasgow to London Pullman express at Berwick-on-Tweed to set down your players and party has been carefully considered, and I am sorry it has not been found possible to meet your wishes in this respect.

I presume it will be your intention, therefore, to travel by the 8-37a.m. express and on hearing from you I shall have pleasure in reserving the required accommodation and supplying the necessary tickets for the occasion.

Yours faithfully,

For JNO. ELLIS

On 19th January, 1929, the club had a Scottish Cup tie at Berwick. To facilitate travel Archie Buchanan wrote to the London & North Eastern Railway Company politely requesting that the Glasgow to London Pullman should make an unscheduled stop at Berwick. Here is the equally polite letter of reply. It was an unconditional refusal.

Biggest away Scottish Cup win (three-way tie)

19th January, 1929: First round: Berwick Rangers 3 Ayr United 9.

Team: Hepburn, Price, Hamilton, Neil, McLeod, Turnbull, Nisbet, Tolland, Robertson, Sharp and McCall.

Berwick Rangers: Patterson, Spence, Crombie, Wilson, Atkinson, Lee, Borthwick, Jefferson, Trainer, Blythe and Johnson.

Goals: Willie Neil (penalty) 0-1; Alex Sharp 0-2; Blythe (penalty) 1-2; Andy McCall 1-3; Alex Sharp 1-4; Willie Neil 1-5; Jefferson 2-5; Willie Robertson 2-6; Jim Nisbet 2-7; Danny Tolland 2-8; Atkinson 3-8; Alex Sharp 3-9.

This result was achieved without the services of record breaking goalscorer Jimmy Smith who remained injured. It was 6-2 at half-time and, just after the sixth goal, Patterson, the Berwick goalkeeper, retired from the match through illness. Right-half Wilson replaced him and the home team completed the tie with ten men. It was a novelty to win a Scottish Cup tie in England. A radio announcer contrived to announce the result as 3-1 to Berwick Rangers.

16th February, 1974: Fourth round: Stranraer 1 Ayr United 7.

Team: Ally McLean, Filippi, Murphy, McAnespie, Fleming, Mitchell, Bert Ferguson, Graham, Alex Ferguson, George McLean and McCulloch; substitutes – Bell and Ingram.

Stranraer: Gallacher, Hopkins, McAuley, McCutcheon, Heap, Hay, McColl, Gray, Flynn, Traynor and Campbell; substitutes – Malone and Bark.

Goals: Davy McCulloch 0-1 and 0-2; Johnny Graham 0-3; George McLean 0-4; Davy McCulloch (penalty) 0-5; George McLean 0-6 and 0-7; Hugh Hay 1-7.

The ex-Ayr United players in the Stranraer team were Ronnie McColl, Denis Gray and Jim Flynn. Davy McCulloch and George McLean both got a hat-trick. Not until 24th January, 1998, did an Ayr United player next get a Scottish Cup hat-trick. That was Ian

Ferguson at Alloa. In the build-up Stranraer boss Eric Caldow had been playing down his team's chances. It was uncertain whether he was playing mind games or whether he was simply a realist.

5th January, 2002: Third round: Deveronvale 0 Ayr United 6.

Team: Nelson, McEwan, Lovering (Sharp 58), Robertson, Hughes, Craig, Crabbe, McGinlay, Annand (McLaughlin 58), Grady and Sheerin (Wilson 62); unused substitutes – Duffy and Dodds.

Deveronvale: Thompson, Dolan, Kinghorn, Chisholm (Urquhart 62), Henderson, Montgomery, More (McAllister), Brown (Mackenzie 80), Murray, Watt and Pressley; unused substitutes – Craigie and Speirs.

Goals: Eddie Annand 0-1 and 0-2; Paul Sheerin 0-3; Pat McGinlay 0-4; Scott Crabbe 0-5; James Grady 0-6.

Staff from a local golf club and an army of Deveronvale fans worked hard to ensure that the pitch was playable but the final outcome must have made them regret their efforts. There was an omen before the game when Willie Grant was introduced. He was the player whose two goals for Elgin City had eliminated Ayr United from the Scottish Cup in 1967. A repeat of that shock did not have the remotest glimmer of happening. It was 4-0 by half-time. At 6-0 James Grady had a penalty saved. Eddie Annand, the usual taker, had already been substituted.

Biggest League Cup win

13th August, 1952: Sectional tie: Ayr United 11 Dumbarton 1.

Team: Round, Willie Fraser, McKeown, Cairns, McNeil, Nesbit, Japp, Robertson, Jim Fraser, Hutton and McKenna.

Dumbarton: Paton, McNee, Ferguson, Shaw, Whyte, Tait, Donegan, Malloch, Maxwell, Scott and Finnie.

Goals: Willie Japp 1-0; Jim Fraser 2-0 and 3-0; Willie Japp 4-0; Jacky Robertson 5-0 and 6-0; Jim Fraser 7-0 and 8-0; Mike McKenna 9-0; Tom Donegan 9-1; Willie Japp 10-1; Joe Hutton (penalty) 11-1.

Eddie Annand

Pat McGinlay

In the year of writing this is the record score in the entire League Cup competition although it is shared with Partick Thistle who beat Albion Rovers by the identical scoreline at Motherwell's Fir Park on 11th August, 1993. When the Ayr team was announced over the loudspeakers there was a great deal of grumbling because it was unchanged from the side that had lost 2-0 at Stirling. The mood was decidedly more chirpy at half-time when it was 5-0. There was no fear of the momentum halting at the break. It was 6-0 by the first minute of the second half. All five forwards scored, the chief contributors being Jim Fraser with four and Willie Japp with a hat-trick.

Biggest away League Cup win

29th July, 2017: Sectional tie: Annan Athletic 1 Ayr United 6.

Team: Hart, Geggan, Reid, Higgins, Boyle, McDaid, Crawford (Ferguson 63), Docherty, McGuffie, Moore (Murphy 69) and Moffat (Gilmour 73); unused substitutes – McCowan and Avci.

Annan Athletic: Atkinson, Brannan, Watson, Krissian, Creaney, Murphy, Sinnamon, Omar (Hooper 83), Orsi, Smith and Stevenson (Pearson 79); unused substitutes – Mitchell, Sonkur, and Swinglehurst.

Goals: Ross Docherty (0-1); Craig McGuffie (0-2), Michael Moffat (0-3), Craig Moore (0-4); Andy Geggan (0-5); Declan McDaid (0-6); Ryan Sinnamon (1-6).

This match spawned a variance of statistics. In addition to being the club's biggest away win in the League Cup, a club record was created for the fastest goal and the win was achieved with six different scorers. Jordan Hart and David Ferguson were ex-Annan players in the Ayr team while James Creaney, Peter Murphy and Ryan Stevenson were ex-Ayr players in the Annan team. A goal up in fifteen seconds, two up inside the third minute and four up by half-time – the contest was very quickly killed off. The crowd was 659 including a rapturous visiting support of 393.

Biggest Scottish Qualifying Cup win

16th September, 1911: Second round: Ayr United 10 Whithorn 0.

Team: Massey, McKenzie, Gardiner, Connell, Tickle, McLaughlan, A.H. Goodwin, Logan, Phillips, Simpson and Dickson.

Whithorn: D. Douglas, J.J. Clark, J. Huxtable, W. Garick, H. Walker, J. Cain, J. Martin, J. Boyce, J. Little, W. Douglas and H. McGinn.

Goals: Harry Simpson 1-0; Charlie Phillips 2-0; Harry Simpson 3-0 and 4-0; Charlie Phillips 5-0; Bert Tickle 6-0; Hugh Logan 7-0 and 8-0; John Dickson 9-0; Hilly Goodwin 10-0.

It was always the custom to publish the initials of players who were on amateur terms. That is why Hilly Goodwin was thus listed (Alex Hill Goodwin) as well as the entire Whithorn team. This tie was one-sided to the point of farce. The *Ayrshire Post* had headlines of FARCICAL FOOTBALL and AYR UNITED TOY WITH WHITHORN. Within the report was a comment that: "Ayr United mercifully restrained from putting in their best efforts." It was 8-0 at half-time. Near the end there was great laughter from the crowd. The source of mirth was the sight of Massey, McKenzie and Gardiner taking it in turns to pose for a photographer with the game in progress. It should be understood that photography in 1911 was far from an instant process.

Biggest friendly win

3rd July 1975: Tour match: Saint Pierre 0 Ayr United 14.

Ayr United's Newfoundland tour in the summer of 1975 did not leave the players unduly stretched. Forty-nine goals were scored in the eight matches with the largest haul being in the French-Canadian town of Saint Pierre. This match was the highlight of a week-long carnival in the town. John Doyle scored four, Johnny Graham scored three, Hugh Cameron scored three, John Dickson scored two and there were single goals for Jim McSherry and Gerry Phillips.

Broadcast media

Hospital radio

The idea of relayed commentaries was conceived by the Ayr United Supporters' Association. Conscious of the fact that many Ayr United supporters had the misfortune to spend varying periods in hospital, it was thought that a system of direct commentaries would create a closer liaison than would be possible via the press. At the time the scheme had already been implemented at other grounds. However there was a financial problem which threatened the possibility of a pilot scheme. In 1952 the Association members had completed the construction of the gymnasium at the foot of Tryfield Place and, although much toil and sweat had been volunteered, building costs still created a red balance. There was also the matter of the incomplete wall between the ground and Walker's premises. In order to proceed with that work further cash was required. The go-ahead to complete the wall was not given until 1954 but the mere anticipation of this work was still a factor in the lack of funding for the Hospital Radio plan. Boldly the project was embarked upon on condition that it did not interfere with the drive for solvency. The Association committee sponsored the scheme by name and two members worked on it on their own. Collections at major works plus private donations solicited the sum of £400 and the installations took place. The hospital authorities consented to the use of existing wiring and equipment. By this means it was possible to cover the male wards in the County Hospital, Heathfield Hospital and the Welfare Home. The first broadcast was on 28th November, 1953, (Ayr United 2 Dundee United 1). On the evening of 12th August, 1959, a new broadcasting studio was opened on the occasion of a League Cup tie (Ayr United 1 Falkirk 1). That studio remains in the same location. That location is on the top of the gymnasium. It is prominent by the window which is angled at forty-five degrees. It was correctly considered that such a design would permit commentators to have a good vantage point for every part of the pitch. The early commentators included Andrew Stevenson, George Hearton, Arthur Stanley and Willie Shields. Willie Shields! He was a legend of the hospital radio service. He did his first commentary in 1954 and continued for more than six decades. Willie recalled that in the pioneering years a few of them would sit in the Stand and pass the microphone between them. Stewart Clark became another longstanding commentator with more than fifty years behind the microphone. John Cameron and Keith McHarg are also commentators of longstanding. The commentaries are shared, each doing fifteen-minute stints. Currently the hospitals served are Ayr, the Ailsa and the Biggart. The service is also popular with visually impaired fans who listen from the Stand.

Ayr United Media

Ayr United Media originated in 2010. It arose from the seed of an idea that the communications between the club and the supporters deserved to be better. Fans had bemoaned that communications were inadequate and that the local newspapers were the only channel for the type of information sought by the public. At the same time that such concerns were being aired Calum Campbell was becoming conscious that many of the fans who craved information happened to live or work abroad including a significant number serving in the military. Could there be an effective means of assisting them to follow Ayr United? Calum was providing assistance to a couple of radio stations and he considered that internet radio broadcasts could be viable. Communication for young fans was also a consideration and it was helpful that Calum assisted in the running of the Panda Pals, an initiative aimed at fostering interest amongst the younger members of the club's fanbase. He discussed ideas with Iain Robb and Michael Lamont. There was a clear consensus between them. All three joined together to create a bid to the Ayr United board in order to produce an online broadcast channel for matches and provide ways for Ayr United to communicate directly to its fans. The overriding intent was to bring the club and its fans closer together.

Prior to the outset of season 2011/12 Ayr United Media made a proposal to the board. The proposal included match broadcasts,

The broadcasting studio on the drawing board. This plan is dated June 1958.

post-match interviews and a new Facebook page which would allow responses. The directors were in accord and it was agreed to create a system for interacting with Ayr United Media via a line of management. Ayr United Media's proposal clarified that the service was to be to the benefit of Ayr United and not to cost the club money. Henceforth Ayr United Media would provide, finance, and develop the service without becoming a burden on the club. Another key element was the decision to provide the service at a discounted rate to those who listened and again this was to be financed by Ayr United Media. It was later financed by advertising and this has persisted until the present day. Ayr United, Ayr United TV and Ayr United Media developed a nice spirit of co-operation. It was agreed that Ayr United Media would co-operate to broadcast and place highlight packages on their own sites. In season 2013/14 former Ayr United player David Kennedy accepted an invitation to become one of the broadcasting team and he has remained since.

Trial broadcasting began in season 2011/12 with the full go-ahead taking place in season 2012/13 when all matches were broadcast. Over the years Ayr United Media has developed and improved its product and now has two key sponsors. These are Ayrshire Medical Services (through diehard Ayr fan Garry Savage) and half-time show sponsor Johnston and Graham (through equally diehard fan Charlie Johnston). The sponsors have greatly assisted in the progression. Development has been immense. There is assistance with the production of both paper and video adverts for the club as well as promotions and help with the organisation and running of events. When it is needed Ayr United Media provides photography for the club and also supplies reports for the local press. In addition the weekly podcast has become a popular feature.

Original member Michael Lamont left to further his career as a journalist while Calum and Iain continued with the running of the service. Calum and Iain developed plans for an extension of the service to include live TV broadcasts and, to this end, presented a proposal to the board. This was accepted and Iain Martin was invited to join in order to provide the technical expertise to allow for TV broadcasting and updating of the web services. 2018/19 saw the first live TV broadcasts for those outside the UK and these will continue in 2019/20. Season 2019/20 will further see expansion to include more regular reports on the reserves and women's football along with its current products.

Responsibility has been taken on to help develop younger people interested in sports journalism and there is assistance with Ayr United's links to the University of the West of Scotland.

As of 2019 the Ayr United media broadcasting and reporting team includes David Kennedy, Sunny Wyrich, Sarah Peddie, George Connolly, Lauren Johnstone, Karen Malcolm, Hugh Maxwell, Iain Martin, Iain Robb, and Calum Campbell.

Midway through season 2018/19, Ayr United created the Ayr United Broadcast Group (ABG) (for Ayr United Media and Ayr United TV). This was done to increase possibilities and assist co-operation at the club while restructuring the management system for broadcasting.

David Kennedy. His debut was on 28th February, 1987, and his last game for the club was on 18th December, 1993. In the present time he assists Ayr United Media.

Captains

The first captain

Ayr United's first ever match was a 4-1 friendly win at home to Hurlford on 17th August, 1910. The captain that night was Sam Graham. On Saturday, 20th August, the first competitive match was a 2-0 home win over Port Glasgow Athletic in a Second Division fixture. This match was played under the captaincy of Bert Tickle.

Youngest captains

The youngest Ayr United captains are, in order, Willie McStay, Nicky Devlin and Jacky McGugan but please refer to the 'Age' section for more precise details.

Largest turnover of captains

The largest number of Ayr United captains in a season is four. Successive injuries in season 2017/18 meant that the captaincy began with Ross Docherty then passed in turn to Chris Higgins, Paddy Boyle and Steven Bell.

Two captains in the one game

If a captain gets substituted he will pass on the armband to a colleague but there was a unique scenario on 19th November, 2016. Paul Cairney's wife had given birth a matter of hours before a Championship fixture at home to Falkirk. He was given the captain's armband and took part in the toss-up. The armband was then passed to regular captain Nicky Devlin.

Championships

Second Division champions

	Played	Won	Drawn	Lost	For	Against	Points
1911/12	22	16	3	3	54	24	35

Winning the Second Division title in the club's second season gave rise to a hope that Ayr United could secure sufficient votes for inclusion in the First Division. At the annual general meeting of the Scottish Football League a motion was passed that the highest club in the Second Division should automatically pass into the First Division. Then there was a u-turn when the St.Mirren delegate complained that the motion would relegate his club after committing themselves to a First Division wage bill.

	Played	Won	Drawn	Lost	For	Against	Points
1912/13	26	13	8	5	45	19	34

Retaining the Second Division title subjected Ayr United once more to the vagaries of the voting system of the Scottish Football League. Again there was no relegation but a decision was made to expand the First Division by two clubs. The clubs voted in were champions Ayr United and sixth-placed Dumbarton.

	Played	Won	Drawn	Lost	For	Against	Points
1927/28	38	24	6	8	117	60	54

After relegation in 1925 it was a source of frustration that it took three attempts to return to the First Division. The dissent amongst the supporters ebbed away in 1927/28. This was the first time an Ayr United team had completed a league programme with a goals

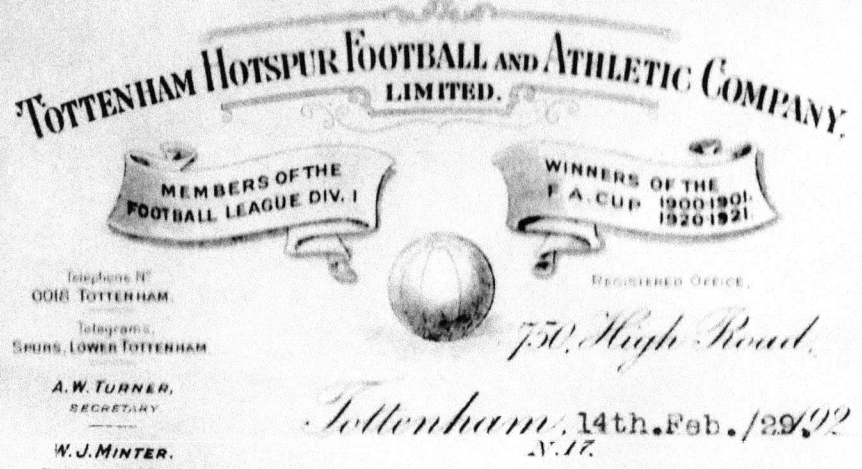

A.Buchanan.Esq.
 Secretary,
  Ayr United F.C.

Dear Mr.Buchanan,

Have you any idea of parting with J.Smith your Centre Forward.

I should be very pleased if you would let me know.

Yours faithfully,

Team Manager.

In February 1929 Tottenham Hotspur made a confidential enquiry regarding the availability of Jimmy Smith. It is confidential no more. Here are the letters showing their initial enquiry and the follow-up.

TOTTENHAM HOTSPUR FOOTBALL AND ATHLETIC COMPANY LIMITED.

MEMBERS OF THE FOOTBALL LEAGUE DIV. I

WINNERS OF THE F.A. CUP 1900-1901. 1920-1921.

Telephone No. 0018 TOTTENHAM

Telegrams, SPURS, LOWER TOTTENHAM.

A.W. TURNER, SECRETARY.

W.J. MINTER, TEAM MANAGER.

REGISTERED OFFICE,
750, High Road,
Tottenham 21st. Feb./ 1922
N. 17.

A. Buchanan, Esq.
Secretary,
Ayr United F.C.

Dear Mr. Buchanan,

I thank you for yours of the 19th. In order to assist me when bringing the matter before my Board, I shall be glad if you will give me some idea of the figure you have in mind,

Yours faithfully,

W.J. Minter
Team Manager.

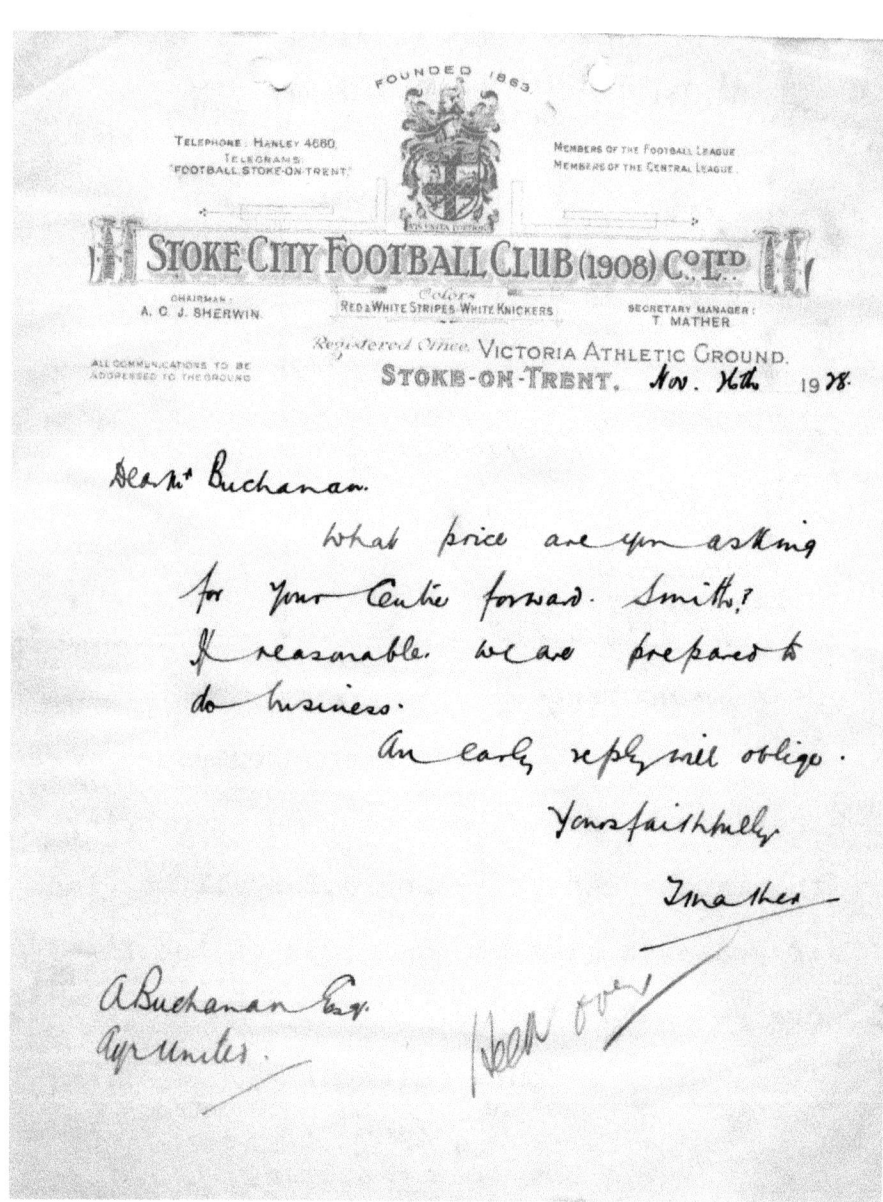

In November 1928 Stoke City asked Ayr United to name a price for Jimmy Smith.

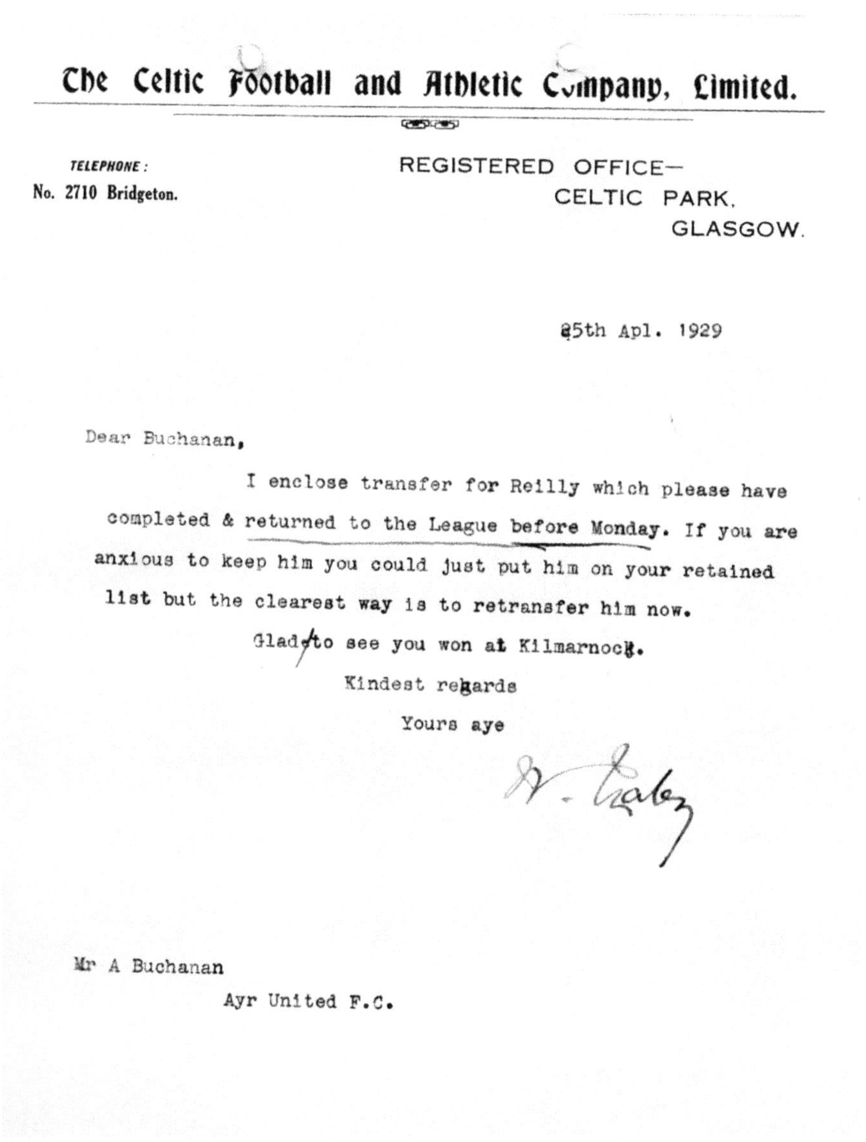

The Celtic Football and Athletic Company, Limited.

TELEPHONE:
No. 2710 Bridgeton.

REGISTERED OFFICE—
CELTIC PARK,
GLASGOW.

25th Apl. 1929

Dear Buchanan,

I enclose transfer for Reilly which please have completed & returned to the League before Monday. If you are anxious to keep him you could just put him on your retained list but the clearest way is to retransfer him now.

Glad to see you won at Kilmarnock.

Kindest regards

Yours aye

W. Maley

Mr A Buchanan
    Ayr United F.C.

This letter dated 25th April, 1929, confirms Joe Riley's loan deal from Celtic. Willie Maley is easily the longest serving Celtic manager of all time (1897 – 1940). However he has signed a letter in which the surname of the player has been mis-spelt Reilly.

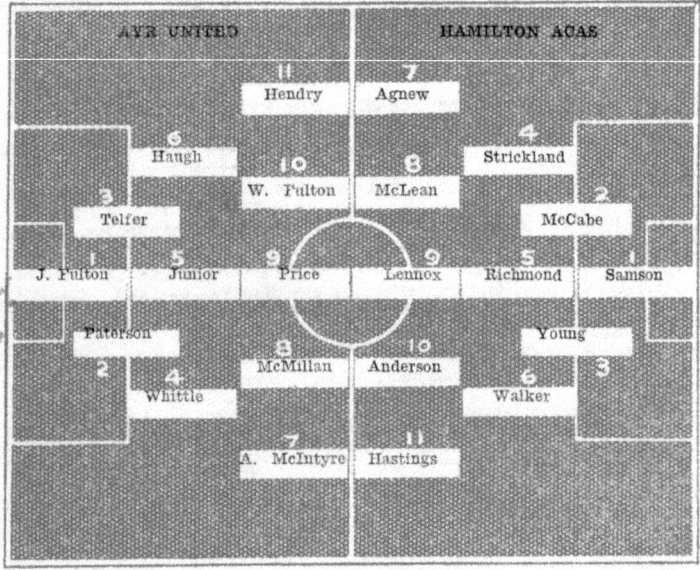

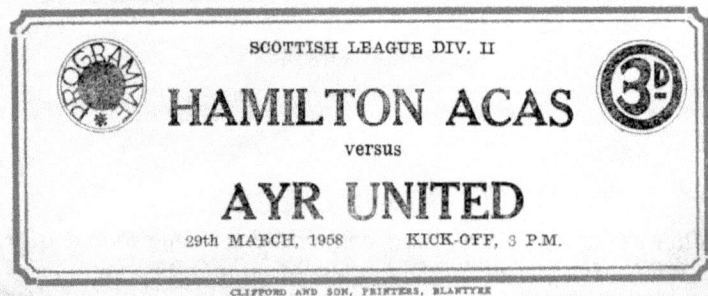

29th March, 1958 – the programme cover for an historic game for Peter Price. 4-1 down until he hit a four-goal burst for a 5-4 win.

ratio exceeding three per game. Jimmy Smith netted sixty-six league goals to create what remains a record in the Scottish and English leagues.

	Played	Won	Drawn	Lost	For	Against	Points
1936/37	34	25	4	5	122	49	54

The tall scoring of 1927/28 was eclipsed in 1936/37 when the eager forwards ran up what remains a club record for league goals in a season. Terry McGibbons struck thirty-nine of those in a campaign of joyous football punctuated by massive victories. Brechin City (8-1), Stenhousemuir (8-3) and Montrose (8-1) bore the brunt. Thirty-three home points were taken from a maximum thirty-four.

	Played	Won	Drawn	Lost	For	Against	Points
1958/59	36	28	4	4	115	48	60

Peter Price remains Ayr United's greatest scoring phenomenon and you would be correct to assume that he got the largest share of that total of 115. He struck thirty-seven. Manager Jacky Cox assembled an efficient unit which was a joy to watch. The standard was set so high that big wins became the expectation with the consequence that a 2-0 home win over Berwick Rangers on 3rd January attracted negative headlines.

	Played	Won	Drawn	Lost	For	Against	Points
1965/66	36	22	9	5	78	37	53

In the summer of 1965 not even the wildest of optimists predicted a title win in the season ahead. The recently finished 1964/65 season remains the worst in our history. Second bottom of the Second Division brought a requirement to apply for re-election to the league. The only two new signings were winger Johnny Grant who had been freed by Hibs and inside-forward Ian Hawkshaw who had been freed by St. Johnstone. Manager Tom McCreath lacked experience in senior football but a major factor in the miraculous transformation was the appointment of Ally MacLeod as a coach.

Alex Glen (left) and Jim McGhee (right) – team mates in the 1958/59 title winning side.

Second Division champions (new style)

	Played	Won	Drawn	Lost	For	Against	Points
1987/88	39	27	7	5	95	31	61

Ally MacLeod's love of attacking football was a major feature of this campaign. John Sludden, Henry Templeton and Tommy Walker got seventy-three league goals between them. The entertaining style was loved by the fans but this had the consequence of Mr MacLeod having to make a request to curb the persistent pitch invasions created by the overall excitement. Such jubilation was a suitable reward for the crushing disappointment of finishing 1986/87 with a defeat at home to Stirling Albion when a draw would have been enough to clinch promotion.

	Played	Won	Drawn	Lost	For	Against	Points
1996/97	36	23	8	5	61	33	77

This was the club's first title win based on three points for a win rather than two. Only one defeat was suffered out of the season's last nineteen league fixtures and that solitary defeat occurred in highly contentious circumstances at Livingston. The late season momentum was crucial because close contenders Hamilton Accies just could not be shrugged off. It went down to the last day when a win at Berwick was required to ensure the title. At least that is what we all thought! Hamilton Accies only drew with Livingston thereby making a draw at Berwick the minimum requirement. Gordon Dalziel's team left nothing to chance in a 2-0 victory.

League One champions

	Played	Won	Drawn	Lost	For	Against	Points
2017/18	36	24	4	8	92	42	76

No clubs in the British senior leagues exceeded Ayr United's total of 124 domestic goals in season 2017/18 but the League One title was won by an uncomfortably narrow margin. One point off the top on the final day! The requirement was to beat Albion Rovers at home and hope that Raith Rovers would fail to beat Alloa Athletic at Stark's Park. Ayr United 2 Albion Rovers 0 – then came the

Ayr United versus Raith Rovers on 25th March, 1989. Henry Templeton is equalising Gordon Dalziel's opener.

Tommy Walker

tortuous wait while Raith Rovers played out the last minutes of a 0-0 draw. It had looked as if losing at Alloa on the previous Sunday would have been fatal. Then came the reprieve.

Second Division runners-up

1910/11

There was no relegation from the First Division and consequently no promotion from the Second Division. Champions Dumbarton had an even stronger grievance. This was attributable to a system which meant that such issues relied on the outcome of a vote. The columns of the *Ayrshire Post* contained a most telling observation: "There is no doubt that the method of automatic promotion in force in the English League competition is the right and proper one."

1955/56

By completing the season as runners-up to Queen's Park, top league football was reinstated for the first time since the war. At least a draw was needed from the final game to clinch promotion. That game was at home to Brechin City on the Monday evening of 30th April, 1956. Johnny Traynor and Sam McMillan scored in a 2-0 win which created frenzied scenes from a crowd variously estimated between 12,000 and 15,000.

1968/69

The season was completed with fifty-three points. Three years earlier the same points total had been sufficient for Ayr United to win the Second Division title but in 1969 it was merely enough to finish thirteen points behind runaway champions Motherwell. The second promotion place was clinched on the bittersweet afternoon of 26th April, 1969. After losing 3-2 away to Queen of the South it emerged that promotion had been won by virtue of defeats for Stirling Albion and East Fife. Most of us were on the road to Thornhill when the news came through by the media of car radio.

First Division (new style) runners-up

2000/01

League reconstruction in 1975 created a situation whereby the league known as the First Division was actually the second tier. To further confuse the scenario you may be told that in 2013 the third tier was rebranded as League One. Yet the item of study here is the First Division in 2001. This was the second tier and Ayr United made a determined attempt at promotion to the Premier League. In the previous season the top two (St.Mirren and Dunfermline Athletic) got automatic promotion. In 2000/01 Ayr United finished as runners-up, seven points behind top-placed Livingston and thirteen in front of third-placed Falkirk. This time there was only one promotion place. Yet even if Ayr United had been the champions there would have been no promotion anyway due to the stadia criteria and with the plans for relocating to Heathfield being strangled in red tape there was no hope.

Second Division (new style) runners-up and play-off winners

2008/09

The main combatants in the battle for the Second Division title were Ayr United and Raith Rovers. A 1-0 defeat at Brechin on 18th April was fatal. On that day we dropped to second place and Raith Rovers held their nerve in the final three games to win the title by two points. At the end of a season in which we had no home league defeats the route to promotion was via the play-offs. The route was safely negotiated. In the semi-finals Brechin City were beaten 5-2 on aggregate. Then, in the final, Airdrie United were beaten 3-2 on aggregate. The second leg at Airdrie was the scene of extreme celebrations when time was blown on a 1-0 win from a Ryan Stevenson goal.

2010/11

The closing weeks of the season lacked incentive. Brian Reid's team was on course to finish second yet this was tempered by Livingston winning the league with twenty-three points to spare. Proper hostilities got resumed when the play-offs were underway. In the semi-finals a 4-1 first leg win at Forfar rendered the second

Catering workers at the club in 1956. Left to right: Miss Janette Martin, Miss Mary Murray, Mrs Thorburn and Mrs McKenzie. Lynne Watson – these are your predecessors.

John Traynor.

leg a formality. It was 3-3 on the day. The first leg of the final saw a 1-1 draw at home to Brechin City and a second leg that was far from a formality, especially when 1-0 down with less than a quarter of an hour to go. Mark Roberts then Michael Moffat then struck for yet more scenes of fan mania.

League One (new style) runners-up and play-off winners

2015/16

As in 2011 the incentive in the closing weeks ebbed away due to the absolute certainty that Dunfermline Athletic would win the title. As evidence you may be told that the final gap at the top was eighteen points. Another comparison with 2011 was a 4-1 away win in the first leg of the play-off finals. That was at Peterhead. It became 6-2 on aggregate. A 1-1 draw in the first leg of the final was another echo of 2011. That happened at Stranraer but only by courtesy of a Ross Docherty goal in the fifth minute of stoppage time. Even after extra time the leg at Ayr was scoreless. Promotion was then won in a shootout in which Greg Fleming had three saves.

Christmas Day Football

1915: First Division: Ayr United 2 Kilmarnock 0.

Team: Kerr, Bell, McStay, Hay, Nevin, McLaughlan, Ingram, McKenzie, Richardson, Jackson (Leeds City) and Gray.

Kilmarnock: Blair, Murray, Mitchell, Fulton, Dickie, McAlpine (Southampton), Armour, Armstrong, Culley, Mackie and McPhail.

Goals: Jimmy Richardson 15 and 87.

This was Ayr United's first win since last playing Kilmarnock at Rugby Park on 23rd October, 1914. Considering the demands of war work and military duty the estimated attendance of 8,000 was reasonable.

1920: First Division: Motherwell 6 Ayr United 1.

Team: Nisbet, Smith, McCloy, Hogg, Gillespie, Gibson, Crosbie, McKenzie, Richardson, Slade and McBain.

Motherwell: Rundell, Brown, McDougall, Paterson, Finlayson, Stewart, Lennie, Rankin, Ferguson, Reid and Ferrier.

Goals: Hugh Ferguson 1-0 and 2-0; Donald Slade 2-1; Lennie 3-1; Bob Ferrier 4-1; Hugh Ferguson 5-1 and 6-1.

The four-goal display from Hugh Ferguson was exceptional. He was destined to score the winning goal for Cardiff City against Arsenal in the 1927 FA Cup final. Another festive scorer against Ayr United in 1920 was Bob Ferrier who would become the first occupant of the manager's office at Somerset Park on the resumption of football at the end of the Second World War.

1926: Second Division: Ayr United 2 Bathgate 2.

Team: Hepburn, Woodburn, Fleming, Kelly, Gillon, Turnbull, Walters, Blair, Tolland, Brae and Pearson.

Ayr goals: Jacky Walters 1-0; Billy Brae 2-2.

Jacky Walters scored with a 15th minute penalty after Danny Tolland had been pushed off the ball. Bathgate equalised before half-time then went ahead with fifteen minutes left. At that point they packed their goal but they could not prevent Billy Brae from rescuing a point.

1930: First Division: Queen's Park 4 Ayr United 1.

Team: Hepburn, Willis, Fleming, Yorke, Young, Turnbull, Suggett, Tolland, McGillivray, McCall and Morgan.

Queen's Park: R.G. Peden, T.K. Campbell, W.O. Walker, R. Grant, R. Gillespie, W.S. King, F.P. Taylor, H.T. Bremner, D. McLelland, J. Donnelly and J.B. McAlpine.

Goals: F.P. Taylor 1-0; D. McLelland 2-0; Charlie McGillivray 2-1; R. Grant 3-1; J. Donnelly 4-1.

In 1930 Christmas Day landed on a Thursday but this fixture was rearranged from New Year's Day so that Queen's Park could play Corinthians on that day. The plethora of initials in the home team's listing was mandatory to denote their amateur status. Amateur they may have been but they had a reputation for being hard. This reputation was endorsed early in the match. McLelland got stretchered off in the third minute. Ten minutes later he resumed playing and twelve minutes after that he put his team 2-0 up.

1937: First Division: Ayr United 0 Arbroath 1.

Team: Smith, Dyer, Strain, Taylor, Currie, Mays, Craig, Dimmer, McGibbons, Steele and Gemmell.

Arbroath: Robertson, Fordyce, Becci, Adams, Gavin, Urquhart, Lowe, McInally, Brand, Devlin and Christie.

Goal: John Lowe.

Sitting third bottom of the twenty-club table, Ayr United were in the throes of a relegation battle which would ultimately end in a last day escape. Arbroath arrived and departed as the seventh-placed club. John Lowe's headed goal came just before half-time. Near the end Christie, the Arbroath outside-left, went down injured and Hyam Dimmer dragged him off the field to prevent a hold-up.

1948: 'B' Division: Dumbarton 0 Ayr United 0

Team: Round, Duncan, Coupland, Thomson, McNeil, Nesbit, Agnew, Ramsay, Miller, McIlwain and Beattie.

Dumbarton: Paton, Jack McNee, Ferguson, Lynch, Donaldson, Grant, Donegan, Cantwell, Stirling, Goldie and Chris McNee.

Goalkeeper Len Round's performance was most eloquently expressed in the columns of the *Ayrshire Post*: "Round can mark Christmas Day, 1948, with a red pencil in his diary. He was the outstanding performer with nary a blemish on his escutcheon." In future years the inarticulate translation of this was to become: 'The boy done great!'

1954: 'B' Division: Ayr United 2 Albion Rovers 2.

Team: Round, Thomson, Leckie, Gallagher, O'Donnell, Lindsay, Beattie, Hepburn, Robertson, McNulty and McKenna.

Albion Rovers: McCracken, Maxwell, Clark, McPhail, Dunn, Hannah, Farquhar, Findlay, Kiernan, Crawford and Hodge.

Goals: Felix Kiernan 0-1; Alec Beattie 1-1; Andy Crawford 1-2; John McPhail own goal 2-2.

Albion Rovers went 2-1 up in the 58th minute then three minutes later Mike McKenna struck the crossbar with a fierce drive that had the goalkeeper beaten. It was starting to look as if the pursuit of an equaliser was going to be frustrating. It was a lucky development when John McPhail headed past his own goalkeeper in the 69th minute.

1956: First Division: Queen's Park 2 Ayr United 0.

Team: Round, Bell, Thomson, Boden, Brice, Haugh, Japp, McMillan, Price, Whittle and Beattie.

Queen's Park: F. Crampsey, L.G. Harnett, W.M. Hastie, R. Cromar, J.C. Valentine, A. Glen, W. Scobie, J. F. Robb, A. McEwan, D. McLean and C. Church.

Goals: Bobby Bell own goal 1-0; Donald McLean 2-0.

This game was scheduled for the previous Saturday but it suffered a postponement until Christmas Day which landed on the Tuesday. Both clubs had been promoted at the end of 1955/56 and now they were both fighting relegation. Bobby Bell was very unlucky with his own goal. It came from a miscalculated clearance and, as if to compound the frustration, the shot from Charlie Church was going wide.

1965: Friendly: Ayr United 2 Celtic reserves 0.

Team: Paton, Malone, Murphy, Thomson, Monan, McAnespie (Moore, midway through the second half), Davy Paterson, Hawkshaw, Balfour, Oliphant and Arthur Paterson.

Celtic reserves: Fallon, Young, McCarron, Cattanach, McNeill, O'Neil, Connelly, Quinn, Divers, Lennox and Auld.

Goals: John Balfour 1-0; Eddie Moore 2-0.

Three of that Celtic team would become Lisbon Lions the following season. They were Billy McNeill, Bobby Lennox and Bertie Auld. Young John Balfour had been signed from Ardeer Recreation in October and this was his debut. He was exceptional against the experienced McNeill. Lennox and Auld both got booked for persistent fouling therefore it was evident that the friendly status did not diminish the commitment.

1971: First Division: Partick Thistle 0 Ayr United 1.

Team: Ally McLean, Murphy, Rough, McAnespie, McFadzean, Filippi, Doyle, Graham, Ingram, McGregor and Robertson; substitute – George McLean.

Partick Thistle: Rough, Hansen, Forsyth, Glavin, Campbell, Strachan, McQuade, Coulston, Bone, Alex Rae and Lawrie; substitute – Tommy Rae.

Goal: David Robertson.

In their previous home match Partick Thistle had beaten Motherwell 8-3. Another warning for Ayr United was a programme cover showing Partick Thistle players at a civic reception to commemorate winning the League Cup. In the 82nd minute David Robertson outwitted John Hansen then beat Alan Rough with a low drive.

Christmas Day summary

League	9	
Friendly	1	
Won	3	Your writer attended two of the three wins. The exception, of course, was 1915!
Drew	3	
Lost	4	
Total	**10**	

Clergy

The first clergyman to join Ayr United was the Reverend John McKenzie. During season 1925/26 he was a regular goalkeeper for the reserves but did not break into the first team. On 10th October, 1925, he was about to start the second half of a match against Queen of the South reserves when a fan presented him with a bouquet of chrysanthemums!

In the summer of 1928 James McPartlin, a winger, was signed. His previous club was Hibs and he was something of a utility player, being able to play at full-back as well. He too was unable to break into the first team. In later life he became the Reverend Father Giles McPartlin. He died at Dundee in December 1959 at the age of 51.

Bill Chalmers was a divinity student while with Ayr United in season 1951/52. In common with John McKenzie he was a goalkeeper confined to the reserves. He went to America to complete his studies. On returning he became a minister in Glasgow in 1954 and in 1955 he accepted a similar position in New York. He settled in Scotland and in 1992 he retired after twenty-six years as the minister at Dunbar Parish Church in East Lothian. His greatest footballing achievement was playing for an American All Stars team which defeated Vienna Rapide.

On 13th February, 1954, Ayr United lost 5-1 at Berwick in a Scottish Cup second round tie. Brian Kingsmore, an Irish divinity student, scored a hat-trick for Berwick Rangers.

Coincidental happenings

The scorer of Somerset Park's first goal and the scorer of Ayr United's first competitive goal both had the name A. Campbell. On 7th May, 1888, the ground was opened with a 3-0 win by Ayr FC over Aston Villa with the first goal being scored by Alex Campbell. On 20th August, 1910, Ayr United beat Port Glasgow Athletic 2-0 in the club's first competitive engagement, a Second Division fixture, also at Somerset Park. The opening goal was scored by Archie Campbell.

On 14th January, 1911, the Lockerbie-based Mid Annandale came to Somerset Park for a Scottish Consolation Cup first round tie. Ayr United won 5-0. That club next played here on 18th January, 1930. The occasion was a Scottish Cup first round tie and again it was a 5-0 Ayr win. In 1911 all of the goals were scored in the first half and in 1930 all of the goals were scored in the second half. There was hilarity at the 1911 match when a shot from Bert Tickle knocked off the visiting goalkeeper's cap. It then flew over the crossbar – the cap not the ball!

In season 1920/21 Ayr United had two identically-named players. Match reports referred to Auchinleck Scott and Falkirk Scott.

On 3rd October, 1913, goalkeeper George Woods signed for Ayr United from Lugar Boswell. At that time the club trainer was Alex Aitken who was known as Sanny. They both died on the same date. That date was 7th February, 1938. Woods was aged forty-six and Aitken was aged sixty-four.

On 25th September, 1948, Ayr United lost 6-1 in a League Cup tie against Airdrie at Broomfield Park. On the same date in 1954 Airdrie again beat Ayr United 6-1 in a League Cup tie at Broomfield Park. Goalkeeper Len Round was the only Ayr player to appear in both matches.

Official Programme = 3ᴅ

1954 — AIRDRIEONIANS FOOTBALL CLUB, Established 1878 — 1955

DIRECTORS:—ROBERT PATERSON, Esq. (Chairman); JOHN HENDERSON, Esq. (Vice-Chairman); PETER BENNIE, Esq., M.C.; GEORGE CARROL, Esq.; DAVID B. FRAME, Esq.; Lt.-Col. J. F. GIBSON, M.C., T.D., D.L.; ROBERT W. SMITH, Esq.

Manager: WM. G. STEEL   Trainer: ANDREW MURRAY

TELEPHONE: AIRDRIE 2067.

Saturday, 25th September, 1954.   Kick-off 3 p.m.

AIRDRIEONIANS
VERSUS
AYR UNITED

✦ **AFTER THE GAME**—Take a Look at Our Window

ALWAYS FIRST with the LATEST in MEN'S, YOUTHS' and BOYS' CLOTHING OF ALL KINDS at

THE MEN'S & BOYS' SHOP
Danskin's
THE CROSS · 32 GRAHAM STREET
AIRDRIE

On the same date six years earlier it was the same result at the same venue in the same competition.

On 17th October, 1953, St.Johnstone won 4-3 in a league fixture at Ayr after having a 3-0 lead. This scenario was replicated precisely on 3rd September, 1994.

On 2nd November, 1996, Ayr United beat Clyde 3-2 in a league fixture at Broadwood Stadium. The attendance was 1,207. Our next league fixture at that ground saw a 1-1 draw on 19th April, 1997. The attendance then was merely one turnstile click more at 1,208.

On 4th November, 2006, 1,003 people witnessed Ayr United winning 3-1 in a league fixture at Stair Park, Stranraer. On 13th September, 2008, both the result and the attendance were identical.

On 24th March, 1962, a league fixture had a result of Ayr United 3 Arbroath 5. On 2nd March, 1963, Arbroath won a league fixture at Ayr with an identical result.

On 30th October, 1915, Third Lanark and Ayr United contested a 1-1 draw in a league fixture at Cathkin Park. On 30th October, 1965, precisely a half-century later, the identical result happened and this was also in a league fixture. This proved to be Ayr United's last ever game at Cathkin Park.

On 11th August, 1962, a League Cup tie at Firs Park had a result of East Stirling 4 Ayr United 1. In the same season East Stirling won 4-1 at Ayr in the league. That was on 30th March, 1963. In the League Cup tie East Stirling's last three goals were timed at 76, 81 and 86. In the league match their last three goals were timed at 76, 81 and 84.

Three consecutive matches were won by an 87th minute goal in February, 1964. These were:

15th February, 1964: Scottish Cup third round: Aberdeen 1 Ayr United 2.
This match was approached in the hope that the damage would be limited to a defeat of sensible proportions. Johnny Kilgannon's late winner seemed like a fantasy.

22nd February, 1964: Second Division: Ayr United 4 Albion Rovers 3.

Kenny Cunningham, scorer of the 77th minute equaliser at Aberdeen, hit the 87th minute winner against Albion Rovers. An injury to Willie Toner meant having to play a man short in the second half.

29th February, 1964: Second Division: Arbroath 0 Ayr United 1.

Again the late winner came from Kenny Cunningham but the circumstances were contentious. The build-up to the goal came from a disputed throw-in. It was given to Ayr United on the referee's decision but the linesman signalled that it was Arbroath's. The protests were furious.

On 7th December, 2002, a crowd of 1,663 watched the 3-3 draw against Inverness Caledonian Thistle at Somerset Park. The next home match was also a league fixture. It was a 4-0 win at home to Arbroath three weeks later. The attendance increased by just one turnstile click to 1,664.

On 12th November, 2013, Stranraer won a league fixture 6-3 at Ayr and the attendance was 986. On 23rd November our next home match took place in front of an identical attendance. On this occasion Stenhousemuir were beaten 4-3 in the league.

At Stranraer on 23rd November, 1968, home centre-half Jim Hannah scored an own goal against Ayr United from forty yards. The further significance of the number forty is that it was the fortieth league own goal in Ayr United's favour since the foundation of the club.

On 13th August, 1952, Ayr United beat Dumbarton 11-1 in a League Cup sectional tie at Somerset Park. 13th August, 2002, marked the 50th anniversary of the annihilation and this date coincided with the clubs meeting in the League Challenge Cup. This time Dumbarton won 3-0 in a tie played at the Strathclyde Homes Stadium.

On 14th December, 1993, Ayr United lost 6-1 in a league fixture away to Dunfermline Athletic and on 10th December, 1994, we lost

6-0 away to Dunfermline Athletic in the league. The dates and results bore a close comparison but you will now be told of an identical comparison. In the 1993 fixture Ayr goalkeeper Cammy Duncan went off injured in the 64th minute and he was replaced by George Grierson. The 1994 fixture saw Ayr goalkeeper Stuart McIntosh go off injured and it was also in the 64th minute. Again the replacement was George Grierson. The 'Groundhog Day' experience was compounded by George Grierson having had no first team action in between those matches.

You will now be told another tale of coincidental happenings in relation to East End Park, Dunfermline. On 25th September, 1999, Ayr United lost 2-1 at that ground and, on our return on 22nd January, 2000, we lost 2-0 there, again in the league. There is nothing spooky about that you may think. However in the first of these matches the Dunfermline Athletic goals were timed at nine and ten minutes. On the next visit their goals were timed at nine minutes and eleven minutes.

On the last Saturday of the 20th century Airdrie played at Ayr and the match programme contained the following: "Today we welcome Airdrie to Somerset Park and herein lies an amazing coincidence. On the last Saturday of last century (30th December, 1899) the visiting team at Somerset Park just happened to be Airdrie. For this our last fixture of the twentieth century the same club are the visitors. In 1899 the Airdrie left-back did not turn up and they played a man short throughout. The advantage was exploited to its fullest effect with Ayr FC winning 5-0. Would it be asking too much for the coincidence to stretch to today's scoreline?"

Airdrie playing a league game at Somerset Park on the last Saturday of consecutive centuries was surely coincidence enough. What type of crazy programme writer would even dare hint that the 5-0 scoreline would be repeated? Oops, that would be me! In a phenomenal example of history repeating itself Ayr United beat Airdrie 5-0. The scorers in 1899 were McAvoy (twice), Kelt and Lindsay (twice). In 1999 the scorers were Marvyn Wilson, Neil Tarrant, Glynn Hurst (twice) and Jens Hansen.

On 27th October, 1956, Peter Price scored a hat-trick of headers in a 4-1 league win at home to Airdrie. On 13th April, 1985, Ian McAllister scored a hat-trick of headers in a 5-1 league win at home to Airdrie. This statistic is qualified with the information that between those dates there were two other matches involving an Ayr United player scoring a headed hat-trick. 22nd August, 1964: League Cup: Ayr United 6 Berwick Rangers 0 and 12th September, 1964: league: Queen of the South 4 Ayr United 3. Eddie Moore was the player who achieved the feat on each of these occasions.

Here is the coincidence that wasn't! Ayr United versus Livingston (league) on 15th October, 2011, was reported across all media sources to have had a crowd figure of 1,390. The next match, also in the league, was at home to Dundee on 22nd October and the crowd figure was again reported as 1,390 by the media. These figures were mistakenly reported. The correct attendances were 1,361 for the Livingston match and 1,392 for the Dundee match.

In opening day league matches at home, Ayr United have had three that remained scoreless. These were in 1924, 1966 and 2008. Each time the gap has been forty-two years.

16th August, 1924: Ayr United 0 Third Lanark 0.

Team: Hughes, Smith, McCloy, Stewart, McLeod, Murphy, Templeton, Kilpatrick, Skinner, McKenzie and Cunningham.

Third Lanark: Jarvie, McCormack, Frame, Gilchrist, Williamson, James Walker, Reid, Findlay, P. Walker, McInally and Archibald.

With Somerset Park still undergoing extensive renovation this First Division fixture took place at Beresford Park. The crowd was estimated at 7,000 and at one time the queue extended across to the Ayrshire and Galloway. It was a poor game characterised by rough play. An injury to Dan Templeton meant that Ayr United had to play the second half with ten men. Third Lanark missed a second half penalty.

Ayr United FC 1924/25. Rear (left to right): Jock Smith, John Anderson, Murdoch McKenzie, Harry Cunningham and John Hughes. Front (left to right): Tommy Kilpatrick, Phil McCloy, Jimmy McLeod, James Murphy, Dan Templeton and Bobby Stewart.

10th September, 1966: Ayr United 0 Dunfermline Athletic 0.

Team: Millar, Malone, Murphy, Thomson, Monan, Mitchell, Grant, McMillan, Ingram, Hawkshaw and Paterson.
Dunfermline Athletic: Martin, Willie Callaghan, Lunn, Thomson, McLean, Tom Callaghan, Fleming, Paton, Hunter, Maxwell and Robertson.

This match was approached with more than a degree of trepidation. After winning the Second Division title the visit of Dunfermline Athletic in the opening First Division fixture was daunting. In the previous season they had finished in fourth place and in the season before that they had finished third despite the fact that one more point would have given them the league title. Paying no heed to their reputation Ayr United outplayed them without being able to create a breakthrough.

2nd August, 2008: Ayr United 0 Raith Rovers 0.

Team: Grindlay, Dempsie, Easton, Walker, Campbell, Stevenson, Borris, Aitken, Prunty, Williams (Gormley 68) and Keenan; unused substitutes – Henderson, Weaver, McGowan and Stewart.

Raith Rovers: McGurn, Wilson, Cook, Campbell, Ellis, Walker, Sloan, Davidson, Weir, Smith (Graham 83) and Ferry (72); unused substitutes – Silvestro, Wedderburn and O'Connor.

There was a rather severe colour clash. Ayr United played in all white with a black trim and Raith Rovers played in light grey with a red trim. At times there was little distinction in the sunlight. This was a hard fought battle between the clubs who would finish first and second in the Second Division in the season just underway. Our route to promotion was via the play-offs.

11th February, 1956: league: Stranraer 3 Ayr United 6.
12th November, 2013: league: Ayr United 3 Stranraer 6.

In the 1956 fixture there were three hat-tricks. They were scored by Peter Price and Alec Beattie for Ayr and Jack Gilroy for Stranraer.

In the 2013 fixture both sides could also lay claim to a hat-trick. They were scored by Michael Moffat for Ayr and Jamie Longworth for Stranraer.

On 15th December, 2012, Kyle McAusland scored in the 17th minute to make it 2-0 against East Fife. The clubs next met on 26th January, 2013, and Kyle McAusland again scored in the 17th minute to make it 2-0. Neither match (both in the league) was won. The first one ended Ayr United 2 East Fife 3 and the next one was East Fife 3 Ayr United 3.

21st April, 1917: league: Ayr United 2 Raith Rovers 1.
28th February, 2017: league: Ayr United 1 Raith Rovers 0.

The two occasions when Raith Rovers turned up at Ayr without a match-fit goalkeeper occurred just short of 100 years apart. In 1917 Sprigger White, the Ayr United reserve goalkeeper, guested for them. In 2017, one of their midfielders, Ryan Stevenson (ex-Ayr United), deputised in goal for them.

In consecutive home games Eddie Malone scored a 60th minute goal at the Somerset Road end and in each of those games the opposition had a goal disallowed in stoppage time. These games were Ayr United 2 Falkirk 2 (league) on 20th August, 2011, and Ayr United 1 Inverness Caledonian Thistle 0 (League Cup) on 24th August, 2011.

24th October, 2015: league: Stenhousemuir 0 Ayr United 1.

To commemorate his recent death the supporters came up with the idea of singing: "There's only one Peter Price." The plan was to sing it in the ninth minute to commemorate the great man's shirt number. Right on cue the fans let rip and, just as they did so, Ross Caldwell scored. The ball entering the net while this was being sung gave rise to a belief that the spirit of Peter Price was alive at Ochilview Park.

Colours

It has to be admitted that Ayr United's first strip was a hotch-potch. It comprised the crimson and gold hooped shirts of Ayr FC and the blue shorts of Parkhouse. There was a strong case for amalgamating the clubs but the argument for amalgamating the kit was less compelling. In August 1914 an eminently sensible announcement was made: "Ayr United will no longer play in crimson and gold. The team will now play in black and white hooped shirts and black shorts." In opting for neutral colours this initiative was respectful to the memory of both Ayr FC and Parkhouse. By the 1920s the shorts were white and for the greater part of the 1930s the shirts were adorned with broad black and white hoops rather than those of a more conventional size. On the Tuesday evening of 24th May, 1938, the Ayr United annual general meeting was held in Young's Tea Rooms. There was vigorous discussion on the topic of changing the club's name to Ayr FC. The discussion was ditched when it was correctly concluded that this would have been disrespectful to the memory of Parkhouse. Yet a radical plan was hatched and implemented in relation to the team kit. Consequently, at the outset of season 1938/39, the team took to the field wearing white open-necked shirts bearing the Ayr coat-of-arms badge, navy blue shorts and blue and white hooped stockings. Speculatively it might be observed that the influence came from Preston North End who had recently won the FA Cup. The immediate post-war era saw that shirt style retained but by then the shorts were black and the stockings were black with white tops. This coincided with the town badge being discarded in favour of a badge with an anchor on it. In October 1949 the club reintroduced the medium sized black and white hoops. This shirt style was worn until the mid-1950s but the plain white shirts were also worn during that time. In the years spanning the 1950s into the 1960s the shirts were white with a black v-neck and the shorts were black with an illusion of being silken.

In November 1962 black and white vertical stripes got introduced with white shorts and white stockings with two black hoops at the top. In the modern age commercial considerations would prevent a during-the-season kit redesign but back then the idea of wearing a football shirt as casual wear had not been thought of. The black and white hoops got reintroduced to coincide with a Scottish Cup tie at Aberdeen in February 1964. At the end of 1968/69 the hoops got discarded.

In the intervening years the style, in the main, has been white shirts with black shorts but with a variety of embellishments including round necks, v-necks, in-filled necks, penguin style, Umbro diamonds on the sleeves, black speckles and a broad black band. Radical exceptions to the predominantly white shirts were the broad black and white vertical stripes introduced during the summer of 1994 and the all-black kit introduced one year later. On 28th October, 1995, East Fife recorded their first ever league win at Ayr. The significance of this result is endorsed by the fact that their first league fixture at Somerset Park took place on 31st October, 1925. Three days short of seventy years to break the hoodoo! The purpose of this digression is to convey the point that, in the wake of this match, the all-black kit was ditched at the behest of manager Gordon Dalziel. He was of the opinion that the strip symbolised everything that was wrong. The course of history dictates an inevitability that shirts of black and white hoops will appear on a recurring basis. Surely enough this style was reintroduced for season 2009/10. The style of 2011/12 comprised shirts which were half black and half white in the style of Blackburn Rovers. For 2016/17 the hoops were half reintroduced! The shirts had hoops on the front only.

Change strips have comprised a complete explosion of colours with the potential of having the Marmite effect of being greatly liked or greatly disliked. The most argued about change strip appeared as something of a shock at Dumbarton's Boghead Park on 5th October, 1996. The team took to the field in jerseys of green and purple halves and shorts of green and purple halves. The socks were purple. The scenario was similar when an all pink change kit was ordered for season 2018/19. It first got an airing on 14th August,

2018, on the occasion of a shootout defeat against Queen's Park at Hampden in the Irn Bru Cup. On 1st September it got its next airing on the occasion of a 5-0 league defeat against Queen of the South at Palmerston Park. In a season which had been otherwise going well there was a school of thought that the pink kit was a jinx. Four weeks later the team wore it for a league fixture at Cappielow Park. This brought forth predictable comments from the 'here we go again' brigade. The result was Morton 1 Ayr United 5. On that afternoon pink looked beautiful. For 2009/10 the change strip comprised shirts of crimson with gold trimmings. The shorts and socks were blue. This was done to commemorate the club's original colours with an eye to the forthcoming centenary. Albeit that the colours were the same you can be assured that the 2009 design was eminently more stylish than the original.

Corner–kicks

In 1924 a law change meant that goals could now be scored directly from a corner-kick. Prior to this a goalkick was the correct award when the ball went directly into the net from a corner-kick without touching anyone. There was a highly controversial incident at Somerset Park on 24th November, 1900. Ayr FC were playing Stenhousemuir in a Scottish Qualifying Cup semi-final. Ayr left-back Tom Wills conceded a corner-kick and when the ball was swung in it became apparent that it was headed for the net so goalkeeper Hugh McDonald ducked and let it go in. By the laws of 1900 the match should have resumed with a goalkick. It is true that a visiting player rushed in and got his head on the ball but by the time he made contact the ball had clearly crossed the line anyway. The referee's interpretation was that contact had been made before it had crossed the line. Palpably this was nonsense. The goal stood. It was now 2-0 to Stenhousemuir, Tom Wills having earlier headed an own goal. Sam Aitken trimmed it back to 2-1 and so it ended. It is said that football fans have short memories. The opposite is true. This particular corner-kick travesty was still being complained about even after Ayr FC got swallowed up in the amalgamation to create Ayr United.

Ayr United's greatest exponent of scoring directly from a corner-kick has been Alec Beattie who achieved the feat on six occasions, five of which were at Somerset Park. The matches were:
27th September, 1947.: Arbroath 2 Ayr United 2: 'B' Division
1st November, 1947. : Ayr United 6 Dunfermline Athletic 2: 'B' Division.
6th March, 1948. : Ayr United 2 St. Johnstone 1: 'B' Division.
9th October, 1948 : Ayr United 2 Dumbarton 1: League Cup.
29th January, 1949 : Ayr United 1 Airdrie 1: 'B' Division.
27th September, 1952: Ayr United 5 Dumbarton 0 : 'B' Division.

It was nearly seven. On 11th February, 1950, Beattie struck the crossbar from a corner-kick in a 'B' Division match at home to Forfar Athletic.

On 18th November, 1922, a First Division fixture ended Ayr United 2 Albion Rovers 2. In this match Ayr United had eighteen corner-kicks and Albion Rovers had none.

In reference to a 'B' Division fixture ending Dumbarton 0 Ayr United 0 on Christmas Day, 1948, the *Ayrshire Post* stated: "Dumbarton secured a phenomenal number of corners."

On 26th October, 1996, a Second Division fixture ended Ayr United 1 Brechin City 0. During the first half Ray Allan, the visiting goalkeeper, threw the ball out for an Ayr United corner-kick when attempting to throw it upfield.

In November 1996 Ayr United scored directly from a corner-kick in consecutive away matches (both in the league). They were scored by Paul Kinnaird versus Clyde on 2nd November, 1996, and Alain Horace versus Stranraer on 16th November, 1996. Ayr United completed the season with three goals directly from corner-kicks. The other, again in the league, was scored by Paul Smith at home to Queen of the South on 8th March 1997.

On 27th November, 2004, a Second Division fixture ended Ayr United 1 Arbroath 1. In the second half Ayr United got fourteen corner-kicks.

On 16th March, 2013, Ayr United got a corner-kick in the closing minutes of a Second Division fixture at home to Stranraer. It was on the Stand side at the Somerset Road end. When the corner was taken not one Ayr United player was located in the penalty area. The ball was played short then back into the corner in order to run down the clock on a 2-1 lead.

On 10th December, 2016, a Championship fixture ended Ayr United 0 Dundee United 1 despite the corner-kick count being 14 – 2 in Ayr United's favour. Eighteen days earlier a 1-1 draw away to

Raith Rovers, also in the Championship, saw a corner-kick count of 14 – 3 in our favour.

Jim 'Tottie' McGhee was reputed to have scored an Ayr United winner at Celtic Park directly from a corner-kick with the last kick of the ball. Ayr United did beat Celtic 3-2 at Celtic Park in the First Division on 7th November, 1959, and McGhee did score the winner directly from a corner-kick. However he executed the feat not with the last kick but with six minutes remaining.

Corruption

Steen versus Hay

On the evening of 27th January, 1926, the Council of the Scottish Football Association met to discuss a dispute between Ayr United manager Jimmy Hay and club director Tom Steen. The dispute originated on the afternoon of 28th March, 1925, when Ayr United won 1-0 in a crucial relegation battle against Third Lanark at Cathkin Park. Ultimately Ayr United did get relegated but a major controversy erupted after Hay accused Steen of attempting to bribe referee Tom Dougray in order to influence the outcome of that match. The accusation was that Steen had arranged for fellow director Alex Stirling to offer Dougray £5 or £10 to make sure of an Ayr United win. Stirling was a friend of Dougray. Compounding the severity of the accusation was Steen's position as treasurer of the Scottish Football Association, his tenure having been unbroken since 1907. The issue at stake was not the accusation but Hay's refusal to tender a written apology. In concluding that the accusation had no foundation, there was a unanimous decision to impose a *sine die* ban on Jimmy Hay. On the evening of 2nd March, 1926, a shareholders' meeting was held in the YMCA Hall in Ayr High Street. This was at the instigation of shareholders who felt aggrieved at Hay's ban. The sole item on the agenda was to consider a signed requisition for the deposition of Tom Steen from the Ayr United board. Douglas Bowie, the club chairman, presided. About 140 shareholders were in attendance. Mr B.W. Chambers put forward the motion for Steen's removal. He then gave a speech outlining why he was doing this. Jimmy Quaite seconded. George Lockhart then moved a direct negative to the effect that Steen should remain on the board and be given a vote of confidence. George Glendinning seconded. Every time Jimmy Hay tried to speak the chairman consistently ruled him out of order. The proceedings were concluded with a vote. A considerable number abstained and the result was: To depose Steen 34; Against 62. The result was met with applause. In September of that year it was announced that Tom Steen had been deposed as an Ayr United director for failing to attend board meetings for several months while failing to state why. However he managed to remain on the board after taking his case to the Court of Session. On 1st February, 1927, Lord Moncrieff pronounced judgement in the case of "Thomas Steen, hotelkeeper, Ayrshire and Galloway Hotel, Ayr, against the Ayr United Football Club Limited and others as directors of the club and as individuals." It was concluded that the pursuer was still a director. The conclusion must be drawn that it must have been awkward sitting at the boardroom table alongside colleagues whom he had taken to court. Within the first week of May he resigned anyway and was voted out of his twenty-year office as treasurer of the Scottish Football Association.

The attempted bribe

Ayr United were due to host St.Mirren in a First Division fixture on 3rd December, 1932. Team captain Andy McCall received a letter with a Manchester postmark. The anonymous writer offered him a £50 cheque if he "could see to it that Ayr United lost." He passed the letter to the Ayr United board then police investigations commenced. The *Ayr Advertiser* had a very candid take on this tawdry episode: "There are rodents associating themselves with football who ought to be exterminated at any cost." On a lighter note Ayr United won 1-0 with a goal from Alex Merrie.

The Russell case

On 9th March, 1935, Ayr United lost 3-2 at home to Falkirk in a result that was potentially fatal in view of the struggle to avoid relegation from the First Division. In light of what happened next the word 'result' is possibly not appropriate. At the time it seemed inconsequential that George Scobbie, rather than Robert Russell, was selected at right-back even although Russell, newly signed from Clyde, had made a debut in a 3-0 home win against St. Johnstone the week before. That victory was described as the best performance of the season. By way of contrasting mood the defeat against Falkirk put the club at the foot of the league three days later because St.Mirren had a 1-0 home win against Airdrie. Sensational news emerged when it was revealed that a joint commission of the Scottish Football Association and Scottish Football League had a meeting scheduled for the Monday evening of 25th March. The purpose of the meeting was to hear the case of the circumstances surrounding Russell's non-appearance against Falkirk. (On the Saturday prior to this there was another sensation when Celtic were beaten 1-0 at Somerset Park. Andy McCall's goal was so late that the final whistle blew while the ball was being retrieved from the net.) At the meeting William Lockhart represented Ayr United and Mr Kirkwood represented Falkirk. In the style of a court room, witnesses were cross examined and the aim was to make the enquiry "as full, fair and exhaustive as possible." The outcome was a statement that the findings would be reported on Wedensday, 3rd April. Again there was an Ayr United win on the Saturday prior. After a 3-2 home win against Dundee the *Ayrshire Post* carried a headline of AYR WIN ROUGHEST GAME IN YEARS (quite an accolade for 1935!). The outcome of the enquiry was as follows:

FOOTBALL SENSATION

Why Russell Did Not Play For Ayr

S.F.A. DECISIONS

That Robert Russell refused to play for Ayr United FC against Falkirk FC on 9th March, 1935, as a result of his visits to Brockville Park on Thursday 7th March and Friday 8th March.

That Robert Russell was improperly paid the sum of £3 by William Orr.

That, although it was not possible to estimate to what extent the result of the match, Ayr United FC v Falkirk FC, on 9th March, 1935, was influenced by the exclusion of R. Russell from the Ayr United team, the latter club were, in fact, prejudiced.

That, in making the said payment, William Orr was acting as the manager for Falkirk FC and that the said payment was made by him in furtherance of the interests of that club.

That, although it has not been proved that Falkirk FC had any knowledge of, or were party to, the payment to the player, they are responsible for the actions of their manager in making said payment.

To couch it in briefer terms Russell had visited the Falkirk ground on each of the two days before the game at Ayr and Orr, the Falkirk manager, had paid him £3 as an inducement not to play in the match. The punishments were a *sine die* ban for Orr and a £10 fine for Russell. Unsurprisingly Russell did not play for Ayr again. The result on 9th March was declared null and void. A replay was ordered for the evening of Wednesday, 10th April. In the event of Falkirk refusing to play, two points were to be deducted from their total. Interest in the replayed match was so high that the crowd was estimated at 10,000. It was just too bad that the receipts, after deduction of expenses, went to the Scottish Football League. Happily, the replayed match ended Ayr United 3 Falkirk 1 with two goals from Jimmy Fleming and one from Fally Rodger. Had the original result stood Ayr United would ultimately have been relegated and St.Mirren would have survived but the reality was the other way round. You have already read details of the Steen versus Hay case. Coincidentally, in the Edwardian era, Jimmy Hay had played in the same Celtic team as William Orr who was a central character in this messy episode in 1935. It is also interesting to reflect on Ayr United's Scottish Cup quarter-final replay at Airdrie in 1924. An Ayr goal was disallowed in the last minute in circumstances so contentious that old fans were still talking about it in the 1970s. Robbed of victory the tie then went to second and third replays on consecutive days at Ibrox, Airdrie eventually winning then going on to lift that year's Scottish Cup. Their manager was the same William Orr.

The *News of The World* story

On 20th March, 1976, Ayr United beat St.Johnstone 2-1 in a Premier League fixture at Muirton Park. This match was the topic of a story in the *News of The World* dated 16th April, 1995. Derek Robertson, the St.Johnstone goalkeeper in 1976, claimed that he had deliberately conceded a goal so that he could collect a £2,000 bribe from a betting syndicate. Coincidentally he had made his St.Johnstone debut in a First Division fixture against Ayr United at Muirton Park. That was on the evening of 26th April, 1967, when he was aged seventeen and his team won 3-0. The allegations surrounding what happened in 1976 seemed flawed. Malky Robertson hit the winner in the last minute and Derek Robertson's claim was that he purposely dived out of the road. He

Fally Rodger when at Northampton Town.

further claimed that a dearth of opportunities had prevented him from letting in a goal at an earlier stage of the match. Even although the winner came so late Ayr United had been expected to win this match anyway. St.Johnstone were hopelessly adrift at the foot of the Premier League. After losing to Ayr they had two wins, two draws and twenty-two defeats out of the twenty-six matches played. At two points for a win they had a miserly points total of six. Their goals conceded column showed '66' which was easily the worst in that division. The point being made is that St.Johnstone were more than capable of losing matches without recourse to match rigging. One less point at the season's end would have relegated Ayr United but we can reflect that the match was won on merit. The *News of The World* story was not taken seriously by anyone in authority.

The *Sunday Mail* story

On 2nd March, 1996, Ayr United had a 5-0 league win at home to Berwick Rangers. The outcome generated plenty of talking points. No Ayr United team had scored as many in a competitive fixture since 21st November, 1992, when Dumbarton were beaten 5-3 at Ayr. Danny Diver got a debut hat-trick against Berwick and it was the club's first hat-trick since Gordon Mair in the Dumbarton fixture just referred to. The first two goals against Berwick were scored by Finnish striker Tommi Paavola. This was another talking point as was Paul Kinnaird's contribution in setting up all five goals. There were talking points aplenty but the biggest one was Kenny Barnstaple going on as a substitute for the last eight minutes. Gregg Hood went off injured and Barnstaple was the only remaining substitute. He was a goalkeeper but got pressed into duty playing on the wing. Great delight was caused by his attempts at mazy runs rather than cautious passing. In the following day's *Sunday Mail* there was a potentially explosive story that threatened to trump all else that was being said about the action. The story indicated that there had been a run of bets in the Edinburgh area for Ayr United to win 5-0. It was generally considered that a betting scam was unlikely. The allegation was ignored.

Yet another alleged betting scam

On 15th May, 2004, the league season concluded with a 1-0 win at home to Raith Rovers. The result did not see an explosion of excessive joy. Having finished in second bottom place the club's fate was straight relegation to the third tier. On 23rd May the *Sunday Mail* carried a story about this match on its front page. It was claimed that £250,000 had been put on an Ayr United win and that the result had triggered payments of up to £500,000 by bookmakers across Europe. The Scottish Football League did consider the story of being worthy of investigation but nothing more was heard on the matter.

Debuts

The highest scoring debut

On 28th March, 1953, Ayr United beat Forfar Athletic 8-1 in a 'B' Division fixture at Somerset Park. A trialist playing under the guise of 'Newman' scored five. Closer enquiry solicited the information that the player was Andy Torrance who was registered with Bridgeton Waverley. He was a nephew of John Rennie, the match secretary of that club. Such predatory largesse made him an obvious candidate for a contract but his feat meant that there were other suitors. Neither Ayr United nor these other clubs could pursue an interest. He had fifteen months of Army service to complete and was stationed in the Shrewsbury area. His Ayr United career thus ended with a ratio of five goals per game.

A hat-trick on a debut

Tom Newall in a 4-1 league win away to Leith Athletic on 22nd February, 1913.

Willie Fleming in a 5-0 league win at home to Arbroath on 22nd August, 1925.

Jimmy Smith in a 4-4 league draw at home to St.Bernard's on 13th August, 1927.

Danny Diver in a 5-0 league win at home to Berwick Rangers on 2nd March, 1996.

Seventeen-year-olds scoring on a competitive debut

Lewis Thow in a 3-0 league win away to Hamilton Accies on 29th January, 1938. He scored two. Born 11th April, 1920. Age 17 years 293 days.

Barry Scott in a 3-1 league win away to Hamilton Accies on 2nd March, 1993. He scored one. Born 27th June, 1975. Age 17 years 248 days.

Gareth Armstrong in a 3-1 League Cup win away to Queen's Park on 1st August, 1998. He scored one. Born 31st August, 1980. Age 17 years 335 days.

Stewart Kean in a 3-1 league defeat away to Livingston on 29th April, 2000. Born 4th March, 1983. Age 17 years 56 days.

Andrew Ferguson in a 4-0 league win at home to Arbroath on 28th December, 2002. He scored one. Born 24th March, 1985. Age 17 years 279 days.

Sixteen-year-old scoring on a competitive debut (see 'Age' section)

The sole entrant in this section is Alan Forrest. He scored one in a 2-1 win away to Queen's Park in a Ramsdens Cup tie on 27th July, 2013. Born 9th September, 1996. Age 16 years 321 days.

Most players making a debut

On 20th August, 1910, eleven players made a competitive debut for the club but you will have correctly surmised that it was Ayr United's initial league match. Port Glasgow Athletic were beaten 2-0 at Ayr and the team, with former clubs bracketed, was: Massey (Partick Thistle), McKenzie (Ayr FC), Black (Parkhouse), Morrison (Ayr FC), Tickle (Parkhouse), McLaughlan (Kilwinning Rangers), Goodwin (Parkhouse), Graham (Ayr FC), Howe (Parkhouse), Phillips (West Ham United) and Campbell (Ayr FC).

Outside of the club's initial engagement the largest number of players to make a debut is seven. This was for a League Cup tie at Berwick on 8th August, 1964. It was a 3-1 defeat. The team, with former clubs of the debut players bracketed, was: Paton, Thomson (Airdrie), Murphy, Nelson (St.Mirren), Monan (Irvine Meadow), MacLeod (Third Lanark), Oliphant (Johnstone Burgh), Billy Kerr (Lochend), Moore, McMillan and Paterson (Irvine Meadow). The significant name in that line-up was that of Ally MacLeod who had an additional role as a coach.

Ayr United FC on 15th August, 1964. Rear (left to right): Dicky Grant, Ally MacLeod, John Murphy, Alastair Paton, Eddie Monan and Drew Nelson. Front (left to right): Billy Muir, Billy Kerr, Bert Whittington, Sam McMillan and Arthur Paterson.

Debut on a birthday

Tom Smith made his debut in a 1-0 league win at home to Livingston on 12th October, 1996, the date of his twenty-third birthday.

Daniel Harvie made his debut in a 3-1 League Cup win at home to Morton on 14th July, 2018, the date of his twentieth birthday.

Defeats

Biggest overall defeat (three-way tie)

16th November, 1929: League: Rangers 9 Ayr United 0.

Team: Hepburn, Robertson, Fleming, Turnbull, Price, McCall, Nisbet, Tolland, Livingstone, Brae and Ferguson.

Rangers: Tom Hamilton, Gray, Robert Hamilton, McDonald, Meiklejohn, Craig, Archibald, Brown, Fleming, Marshall and Morton.

Goals: Fleming 1-0 and 2-0; Marshall 3-0; Fleming 4-0 and 5-0; Archibald 6-0; Brown 7-0; Marshall 8-0; Archibald 9-0.

The Ibrox pitch was frozen but Jimmy Fleming seemed to revel in the awkward conditions and he netted four. As a youth he had played a trial for Ayr United and was not offered terms. He signed for St.Johnstone from whom Rangers captured him. Fleming eventually did sign for Ayr United, and he scored twice on his debut. That was in a 5-4 league defeat away to Dundee on 10th November, 1934.

28th February, 1931: League: Hearts 9 Ayr United 0.

Team: Hepburn, Willis, McBain, Yorke, McLeod, McCall, Ferguson, Tolland, McGillivray, Brae and McLean.

Hearts: Harkness, Anderson, O'Neil, Herd, Johnston, Bennie, Massie, White, Battles, Chalmers and Murray.

Goals: Barney Battles hat-trick; William Chalmers; Willie Murray two; Jock White two; John Johnston.

A letter from Stoke City enquiring about the availability of Billy Brae in May 1929. It is curious that they are willing to pay for a player while asking for clarification about his best position. Brae had been at Ayr since 1923 and his eventual move in 1935 took him to Swindon Town.

Battles had his hat-trick by half-time at which stage it was 4-0. The second half became so farcical that many of the spectators began to lose interest and it was estimated that about half of the crowd had left before the end.

4th December, 1954: League: Third Lanark 9 Ayr United 0.

Team: Round, Govan, Leckie, Gallagher, O'Donnell, Lindsay, Beattie, Traynor, Tracy, Finnie and McKenna.

Third Lanark: Bickerstaff, Balunas, Phillips, Kennedy, Forsyth, Muir, Brolls, Miller, Dick, Armstrong and Barclay.

Goals: Wattie Dick 1-0; Norman Brolls 2-0; Wattie Dick 3-0; Norman Brolls 4-0; Wattie Dick 5-0; Willie Barclay 6-0; Ally Miller 7-0 and 8-0; Wattie Dick 9-0.

Gazing at the result could give the impression that it could not have been worse. It actually could! It was 6-0 at half-time and 7-0 one minute into the second half. Goal nine came with fourteen minutes left therefore the threat of double figures was real. The *Ayrshire Post* report stated: "Ayr United were well and truly beaten but they did not disgrace themselves." It must be assumed that this was a reference to the sportsmanship displayed. Goalkeeper Len Round commented that he was glad he was no longer working in the Stampworks.

Biggest home defeat (two-way tie)

24th September, 1966: League: Ayr United 0 Dundee United 7.

Team: Millar, Malone, Murphy, Thomson, Monan, Mitchell, Grant, McMillan, Ingram, Hawkshaw and Paterson; substitute – Oliphant.

Dundee United: Davie, Millar, Briggs, Munro, Smith, Wing, Persson, Hainey, Dossing, Gillespie and Mitchell; substitute – Neilson.

Goals: Eddie Monan own goal 0-1; Finn Dossing 0-2; Orjan Persson 0-3 and 0-4; Ian Mitchell 0-5 and 0-6; Finn Dossing 0-7.

From personal testimony you may be told that this was a hard game up until the 52nd minute opener when Eddie Monan conceded an own goal. It was 7-0 by the 79th minute. A competitive match degenerating into a one-sided farce was as devastating as it was incomprehensible.

24th April, 2010: League: Ayr United 0 Inverness Caledonian Thistle 7.

Team: Samson, Mitchell, Easton, Gibson, Campbell, McGowan, Connolly (Mendes 66), Keenan (Bowey 78), McManus (Roberts 78), McKay and Lafferty; unused substitutes – Woodburn and Grindlay.

Inverness Caledonian Thistle: Esson, Proctor, Tokely, Munro, McBain (Bulvitis 26), Morrison, Odhiambo (Eagle 71), Duncan, Foran (Sanchez 64), Rooney and Hayes.

Goals: Jonny Hayes 0-1; Adam Rooney 0-2; Richie Foran 0-3; Eric Odhiambo 0-4; Danni Sanchez 0-5; Robert Eagle 0-6; Gavin Morrison 0-7.

There was no incentive whatsoever for Inverness since they had already clinched the First Division title. The home team was in a relegation fight but there was no sign of desperation. Inverness even had the luxury of seven different scorers. Assistant manager Scott MacKenzie said: "I am speechless. I can't believe what I have seen out there." He was not alone. None of us could believe what we had just seen.

Biggest Scottish Cup defeat

8th February, 1947: Second round: Aberdeen 8 Ayr United 0.

Team: Barbour, McNeil, Kelly, Stewart, Smith, Nesbit, McGuigan, Ouchterlonie, Tyson, Wallace and Beattie.

Aberdeen: Johnstone, Cooper, McKenna, McLaughlin, Dunlop, Taylor, Botha, Hamilton, Williams, Harris and McCall.

Ayr United FC on 27th April, 1966. Rear (left to right): Adam Thomson, Charlie Oliphant, Dick Malone, Ian Millar, Eddie Moore and John Murphy. Front (left to right): Davy Paterson, Johnny Grant, John Pullar, Sam McMillan and Arthur Paterson.

Goals: George Hamilton hat-trick; Tony Harris hat-trick; Stan Williams; Ray Botha.

The opening goal happened in the final minute of the first half. This raises the question of why seven goals were conceded in the second half. Ayr centre-forward John Tyson once told the author that the wind rose tremendously in Aberdeen's favour in that period. He said that it was an effort to stand up against it far less play football in it. Aberdeen went on to lift the Scottish Cup that year.

Biggest League Cup defeat

10th **August, 1993:** Second round: Ayr United 0 Motherwell 6.

Team: Duncan, Burley, Robertson, Shotton, Traynor, George (Kennedy 26), Walker, Bryce, McGivern, McNab and Scott; unused substitutes – Burns and Grierson.

Motherwell: Dykstra, Shannon, McKinnon, Krivokapic, Martin, McCart, Ferguson, Angus, Arnott, O'Donnell and McGrillen; substitutes – Dolan, Graham and Thomson.

Goals: Paul McGrillen 0-1; Dougie Arnott 0-2 and 0-3; Paul McGrillen 0-4; Ally Graham 0-5; Iain Ferguson 0-6.

Malky Shotton was harshly sent off for supposedly fouling Dougie Arnott but by that stage the team was four down with twenty minutes to go. Goals conceded in 88 and 89 minutes emphasised just how bad a night it was. Ally Graham, our former striker, hit number five.

Fortress Somerset assailed

Over the course of seasons 2012/13, 2013/14 and 2014/15, Ayr United lost twenty-three league matches at home. Compounding the severity of the statistic is the fact that these seasons were all spent in the third tier. The breakdown was seven, seven, then nine respectively. Excluded from this statistic is the play-off defeat at home to Cowdenbeath on 7th May, 2014, and the Peterhead defeat on 15th November, 2014, since that match was later declared void.

Consecutive defeats

The club's worst run of defeats is eleven, dating from 17th December, 1966, until 11th February, 1967. These games comprised ten in the league in addition to a Scottish Cup tie.

Happy (?) New Year

The club's worst run of defeats at the start of a year is eight. That happened when Ayr United lost the first games of 1929, 1930, 1931, 1932, 1933, 1934, 1935 and 1936. The next worst run of defeats in a new year is six. These defeats were at the start of 2012, 2013, 2014, 2015, 2016 and 2017.

Up to and including 2019 the club has started a calendar year with a defeat of four goals or more on eleven occasions. 2013 and 2014 is the only instance of it happening in consecutive years. Ten of those were away from home, the exception being Ayr United 1 Queen of the South 5 on 2nd January, 2013. The record defeat at the start of a year remains Queen of the South 7 Ayr United 1 on New Year's Day 1935.

Biggest second half fadeouts

14th December, 1946: League: Ayr United 2 Dundee 6: Ayr took a 2-0 lead in 54 minutes. The Dundee goal times were 67, 68, 78, 82, 87 and 89.

8th February, 1947: Scottish Cup: Aberdeen 8 Ayr United 0: The only goal before the interval was scored in the final minute of the first half.

9th April, 1949: League (half time score in brackets): Cowdenbeath (1) 9 Ayr United (2) 2.

2nd January, 1964: League: Alloa Athletic 5 Ayr United 1: Alloa Athletic equalised in the 74th minute.

24th September, 1966: League: Ayr United 0 Dundee United 7: The goal times were 52, 53, 60, 64, 69, 71 and 79.

Ally Graham

Malky Shotton

16th September 1978: League: Ayr United 2 Dumbarton 5: Ayr took a 2-0 lead in 48 minutes. Dumbarton's goal times were 51, 52, 65, 71 and 76.

5th September, 1979: League (half time score in brackets): Airdrie 6 (1) Ayr United (2) 2: Airdrie's second half goal times were 55, 59, 72, 80 and 89.

27th January, 2001: Scottish Cup: Inverness Caledonian Thistle 4 Ayr United 3: This entry is merited not for the volume of goals lost but the fact that it remains the only competitive match which an Ayr United team has lost after achieving a three-goal lead. That 3-0 lead was held at half time.

11th February, 2018: Scottish Cup: Ayr United 1 Rangers 6. It was 1-1 at half-time. The second half goal times were 66, 69, 72, 81 and 88.

Discipline (Loss of!)

The largest number of Ayr United players sent off in one match is three. This happened during a 2-1 league defeat at Stranraer on 27th August, 1994. First off was Cameron Connie. In the 77th minute, with the score at 1-1, he tripped Darren Henderson from behind. This was a yellow card offence but it was his second yellow. Next off was goalkeeper Cammy Duncan. He brought down Billy Ferguson outside the penalty area and this was his second yellow card having handled the ball outside the box earlier in the second half. Five minutes remained and before the resultant penalty was taken trouble broke between Ayr's Tom Woods and Stranraer's Graham Duncan. Referee Jim O'Hare sent them both off. The contest was now ten versus eight. After much delay former Ayr United player Jim Hughes beat substitute goalkeeper Stuart McIntosh from the spot

The club had a player sent off in each of the first three league fixtures in 1999/00.

- In the league opener on 7th August a 1-1 draw was contested away to St.Mirren. With the game in the 62nd minute Hugh Murray brought down Barry Prenderville with a tackle from behind. Prenderville got up and pushed Murray at the cost of a red card. Murray was shown a yellow card.
- On 14th August we had a 2-1 defeat at home to Livingston. In the 31st minute Glynn Hurst was sent off for the first time in his professional career. It happened after a linesman brought an incident to the referee's attention. Hurst's explanation was: "Allan (McManus) fell on top of me and I pushed him away with my feet. That is all that happened. I am not an aggressive player and I think he was as gobsmacked as me when the referee sent me off."

Barry Prenderville

Jim Hughes.

On 21st August a 2-1 defeat was suffered at Falkirk. In the 25th minute Dave Rogers caught Scott Crabbe with a late tackle. A yellow card was expected but referee Jim Herald displayed a red card. Manager Gordon Dalziel and his assistant Iain Munro both got spoken to for being unable to contain their disgust at the sending-off.

The club worst for consecutive games with a sending-off is four (all league). These games spanned September and October 2004.

On 11th September the visit of Forfar Athletic resulted in a 3-3 draw. In the 13th minute goalkeeper Ludovic Roy was the victim of a bad challenge from Alan Rattray. The normally mild mannered Roy responded by headbutting his opponent. Rattray then got stretchered off after four minutes of treatment. It was wrongly assumed that referee Michael McCurry would restart the match with a free-kick to Ayr United. He gave a penalty to Forfar which substitute goalkeeper John Hillcoat saved. Roy returned to the team after a one-match ban only to be hit with a further six-match ban after being recalled to a hearing.

On 18th September a 0-0 draw at Arbroath was spoiled by a strong wind. Ayr United fans of longstanding will tell you that this is not an isolated occurrence at a ground that juts out into the North Sea. The game further deteriorated as a spectacle with five minutes remaining. Willie Lyle was shown a yellow card for bodychecking Paul Farquharson. It being a second yellow a red card was immediately produced.

On 25th September Brechin City had a 1-0 win at Ayr. In the 72nd minute Stewart Kean contested a loose ball with visiting goalkeeper Craig Nelson. To everyone except referee Chris Boyle it was a fair challenge. Kean got shown a yellow card, his second of the match. On the way off he got a further yellow card for lifting his shirt even although he did not remove it. In stoppage time Brechin's Kevin McLeish got sent off after being on the field for fifteen seconds. A visit from Peterhead on 9th February, 2008, saw the same referee award two nonsensical penalties and a red card to Eddie Forrest, all in the closing minutes. These incidents were so contentious that the stewards had to hold back enraged fans.

In the 66th minute of a 1-1 draw away to Stirling Albion, Jamie Doyle was sent off for a lunging challenge on Scott McLean. The decision was beyond dispute. Four minutes afterwards Robert Burgess was stretchered off with a knee injury by which time the quota of substitutes had been exhausted. Burgess returned but was clearly unfit. With nine fit players and a passenger the Ayr equaliser came in the 79th minute, the scorer being Andrew Ferguson.

The club record for the quickest yellow card lies with Garry Paterson. For 'yellow card' you may also read 'booking'. In bygone days the name of the errant player went into the referee's black book but the concept of yellow and red cards brought greater clarity. To both the player and the spectators it became extremely clear that an offence had been committed. On the night of 4th October, 1994, Ayr United lost 2-0 to Airdrie in a B & Q Cup quarter-final played at Broadwood Stadium, Cumbernauld. Paterson's offence was a wayward tackle on Tommy McIntyre. The game had been in progress for nine seconds. In the 22nd minute John Sharples was sent off for a high challenge on Sandy Stewart. There was a popular view that the Paterson tackle was worse.

There is ample historical precedent for three players being sent off in an Ayr United match. In this context we are talking about three including the opposition. However the distinguishing factor relating to 17th July, 2010, is that the match was a friendly (in name only!). It was against Annan Athletic at Galabank. Despite the ground name there was nothing approaching a gala atmosphere. In the 21st minute Ayr's William Easton got sent off for some ill-chosen words to referee John Beaton. When the teams were making their way in at half-time some hostile exchanges culminated in Dean Keenan and Annan Athletic's David Cox getting a red card each for fighting. This rendered the second half ten versus nine. The match was lost 4-0. An Ayr United trialist on that afternoon was Fabio Ferreira who had been transferred from Sporting Lisbon to Chelsea in 2005. He failed to impress at Annan.

There are two instances of opposition teams finishing with eight men when Ayr United have finished with a full complement.

Ludovic Roy

Left to right: Joe Love, Ross Scott and Davy Wells.

On the evening of 10th May, 1988, a crowd of 3,828 attended Rugby Park to see Ayr United win 2-0 to lift the Ayrshire Cup. Ross Scott scored after fifteen minutes and by the time the match reached the final twenty minutes the nets had not been further tested. Then came a run of sendings-off for the home team. Ian Bryson got dismissed first for a rash tackle on Stevie McIntyre. Stuart McLean was next to go for something he said then Louis Thow sent off Colin Harkness for a lunge on Willie Furphy. The numerically advantaged Ayr team then proceeded to stroke the ball from man to man and Tommy Walker scored six minutes from the end.

On 5th December, 1992, St.Mirren visited for a league fixture. In the final minute of the first half we took the lead. The scorer was Ally Graham, who netted with a header from a George Burley free-kick. As the game entered the closing stages it remained 1-0 to the delight of the home fans in the 2,516 crowd. Then came an explosive spell. In the 82nd minute Joe Timmons sent off Paul Lambert for a bad challenge on Gordon Mair. The challenge was so bad that the shinpad was split in two. Two minutes later Barry Lavety made the walk of shame after elbowing Gordon Mair. When two more minutes elapsed it became 2-0 when Tommy Walker rifled the ball home after his initial shot had been blocked on the line by full-back Stuart Taylor. The drama reached a climax in the final minute of regulation time at which point St.Mirren went down to eight after Jim 'Chic' Charnley spat at Duncan George.

In season 1987/88 Ayr United had one red card in comparison to ten for our opponents. The opposing players dismissed were Joe Carson (Stranraer), Neil Forbes (Montrose), Graeme Elder (Queen's Park), Derek Edgar (Albion Rovers), Mike McCabe (Stranraer), Garry Wilson (Stranraer), John Holt (Dunfermline Athletic), Ross Jack (Dunfermline Athletic), Gary Murray (East Stirling) and John Ward (East Stirling). The solitary Ayr United red card was brandished to Jim McCann. These incidents occurred between the league and the Scottish Cup.

On 17th November, 1928, Ayr United's Willie Robertson and Kilmarnock's Willie Connell were sent off in a First Division fixture at Ayr. Robertson was punished with a severe censure and a £3 fine. Here is the actual report as typed up by referee Tom Dougray on the Monday.

COPY OF LETTER FROM MR. T. DOUGRAY.

139, Calder Road,
Mossend,
Bellshill.

19/11/28

Dear Sir,

AYR UNITED V KILMARNOCK.

In connection with above game I herewith report two players whom I had occasion to order off the field for fighting, namely, William Robertson and William Connell, of Ayr United and Kilmarnock F.C. respectively. The incident happened thus:- During first half and nearing half-time, when Kilmarnock were attacking, the ball was crossing the goal line and was being sheperded over by the Ayr player when the Kilmarnock player dashed in, with I presume, the hope of gaining possession. Both players came in contact and fell. On rising to their feet an altercation took place between them, and blows were exchanged. I had no alternative but ask them to leave the field, which they did without demur. I had no occasion previously to foul or caution either player regarding their play and their outburst of temper was quite unjustifiable. This is a description of the incident and my report in full. Leaving the matter in the hands of your Committee, when I trust my action in putting them off will be endorsed by their decision.

Yours faithfully,
(sgd.) T. Dougray.

Referee's report from 1928

Ross Scott.

Jim McCann.

Draws

Longest run without a draw

The club record for consecutive league games without a draw is twenty-six. These games were played between 31st August, 1946, and 20th September, 1947. However that sequence was broken when all competitive matches are taken into account. Including all competitive matches the record drawless sequence is also twenty-six. These matches were played between 14th November, 2015, and 7th May, 2016. They comprised twenty-three league matches, one Scottish Cup tie and two play-off matches.

Consecutive draws

The club record for consecutive league draws is five. These games were played between 18th November, 1922, and 16th December, 1922.

Drawless run

In season 1957/58 Ayr United did not draw in either of the first twenty league matches. The club's first league draw of the season was at Stranraer on 1st January, 1958.

Cup ties extending to four games

The following cup ties required three replays in addition to the initial tie:
September 1912: Scottish Qualifying Cup versus Galston.
March 1924: Scottish Cup versus Airdrie.
February 1935: Scottish Cup versus King's Park.

Three times 3-3

In 2005/06 Ayr United had three consecutive away 3-3 draws (all league). They were against Raith Rovers (17th September), Stirling Albion (1st October) and Peterhead (8th October).

Highest scoring draw (thirteen-way tie)

On 13th September, 1950, the Norrie McNeil testimonial resulted in a 5-5 draw against Hibs but this does not fall within the definition of a competitive match.

14th September, 1910: Ayrshire League: Ayr United 4 Kilmarnock 4.

Team: Massey, McKenzie, Shearer, Morrison, Fraser, Black, J.L. Goodwin, Graham, Howe, Muir and Campbell.

Goals: Archie Campbell 1-0; Charlie Howe 2-0; Howie 2-1 and 2-2; Chalmers 2-3; Jacky Goodwin 3-3; Howie 3-4; Muir 4-4.

The Ayrshire League was viewed with apathy by the fans and the clubs. This match was played on a Wednesday morning with a kick-off time of 10.45 am. It was the forenoon of Ayr Races. The goal action fell almost exclusively in the first half. It was 4-3 to Kilmarnock at half-time. The only goal of the second half came shortly after the resumption. Archie Campbell got injured shortly before half-time so the home team played the second half with ten men.

26th October, 1918: First Division: Falkirk 4 Ayr United 4.

Team: "Ballantyne", Semple, McCloy, Hogg, Gillespie, McLaughlan, Devine, "Thomson", Agnew, McBain and Middleton.

Falkirk: Hickie, Laird, McLeod, Scott, Comrie, McCulloch, Harvie, Croall, Main, Martin and Simpson.

Goals: Jocky Simpson 1-0; Willie Agnew 1-1; John Harvie 2-1; "Thomson" 2-2; Billy Middleton 2-3; "Thomson" 2-4; Davie Main 3-4 and 4-4.

The punctuation indicates that the goalkeeper and the scorer of two goals both had their identities concealed. This was common practice during the Great War. It was a form of censorship in order not to reveal a clue as to where the individual was based. It was 4-2 to Ayr United at half-time. Although Davie Main scored two second half goals to get Falkirk a draw, he must have been frustrated at the close of play. With the score at 4-4 he contrived to miss an open goal.

13th August, 1927: Second Division: Ayr United 4 St.Bernard's 4.

Team: Hepburn, Woodburn, Dean, Robertson, Fleming, Melville, Nisbet, Tolland, Smith, McCosh and Walters.

St.Bernard's: Boyne, Swanson, Mitchell, Raeburn, McKnight, Brown, Dickson, Duke, Drummond, McCaig and Walker.

Goals: Dickson 0-1; Duke 0-2; Jimmy Smith 1-2; Jim Nisbet 2-2; Jimmy Smith 3-2; Duke 3-3; Jimmy Smith 4-3; McCaig 4-4.

This was the opening league game of the season and there was nearly an early breakthrough when Danny Tolland hit the crossbar. There was a dramatic turnaround. St.Bernard's went 2-0 up then got awarded a penalty which was struck far too high. Jimmy Smith narrowed the deficit before half-time. Jim Nisbet levelled it at 2-2 and Jimmy Smith looked to have settled matters when the home team took the lead for the first time. The lead lasted for a minute. Smith re-established the lead only for it to be levelled again. A debut hat-trick for Smith marked a fine individual performance.

18th February, 1935: Scottish Cup second round, second replay: Ayr United 4 King's Park 4 after extra time.

Team: Hepburn, Scobbie, Ure, Taylor, Currie, McCall, McGibbons, Brae, Fleming, Fitzgerald and Rodger.

King's Park: Milton, Temple, Soutar, Fowler, Baird, Hillan, Andrew, Young, Bryce, Laird and Lang.

Goals: Lang 0-1; Young 0-2; William Ure (penalty) 1-2; Terry McGibbons 2-2; Lang 2-3; Leslie Fitzgerald 3-3; Terry McGibbons 4-3; Fowler 4-4.

After a 1-1 draw at Ayr a 2-2 draw was fought out at Stirling after extra time. This second replay took place at neutral Firhill on a Monday afternoon. It was 3-3 after ninety minutes. When Terry McGibbons made it 4-3 ten minutes into extra time the lead lasted only for one minute. On the following afternoon King's Park won 2-1 in the third replay at Hampden despite missing two penalties when it was 1-0 to Ayr. Ayr United had never won a Scottish Cup replay to this point of history.

11th May, 1940: Regional League: Ayr United 4 Dumbarton 4.

Team: Hall, Craik, Dyer, Cox, Dykes, Johnson, Clark, Hamilton, Rodger, Marshall and Thow.

Dumbarton: Hill, Soutar, McLean, Mather, Wilson, Browning, Speedie, Dunn, Stewart, Shields and Collins.

Goals: Shields 0-1; Fally Rodger 1-1; Jacky Clark 2-1; Shields 2-2; Fally Rodger 3-2 and 4-2; Stewart 4-3 and 4-4.

Ayr United legend Jimmy Smith was back at Somerset Park as the manager of Dumbarton. This was the season's final Regional League fixture and the completed table showed Ayr United to be second bottom of the sixteen-club league. That day's opponents Dumbarton had the wooden spoon. Fally Rodger was the star performer with a hat-trick. These were extraordinary times with the war situation getting increasingly worrying. Team selection was consistently hampered by players being conscripted.

1st January, 1948: 'B' Division: Kilmarnock 4 Ayr United 4.

Team: Fraser, Rowe, Hunter, Elliott, McNeil, Nesbit, McGuigan, Ramsay, Morrison, Wallace and Beattie.

Kilmarnock: Lamont, Mennie, Hood, Turnbull, Thyne, Maxwell, Pattison, Cavin, Collins, McLaren and Drury.

Goals: Malky Morrison 0-1; Alec Beattie 0-2; Jimmy Drury 1-2; Kenny Pattison 2-2; Frank Mennie 3-2; Allan Collins 4-2; Norrie McNeil (penalty) 4-3; Tommy McGuigan 4-4.

2-0 up then 4-2 down and it took a last minute equaliser to get a draw. At 4-2 an Ayr penalty was squandered. Alec Beattie was fouled then Andy Nesbit had his spot attempt saved. Norrie McNeil later atoned by converting a penalty after a Bob Thyne handling offence. Kilmarnock full-back Frank Mennie's goal was scored from his own half.

10th January, 1948: 'B' Division: Alloa Athletic 4 Ayr United 4.

Team: Fraser, Hunter, Kelly, Elliot, McNeil, Nesbit, McGuigan, Ramsay, Morrison, Wallace and Elliott.

Alloa Athletic: McQueen, Lamb, Frew, Rowan, Laird, Dempster, Hart, Gordon, Jordan, Mackie and O'Sullivan.

Goals: Lewis Gordon 1-0; Malky Morrison 1-1; Jock Wallace 1-2; Jim Rowan 2-2; Tommy Ramsay 2-3; Martin Dempster 3-3; Malky Morrison 3-4: Lewis Gordon 4-4.

In comparative terms there has been a scarcity of 4-4 draws in Ayr United's history but in early January 1948 it happened in consecutive away games. On the Saturday between there was a 3-3 draw with East Fife therefore after the third match of 1948 the tally was played three, drawn three, goals for eleven, goals against eleven. Just before half-time at Alloa, Malky Morrison "dropped like a log" after heading the heavy ball. He carried on then collapsed again in the dressing room at the break. He was revived just in time for the restart.

19th April, 1957: First Division: Ayr United 4 Queen's Park 4.

Team: Travers, Bell, Thomson, Strickland, Brice, Whittle, McIntyre, Paton, Price, McMillan and Beattie.

Queen's Park: F. Crampsey, I. Harnett, W. Hastie, R. Cromar, D. McLean, A. Glen, G. Herd, W. Omand, A. McEwan, J. Devine and T. Heron.

Goals: Bert Cromar 0-1; Willie Omand 0-2; Tommy Heron 0-3; Sam McMillan 1-3; John Devine 1-4; Peter Price 2-4; Bobby Thomson (penalty) 3-4; Peter Price 4-4.

This game was played on the Friday evening in order not to clash with the Scottish Cup final between Falkirk and Kilmarnock on the Saturday. It was 4-1 to Queen's Park at half-time. When Peter Price made it 4-4 there was a quarter of an hour left. Both clubs were promoted in 1956. By now Ayr United were doomed to relegation as the bottom club. The scramble continued to avoid the second bottom position that would also ensure relegation. It transpired that Dunfermline Athletic were on the point of going down too.

27th December, 1958: Second Division: Ayr United 4 Stranraer 4.

Team: Hamilton, Paterson, Telfer, Willie McIntyre, McLean, Glen, Alastair McIntyre, Paton, Price, McMillan and McGhee.

Stranraer: Travers, Mason, McLean, King, Simpson, McKnight, Small, McKechnie, Imrie, Moore and Egan.

Goals: Alastair McIntyre 1-0; Adam Imrie 1-1; John Egan 1-2; Willie McIntyre (penalty) 2-2; Adam Imrie 2-3; Peter Price 3-3; Willie McIntyre (penalty) 4-3; Adam Imrie 4-4.

The Stranraer goalkeeper was Willie Travers who had been released by Ayr United at the end of the previous season and their centre-half Bobby Simpson was on loan from Ayr. Willie McIntyre's last minute penalty looked to have won the match but Adam Imrie completed his hat-trick when he equalised in the little time that was left.

2nd September, 1961: League Cup sectional tie: Falkirk 4 Ayr United 4.

Team: Gallacher, Frew, George McIntyre, Willie McIntyre, McLean, Curlett, Alastair McIntyre, McMillan, Price, Fulton and McGhee.

Falkirk: Whigham, Rae, Hunter, Murray, Milne, Pierson, Wyles, Reid, Oliver, Tulloch and Ormond.

Goals: Jim Pierson 1-0; Willie Wyles 2-0; Billy Fulton 2-1; George Tulloch 3-1; Jim McGhee 3-2; Willie Ormond 4-2; Ian Rae own goal 4-3; Jim McGhee 4-4.

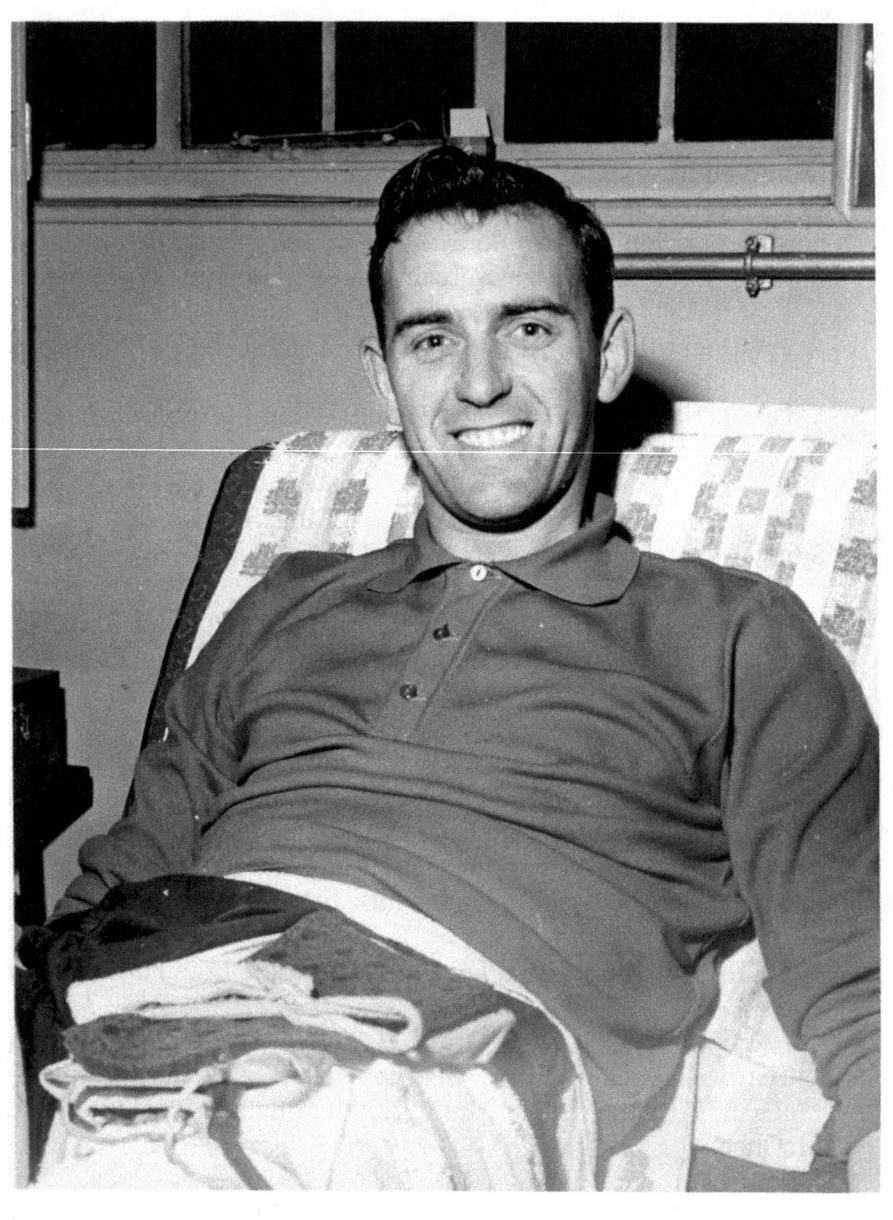

Dave Curlett on the treatment table. Within a year he played in two 4-4 draws.

2nd September, 1961. Programme cover for a 4-4 draw at Falkirk.

The picture looked bleak with twenty minutes to go. At that point Falkirk had a 4-2 lead and the ball was on the penalty spot with the likelihood of it reaching a surely uncatchable 5-2. John Gallacher succeeded in saving the penalty but Jimmy Murray, the taker, latched onto the rebound whereupon he struck the post to create a mad rush in which the ball got thumped out for a corner-kick. Two goals in a minute (75 and 76) brought the draw which won the section for Ayr United. Leg one of the quarter-final resulted in a 4-2 win at home to Stirling Albion. The second leg was lost 3-0 after extra time.

18th August, 1962: League Cup sectional tie: Hamilton Accies 4 Ayr United 4.

Team: Gallacher, Burn, George McIntyre, Willie McIntyre, Frew, Curlett, McCubbin, Kilgannon, Herron, McMillan and Hubbard.

Hamilton Accies: Tait, Japp, McQueen, Strickland, McKechnie, Stewart, Hutton, King, Forsyth, Fearns and Hastings.

Goals: Johnny Kilgannon 0-1; Billy Forsyth 1-1; Bert McCubbin 1-2; Des Herron 1-3; Billy Forsyth 2-3; Sam McMillan 2-4; Billy Forsyth 3-4 and 4-4.

In their previous match Hamilton Accies had drawn 4-4 at home to East Stirling, also in a League Cup sectional tie. The result being replicated was attributable to Billy Forsyth hitting four for the Accies. Two of his goals were in the last five minutes, the last one being right at the end.

8th December, 1984: First Division: Ayr United 4 Clydebank 4.

Team: Sproat, McIntyre, Buchanan, Morris, Irons, Collins, Murphy, McNiven, Grant, Shanks and Anderson; substitutes – Evans and Adams.

Clydebank: Gallagher, Dickson, Given, Fallon, McGhie, Treanor, Shanks, Hughes, Larnach, Conroy and McCabe; substitutes – Ronald and Bain.

Eric Morris

Gerry Collins

Goals: Mike Larnach 0-1; Jimmy Murphy 1-1; Mike Larnach 1-2; Gerry McCabe 1-3; Jim Given 1-4; Gerry Collins 2-4; Eric Morris 3-4; Davy Irons 4-4.

Tenth place out of fourteen in the second tier may not have been particularly illustrious but Somerset Park was deserving of a better attendance than 852. Clydebank, in second place, were a point behind leaders Airdrie both before and after the match. 4-1 down at half-time! Yet manager George Caldwell was rightly more concerned with the first half defensive blunders rather than the second half comeback.

24th December, 2016: Championship: Ayr United 4 Dumbarton 4.

Team: Fleming, Rose, Meggatt, Crawford, Nisbet (Boyle 25), Harkins, Cairney, O'Connell (Forrest 66), Docherty, Balatoni and McKenna; unused substitutes – Gilmour, Murphy, McGuffie, Donald and Hart.

Dumbarton: Martin, Joe Thomson, Buchanan, Barr, Docherty, Robert Thomson, Smith, Harvie, Stirling, Todd (Stevenson 81) and Fleming; unused substitutes – Pettigrew, McCallum, Wright, Crawford and Brown.

Goals: Scott McKenna 1-0; Gary Harkins 2-0; Robert Thomson 2-1; Daniel Harvie 2-2; Alan Forrest (penalty) 3-2; Joe Thomson 3-3; Paul Cairney 4-3; Ryan Stevenson 4-4.

The wind made for extremely difficult conditions. In the second half there was a sense of panic whenever Dumbarton got corner-kicks. The swirling wind made them very dangerous. With six minutes left Joe Thomson score directly from a corner-kick to get his team back in the match at 3-3. Paul Cairney re-established the lead within a minute then, with two minutes to go, Thomson came close to scoring directly from a corner-kick again. However he left Ryan Stevenson the simple task of scoring with a header from point blank range. After being 3-2 then 4-3 up against ten men it was a dispiriting finale.

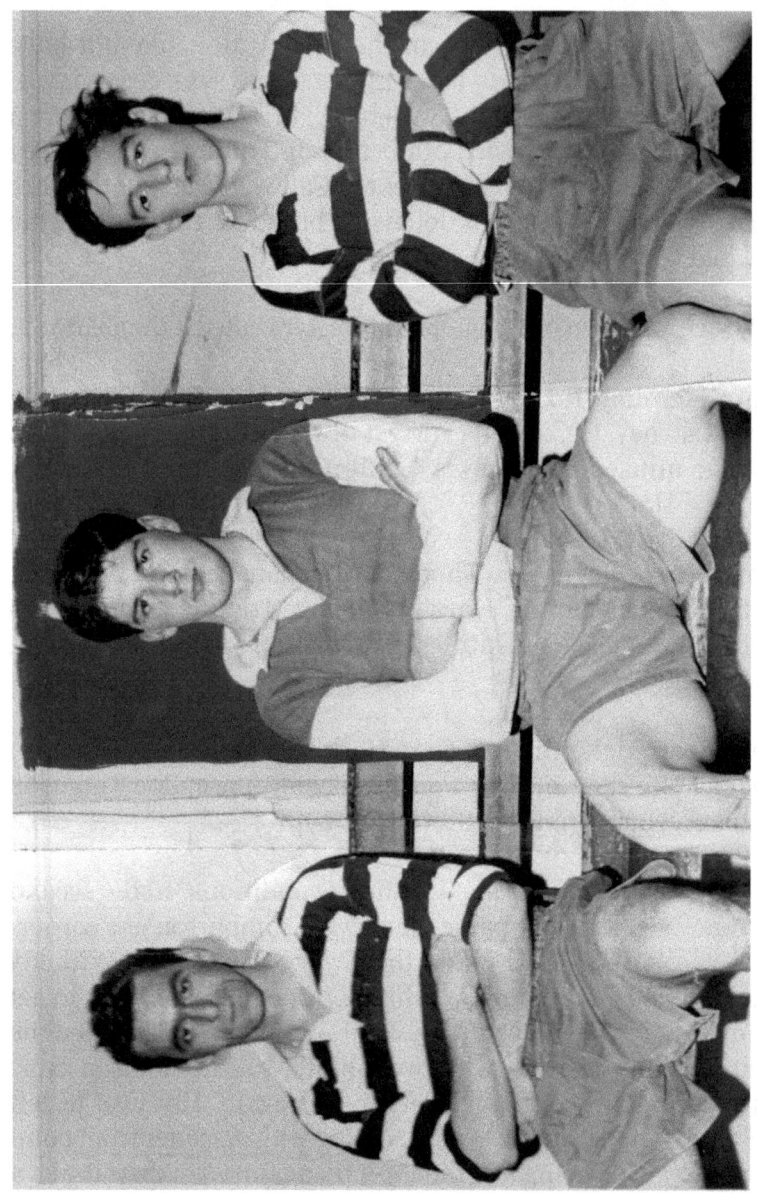

Left to right: Willie Bradley, Ian Hamilton and Ramsay Burn.

Des Herron

John McNiven.

Norrie Anderson – he played in the epic 4-4 draw at home to Clydebank on 8th December, 1984.

18th February, 1976: A Scottish Cup fourth round replay was sitting at Queen of the South 4 Ayr United 4 after ninety minutes. This is excluded from the list of 4-4 draws because the tie had not reached a conclusion. It was 5-4 for Queen of the South after extra time.

John Milton – a full-back signed from Crosshill Thistle in the summer of 1962. One year later he was one of the three Ayr players who moved to Hartlepool United (the others were Bert McCubbin and Willie Bradley). After one season there he rejoined Ayr United.

The programme cover for the marathon Scottish Cup replay at Palmerston Park on 18th February, 1976.

Family connections

The first occasion of two brothers playing in the same Ayr United team occurred on 13th February, 1915. They were Jacky and Hilly Goodwin (Alex Hill Goodwin). It was a First Division fixture with a result reading Rangers 1 Ayr United 3. Jacky scored against his former club in this match. He had played in Ayr United's first ever competitive game and he was transferred to Rangers in time to make a debut at reserve level on 26th November, 1910. His transfer back took place in time for the start of season 1914/15.

In season 1916/17 Willie Cringan and his younger brother Robert played in the same Ayr United team.

In August 1919 cousins Johnny Crosbie and Billy Crosbie appeared in the same Ayr United team for the first time. A further cousin of theirs, Jim Nisbet, made his debut for the club in October 1926. Johnny Crosbie and Jim Nisbet both played for Scotland while still connected to Ayr United. All three were natives of Glenbuck.

In 1929 Jim Nisbet's next door neighbour in Glenbuck played in both of Ayr United's pre-season trial matches. The player was inside-forward Bob Shankly whose older brother Alex, an outside-left, had signed for the club from Glenbuck Cherrypickers, his Ayr debut being on 9th December, 1916, at Celtic Park. Alex remained until the end of 1917/18. In time younger brother Bill, the King of the Kop, would become the more illustrious of the Shankly siblings. Bob Shankly and Ayr United did not agree terms and his first senior club became Alloa Athletic. He became legendary as the manager who won the league title with Dundee in 1961/62 then took them to the semi-finals of the European Cup in 1962/63. On the next page is the letter he wrote agreeing to appear on trial for Ayr United. Pedantically it may be pointed out that it was not written at his home address.

Blue Tower.
Douglas.
Lanarkshire,
15 July. 1929

Dear Sir,

In reply to your letter received on the 12th inst. it is with ready acceptance that I avail myself of the opportunity to play in one of your trail games.

Regarding the most suitable date I think the 27th July will be the most convenient date but I have no doubt I could make the other date available too. The only condition attached to it is that I get compensated for any time lost at work.

I shall be glad to hear from you before that date so there can be no misunderstanding —

Agreed to compensate for loss of work and he requires to be here at 1.30 on 27/7/29. AB/

Yours Truly
Robt Shankly

Letter from Bob Shankly

George McIntyre – he appeared in the same Ayr United team as the brothers Willie and Alastair McIntyre but was not related.

Jock Newall was signed from Burnfoothill Primrose in the summer of 1936. In December 1912 his father Tom signed for the club from Annbank.

In May 1939 Jock Whiteford was signed from Rutherglen Glencairn who had recently won the Scottish Junior Cup. Derek Whiteford, his nephew, signed for Ayr United in July 1980. He played at reserve level only and became a coach at the club.

Alec Beattie was an Ayr United player from 1946 until his death in 1957. His grandson, Stephen McCloy, played in the Ayr United team that lost to Hibs in the final of the BP Youth Cup in 1992. Stephen's father was Peter McCloy, a former Rangers and Scotland goalkeeper who, in the summer of 1991, became a goalkeeping coach at Ayr United. Peter McCloy's uncle, Henry McCloy, was a goalkeeper who signed for Ayr United in the summer of 1937. In August of that year he made his one and only first team appearance for the club.

After signing from Irvine Meadow, Alastair McIntyre made his Ayr United debut on 23rd March, 1957. In November of that year his brother Willie was acquired from Port Glasgow Juniors. On 7th December, 1957, the two brothers were in the same Ayr team for the first time.

Alex McAnespie signed for Ayr United in the summer of 1964 and remained at the club until the end of season 1977/78. His son-in-law, Darren Henderson, had two spells at the club. In February 1996 he was acquired from Stranraer and scored on his debut. He remained until the summer of 1998 when he signed for Hamilton Accies. In May 2004 he rejoined Ayr United and left at the end of season 2004/05.

Stan Quinn was signed from Shettleston Juniors in the summer of 1966 and remained for seven years. He was an uncle of John Kerr who was the club physio from 1995 until 2006.

After signing from Maybole Juniors, Bert Ferguson broke into the first team in November, 1973. He was the brother of Jacky Ferguson who had been an Ayr United player from 1968 until 1971.

In August 1979 Ian Cashmore was signed from Blacklands Boys' Club. After being loaned to Berwick Rangers he broke his neck in a training accident at Somerset Park. The onset of paralysis meant that he was confined to a wheelchair for life. He died on 28th April, 2014, at the age of fifty-three. His nephew, John Bradford, became an Ayr United player in 1996/97 as did Ian Cashmore junior in the summer of 2005. All three were strikers.

Ally MacLeod's son Andrew was the club physio between September 1992 and close season 1993, then again from close season 1994 until close season 1995.

Jock McStay was signed from East Fife in October 1996. His father's uncle, Willie McStay, was an Ayr United player while on loan from Celtic between November 1912 and the end of 1915/16.

James Latta, released by the club in the summer of 2004, was the son of Brian Latta who was released in the summer of 1977.

Mark Campbell was signed from Stranraer and was an Ayr United player between 1999 and 2004. He was the brother of Martyn Campbell who played for the club from 2005 until 2014.

After signing from Stranraer, John Robertson was an Ayr United player between 1997 and 2000 then again in season 2001/02 and yet again from 2011 until 2013. His brother Chris signed for the club in the 2005 close season and remained until the end of season 2007/08.

Scott Agnew signed for Ayr United in May 2008. His brother Steven was a former Ayr United player who signed for the club in February 1995.

David Winters signed for Ayr United in the summer of 2012. His brother Robbie played one game for the club (league) in August 2009.

Jock Mays played for Ayr United between October 1936 and September 1939. His brother Gerry was the club manager from December 1961 until December 1962.

Derek Whiteford

Alex McAnespie.

Farmers

The following players have worked as farmers while attached to Ayr United.

Jock Smith (1919 – 1926).
Tommy Steel (1995 – 1996).
Stuart Boyd (2005 – 2006).
Jamie Adams (2015 –).

Mark Campbell

Ian Cashmore senior.

Film

Cinema and TV

In 2004 your writer paid £12 to the National Library of Scotland for six and a half minutes of video footage. This particular footage comprised the earliest known film of an Ayr United game. It was necessary to sign a sternly worded statement to the effect that it would not be shown in public. Being in VHS format it is not now possible to show it anywhere! The footage was captured by Green's Cinema and it was for a Scottish Cup third round second replay against Motherwell at neutral Celtic Park on the Wednesday afternoon of 2nd March, 1921, the clubs having already played 1-1 draws at Ayr then at Motherwell. The footage showing Motherwell emerging from the pavilion was very clear. Equally clear was the footage of Neil McBain leading out the Ayr United team. The match action was sadly obscure by comparison. Motherwell won 3-1 but the only goal captured by the Green's cameraman was the Ayr one. It was an equaliser from Donald Slade from a Johnny Crosbie cross five minutes after half-time. Motherwell had taken the lead just a minute earlier.

Green's Cinema sent their man to Somerset Park on 22nd September, 1923. On this day Celtic were beaten 4-2 in a First Division fixture. The camera was located in front of the Stand. Later that season the Green's Cinema man was back at Ayr. That was for our 2nd round Scottish Cup tie against Kilmarnock on 9th February, 1924. Ayr United won 1-0 through an 85th minute goal from Harry 'Peerie' Cunningham . The crowd comprised what was then a ground record, the attendance of 16,271 eclipsing the previous best which amounted to 15,853 for a 2-0 Scottish Cup win over Rangers on 27th January, 1923. There was a time when a trip to the cinema meant seeing 'the big picter' and 'the wee picter'. These football clips would have been shown in the gap between the two and they would have been screened weeks after the actual match.

The first televised match involving Ayr United was a 5-2 league win at home to Arbroath on 15th November, 1958. Highlights were shown on Scotsport that evening at 10 pm. A potential danger man in the Arbroath team was Dave Easson who had scored all of the Arbroath goals in their 5-4 win at home to Dumbarton a week earlier. Extraordinarily Hughie Gallacher scored all four for Dumbarton and this was against his former club. True to form Dave Easson (13) got the opener at Ayr. Willie Paton (40), Jim McGhee (46), Alastair McIntyre (58 and 60) and Peter Price put Ayr 5-1 ahead before Easson netted a penalty. The TV images were grainy but there was the satisfaction of topping the Second Division that night with twelve wins and one defeat from the thirteen matches played.

1.15—News. 1.20—Racing from Lingfield. 3.15 — Dog Show and Half-time football scores. 4.40—Disneyland. 5.30—Scotsport News Service. 5.40—Sports Results and News. 6.0—Oh Boy! 6.30—Mary Britten, M.D. 7.0 — Cheyenne. 7.55 — Saturday Spectacular: The Bob Monkhouse Hour. 8.55—News. 9.0—Highway Patrol. 9.30—Dial 999. 10.0—Scotsport. 10.15—All Star Movie: Together Again. 11.45—Close.

STV schedule on 15th November, 1958. Ayr United on at 10 o'clock.

Spanning the sixties into the seventies Ayr United games occasionally had televised highlights shown on STV's Scotsport or BBC's Sportscene. The commentators of old included Arthur

Montford, Alex Cameron, Archie Macpherson, Bob Crampsey and George Davidson. However it took until 22nd August, 1990, for the first Ayr United game to be televised live in its entirety. That was for a 4-0 Skol Cup defeat away to Celtic on 22nd August, 1990. The broadcast was overseen by Adam Fullarton of B Sky B. His grandfather, Ned Fullarton, had played for the pre-amalgamation Ayr FC. It cost B Sky B £25,000 to mount the broadcast. Nine cameras were used. The pictures were beamed from Celtic Park to Kirk of Shotts by a microwave signal. They were then transferred to British Telecom who transmitted them to the B Sky B studios who passed them on to the satellite situated 36,000 kilometres in orbit. The pictures were then re-transmitted down to our television sets. That was how it was done in 1990. Seven decades earlier the Green's man captured his film by furiously turning the handle on a hand-cranked camera.

The first Ayr United home match to be televised live in its entirety was a 2-0 Scottish Cup defeat against Inverness Caledonian Thistle on 16th January, 2006.

Only two Ayrshire derbies have been televised live in their entirety. The first one was Kilmarnock's 3-1 win in a Scottish Cup replay at Rugby Park on 22nd January, 2009. The next one was a 1-0 Ayr United win in a League Cup tie at Somerset Park on 14th July, 2017.

On 20th May, 2009, BBC Alba screened Ayr United versus Airdrie United in the first leg of the First Division play-off final. The historical consequence was that this was the first Ayr United match to be covered with a Gaelic commentary. It was 2-2 on the night and we won 1-0 in the second leg, again with a Gaelic commentary.

The greatest number of Ayr United matches broadcast live on television in a season is eight. This occurred in 2018/19 and it comprised seven league fixtures plus one Scottish Cup tie. The league visit of Inverness Caledonian Thistle on 7th December, 2018, would have been televised live had it not been for a postponement forty minutes before the scheduled kick-off time. It was not televised when eventually played on 29th January, 2019.

The Ayr United film man

The Ayr United film man is Willie Craig and you cannot fail to have seen examples of his match highlights. It exists in archival form from season 2007/08 through to the present day on YouTube. He describes it as "a reasonably full archive." For the fans these highlights are hugely appreciated. The work Willie does for the club is most impressive. Here is a summary of what it entails.

Most of the internal video work with the exclusion of interviews and footage of events which Ayr United Media cover.

DVDs and digital downloads for staff and players.

The distribution of footage to other organisations. These are:
The Scottish Professional Football League. In return the club gets access to the Wyscout coaching platform. Wyscout claim to have the widest football video archive in the world.
The BBC. Since the launch of the BBC Scotland channel Willie's footage has been used at half-time during the Friday night games. **SKY/BT Sports**. Both have used clips in various shows and news features. **The Professional Footballers' Association**. This body has used the footage at awards' nights.

In his own words here is some information on Willie's background. "I am from Ayr and I went to home games with my Dad James between 1985 and 1993. We were both season ticket holders. I think my Dad had been going since at least the 1960s. Having studied and worked away from Ayr I moved back in 2005. Around January 2006 the club asked on the website if anyone was interested in filming games. Video was a hobby of mine and by chance Lachlan Cameron was the new MD at Ayr and he was very keen for first team games to be regularly recorded. Since the 2007/08 season I have been trying to cover most home and away matches. The club have been fantastic. Lachlan is very helpful and accommodating. In fact all club employees, both playing and office staff, have been excellent. I should single out Tracy Ashdown, Graeme Miller and, of course, Lewis Grant for special mentions though. All managers have been great as well, excluding Neil Watt whom I don't think I met. I'm fortunate to be allowed on the team bus. Indeed, in the early days I would often get a lift to away games from various club directors. There has even been the occasional overnight trip, most notably sharing a room with Lewis Grant in a Fawlty Towers-esque hotel in Lossiemouth prior to a cup game at Deveronvale (Ryan Stevenson saved our blushes that day). I have mostly been a one-man band although on a couple of occasions I have asked for help on the Ayr United website. Both times fans have come forward and helped out."

First Kick

Somerset Park's inaugural game took place on the Monday evening of 7th May, 1888. At centre-forward for Aston Villa was Archie Hunter, an Ayr native, who had been a full-back with Ayr Thistle prior to signing for Aston Villa in 1878. In fact he had been in the Ayr Thistle team that reached the semi-final of the Scottish Cup in 1876/77. That occasion was a 9-0 defeat against Vale of Leven at Kinning Park but he later had the distinction of being the first Aston Villa captain to lift the FA Cup (in 1887). He also had the distinction of being the first player to kick a ball at Somerset Park. It was reported that: "Archie set the sphere a-rolling for the Villans against a very stiff gale of wind." Ayr FC won 3-0.

The first player to kick a ball in the Scottish Premier Division was our own Alex Ingram. On 30th August, 1975, the first batch of matches took place in the new league set-up. The Ayr match at Motherwell kicked-off marginally before 3pm and that is the basis for the claim that Alex Ingram was the first player from any club to kick a ball in that division. The result was 1-1.

Floodlights

The first floodlit match in Ayr took place on Thursday 7th November, 1878. Ayr Academicals played Glasgow University at Springvale Park. A large centre light was placed at the far end of the field with two lesser lights being placed at each corner at the Midton Road end. The large light was equal to 6,000 candles. Portable engines were used to work the electricity. Shortly after half-time, rain caused the engine belts to slip thereby breaking the current of electricity and the lights went out one after the other. It was abandoned with Glasgow University winning 3-1.

On Thursday 17th November, 1892, there was a more successful experiment with electric light at Carrick Street Oval. Competitions for cycling and five-a-side football took place.

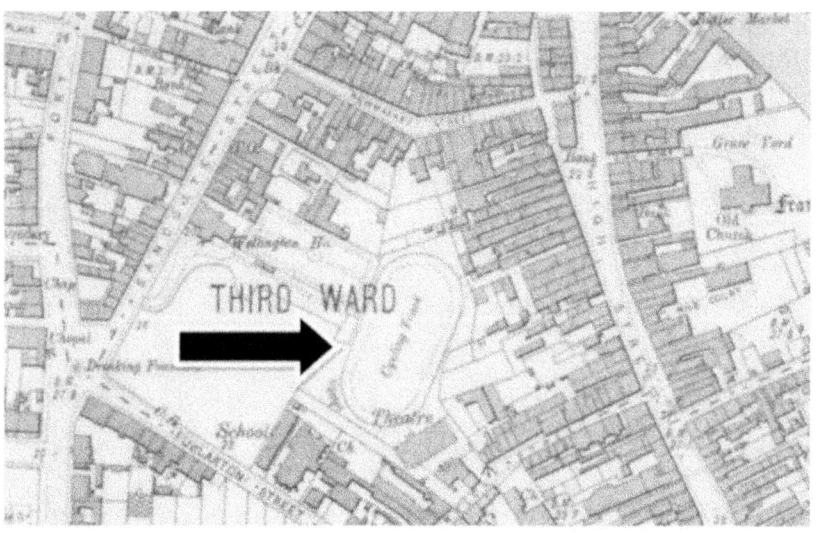

Carrick Street Oval

Jim Gilmour – on 8th October, 1970, he was the goalkeeper for Ayr United reserves in Somerset Park's first floodlit action.

On Tuesday 25th October, 1955, Ayr United played in the club's first-ever floodlit match. It was a testimonial at Rugby Park for Jimmy Middlemass of Kilmarnock. In a 4-1 defeat the Ayr team had two trialists in the starting line-up and at half-time there were either four changes or six according to which newspaper you cared to believe. Peter Price was the Ayr scorer. Future Ayr United player Dave Curlett got a hat-trick and the other Kilmarnock scorer was Adam Imrie. The Ayr team in the first half was: Round, Leckie, Rodger, Traynor, Gallagher, Haugh, McMillan, Stevenson, Price, 'Junior' and 'A.N. Other'. Kilmarnock, with no reported mid-match changes, lined up as follows: Brown, Watson, Rollo, Taggart, Hill, MacKay, Mays, Imrie, Curlett, Beattie and Black.

On Thursday 8th October, 1970, Ayr United reserves played Partick Thistle reserves in a 2nd XI Cup first round tie at Somerset Park. The kick-off time was 5.30pm. After seventy-eight minutes the floodlights were switched on. This was the first floodlit football in the town in modern times. John Cassidy scored in a 1-1 draw. Representing the home team in Somerset Park's first floodlit action, albeit for just twelve minutes, were: Gilmour, Wells, Aitken, McAnespie, McFadzean, Mitchell, Cassidy, McGregor, Filippi, McCulloch and Kinsella; substitute – Rough. The replay ended 3-3 after extra time. Then the second replay reverted to Ayr on Wednesday 21st October, 1970. This was the first game at Somerset Park with the lights on throughout. Ayr United reserves won 2-0 with goals from Tommy Reynolds and John Cassidy.

The official switch-on took place on Wednesday 18th November, 1970, Ayr United beating Newcastle United 2-0.

Team: Stewart, McFadzean, Murphy, Fleming, Quinn, Mitchell, Young, Reynolds, McLean, Whitehead and Doyle; substitutes – McAnespie, Lannon and McGovern.

Newcastle United: McFaul, Craggs, Clark, Elliott, Craig, Moncur, Robson, Hindson, Dyson, Smith and Nattrass; substitutes – Ford, Foggan and Barrowclough.

Goals: Cutty Young and George McLean.

In the 52nd minute George McLean was brought down for a penalty. Cutty Young had his effort saved but he followed up to net the rebound. In the 67th minute a short passback from John Craggs allowed George McLean to intercept and fire in the second goal.

Construction of the floodlight towers at Somerset Park began in June 1970. The £18,000 cost was offset by £12,201: 14s: 11d being raised by the public. Apart from a raffle, the main event was a Free Gift Sale at Ayr Cattle Market on Friday 27th February, 1970. A Friesian bullock made the top price at £101. The first item sold was a West Highland terrier with a pedigree. It fetched £15. The auction sale made £2,300 to boost the fund to £10,500 at that point.

The pylons constructed in 1970 were dismantled between 31st May and 1st June, 2011. The first match played under Somerset Park's next floodlight installation was a second round League Cup tie against Inverness Caledonian Thistle on 24 August, 2011. It was a 1-0 home win.

Team: Cuthbert, John Robertson, Malone, Smith, Campbell (Armstrong 10), McKernon, McGowan, Geggan, Wardlaw, Roberts (Tiffoney 65) and Moffat (Ross Robertson 85); unused substitutes – Burke and McWilliams.

Inverness Caledonian Thistle: Tuffey, Piermayr, Tokely, Sutherland (Andrew Shinnie 65), Hogg, Doran, Hayes (Ross 22), Morrison (Tade 77), Foran, Graeme Shinnie and Golobart; unused substitutes – Laing and Esson.

Goal: Eddie Malone.

Inverness were the first of three Premier League clubs who would fall victim to Ayr United in the run towards the League Cup semi-finals. The others were Hearts and St.Mirren. Eddie Malone's goal came in the 60th minute when he shot home a Michael McGowan corner-kick.

During an Ayr United versus Crusaders friendly in 2014 there was a sustained period of torrential rain. As a result of the gathering gloom the floodlights were switched on at 3.20 pm. This was remarkable because it was a summer's afternoon. It was 19th July.

Foreign players

Football in Ayr dates back to 1872 at which time parochial attitudes prevailed and would remain to do so for generation after generation. The Scottish word 'interlouper' is a reference to someone living in a district in which they were not born, albeit that they may have been living there for a considerable time. Any mention of interloupers is made in such a tone as to imply suspicion. In the modern age the issue is not so pronounced but in the days of long ago an interlouper was unlikely to be accepted in their adopted community. Ayr FC, founded in 1879, attracted criticism for signing players who were not local. The popular view was that anyone playing for Ayr Football Club should live within the boundaries of the burgh. A decade into their existence a letter appeared in the *Ayr Observer* dated 19th February, 1889. The writer complained that: "It is quite absurd to get Maybole or other players into the team when we can get better in our own circles. The expense of the Maybole players is also a little against the funds, and as the name is Ayr Football Club, I think as far as the name is concerned it generally means that the club is formed of Ayr players." To put this into context you must understand that Maybole is only about eight miles from Ayr.

The earlier assertion that parochial attitudes would prevail well into the future will now be proved. In the *Ayrshire Post* dated 8th September, 1961, a letter pleading for team strengthening appeared. Fair point, you may think. However it contained the proviso that local players should be recruited. It read:

"Sir, – I trust you may judge it pertinent my inquiring of the management of Ayr United when they are going to strengthen the team's defence. It has long been obvious to all outside the directors' box that a full-back and a half-back are urgently needed. Ample warning was given last season but apparently even relegation was not sufficiently serious to rouse those in control from their lethargy. The fact that not a single player was added to the playing staff during the close season bears this out. How can enthusiasm be reasonably expected of the players when so little is displayed by those behind the scenes? Their inaction might be excused if no local talent was available but Kilmarnock have clearly shown how a team composed mainly of county lads can match the best."

The writer used the pen name "Disgusted". On the point that there were no close season signings he or she was correct. However the point in reproducing the letter here is to emphasise a recurring desire for signing, in the words of the writer, "local talent."

Harking back to the real olden days, match reports habitually referred to the opposition as being strangers. More than a century would pass before foreign players in local football would occur on a meaningful scale. There was actually a time when foreigners could not enter Ayr far less play football in the district. The Aliens Restriction Order of 1916 compelled that aliens could only enter restricted areas with the permission of the registration officer and even then only if in possession of an identity book. Ayr was named as one of the restricted areas.

Who was the first foreigner to play for Ayr United? On 6th October, 1917, a Dubliner called Webb played in a 1-1 league draw away to St.Mirren. He had a poor display at centre-forward but, due to the difficulties of the times, he was retained for a 2-0 league defeat away to Hearts and at this point his Ayr career ended. Dublin is not in Britain now, but it was in 1917 so this disqualifies him from the title of the club's first foreigner. There was an historical precedent. On 29th September, 1906, goalkeeper James Sherry had played for Ayr FC in a Scottish Qualifying Cup tie against Lanemark at Connel Park, New Cumnock. The tie was won 5-2. He too was a Dubliner. It was a one-off match. He was registered with Bohemians. Let us move on. Dubliners of that era were British.

The first foreign player to make a first team appearance for Ayr United was Mike Gallagher. In October 1954 Ayr United paid Hibs

Brian Kristensen.

"just under £3,000" for the combined purchase of Gallagher and Jock Govan. Gallagher was a native of Donegal who had played for Eire in World Cup qualifiers in the previous season. He was not the first player from the Republic of Ireland to play for Ayr United but he was the first to do so since independence from Britain.

Richie Williams, an American, was the next non-UK player to appear. On 14th May, 1994, he went on in the 39th minute of a 1-0 league defeat at home to St.Mirren. Another American, Kevin Welsh, had been an Ayr United player in 1976/77 but, although being called up for the USA World Cup squad at that time, he did not make a first team appearance for the club.

The concept of signing proper foreigners took hold spectacularly in 1994. By 'proper foreigners' the meaning is taken to be those who were not native English speakers. Here is the list of non-UK players to have played at first team level since then (including native English speakers).

Farid El Alagui (born Bordeaux but described as French Moroccan), Jean-Yves Anis (Ivory Coast), Mohammed Benlaredj (French), Fabien Bossy (French), David Castilla (French), Marco Ciardi (Swedish), Laurent D'jaffo (French), Kristjan Finnbogason (Icelandic), Jose Fortes (Portuguese), Thomas Gill (Norwegian), Regis Gorgues (French), Jens Hansen (Faroese), Alain Horace (French), Jens Knudsen (Faroese), Brian Kristensen (Danish), Peter Lindau (Swedish), John Maisano (Australian), Willie Mainge (French), Ryan McGowan (Australian), Peter Murphy (Irish Republic), Bruce Murray (American), Niclas Nylen (Swedish), Maamria Noureddine (Tunisian), Andy O'Connell (Irish Republic), Kelechi Okorie (Nigerian), Tommi Paavola (Finnish), Jean Francois Peron (French), Barry Prenderville (Irish Republic), Franck Rolling (French), Marius Rovde (Norwegian), Ludovic Roy (French), Luc Sonor (French), Mohammed Sylla (Guinea), Claudio Valetta (Italian), Jerome Vareille (French), Rocky Visconte (Australian), Rune Warholm (Norwegian), Richard Watson (Australian but born in South Africa to a Danish mother. He held a British passport).

Some prospective entrants to the list have been excluded. They are: Colin Miller who played for Canada but was born in Lanark;

Lee Power who played for the Irish Republic at under-21 level despite being a native Londoner; Neil Duffy, Andy McMillan and Johnny Hubbard, all of whom were born in South Africa but could not be said to have foreign traits (apart from Johnny Hubbard's accent!). Similarly manager Neil Watt was born in Germany but had no German traits. On the same argument the players from the Irish Republic might also have been excluded. For example Peter Murphy hardly seemed like a foreigner.

Simon Stainrod was the first Ayr United manager to actively engage in the foreign market. He had played for Strasbourg and could easily converse in French. The largest number of foreign players on the pitch for Ayr United at the same time is five and this dates to Stainrod's reign.

The details are: St.Mirren 1 Ayr United 0 - League – 5th November, 1994. They were Niclas Nylen, Claudio Valetta, Franck Rolling, Bruce Murray and Regis Gorgues.

Then, on 12th November - League - Ayr United 0 Airdrie 3 when we had five again i.e. all of the above except Bruce Murray but including Jose Fortes. By the last game in the month (1-1 against Dundee at Dens Park) on 26th November, Franck Rolling was the only foreigner in the starting eleven.

Colin Miller

Johnny Hubbard.

Foreign tours

Ayr United have played in the following non-UK countries.

Norway and Sweden 1928

All games were in Norway with the exception of the one against the Swedish international team in Stockholm.

Gjøa Crana 1 Ayr United 2. Goals: Jim Nisbet and Jimmy Smith.
Sweden 1 Ayr United 3. Goals: Jim Nisbet and Jimmy Smith with two.
Gjøa Crana 0 Ayr United 4. Goals: Jimmy Smith hat-trick and Billy Brae.
Ooestfold 4 Ayr United 3. Goals: Danny Tolland, Jocky Simpson and Billy Brae.
Drammen 3 Ayr United 6. Goals: Jimmy Smith with four and Billy Brae with two.

Canada 1973

St.John's All Stars 1 Ayr United 5. Goals: Alex Ingram with two, John Doyle, Johnny Graham and Davy Wells.
Burin Peninsula All Stars 2 Ayr United 5. Goals: George McLean with two, Alex Ingram with two and Davy McCulloch.
Newfoundland All Stars 1 Ayr United 9. Goals: George McLean with five, Alex Ingram hat-trick and Davy Wells.
Newfoundland Canada Summer Games Team 2 Ayr United 8. Goals: Alex Ingram with four, George McLean hat-trick and an own goal.

France 1973

These games in Brittany were in the Lorient Festival Trophy which Ayr United succeeded in winning.

St. Lorient 0 Ayr United 2. Goals: Alex Ingram and George McLean.

Concarneau 1 Ayr United 2. Goals: Johnny Graham and Alex Ingram.

Cork Hibs (Ireland) 1 Ayr United 3. Goals: Rikki Fleming and George McLean with two.

Canada 1975

Ontario – Quebec Select 2 Ayr United 3. Goals: Johnny Graham, Gerry Phillips and John Doyle.

Quebec – Ontario Select 0 Ayr United 2. Goals: Johnny Graham and Gerry Phillips.

Corner Brook 0 Ayr United 7. Goals: Johnny Graham with two, Hugh Cameron, Gerry Phillips with two, John Dickson and Alex Ingram.

Canadian All Stars 2 Ayr United 2. Goals: Rikki Fleming and Stevie Joyce.

St. John's All Stars 1 Ayr United 8. Gerry Phillips with four, Hugh Cameron hat-trick and an own goal.

Saint Pierre 0 Ayr United 14. Goals: John Doyle with four, Johnny Graham hat-trick, Hugh Cameron hat-trick, John Dickson with two, Jim McSherry and Gerry Phillips.

St. Lawrence Select 0 Ayr United 8. Goals: Johnny Graham with four, John Doyle with two, Hugh Cameron and Jim McSherry.

Grand Bank Select 0 Ayr United 5. Goals: John Doyle with two, Alex Ingram, Gerry Phillips and John Dickson.

Nigeria 1976

FC Stationary 1 Ayr United 3. Goals: Gerry Phillips with two and John Gray.

Enugu Rangers 0 Ayr United 3. Goals: Gerry Phillips with two and Rikki Fleming.
The Mighty Jets of Kaduna 1 Ayr United 0.

Republic of Ireland 1994

St. James Gate 0 Ayr United 2. Goals: Ian Gilzean with two.

University College Dublin 3 Ayr United 0.

Galway United 1 Ayr United 3. Goals: John Sharples, Sam McGivern and Justin Jackson.

Drogheda United 1 Ayr United 1. Goal: Neil McKilligan.

Sweden 1998

Vasalunds 1 Ayr United 2. Goals: Glynn Hurst and Billy Findlay.
Djurgarden 4 Ayr United 0.
Café Opera 0 Ayr United 0.
Gefle 2 Ayr United 1. Goal: Billy Findlay.

Sweden 2000

Vasalunds 0 Ayr United 3. Goals: James Grady, Pat McGinlay and Glynn Hurst.
I.K. Sirius 0 Ayr United 2. Goals: James Grady and Glynn Hurst.
Sandvikens I.F. 0 Ayr United 2. Goals: James Grady and Glynn Hurst.
Gefle 1 Ayr United 0.

Austria 2009

Wacker Burghausen (Germany) 0 Ayr United 3. Goals: Chris Aitken with two and James Lindie.

United States and Canada 1929 – the aborted plan

When the club announced a summer tour across the Atlantic there was nothing ambiguous. It was definitive.

The resultant publicity came to the attention of the United States Football Association whose secretary wrote to Ayr United *(letter on page 175)* stating that they would give permission for only one foreign team to visit and that no final decision had been made. In the final analysis the decision did not favour Ayr United.

The correspondence came from New York, the scene of the Wall Street crash in October of that year. It would be uncharitable to suggest karma!

The Dominion of Canada Football Association wrote *(letter below)* to Ayr United stating that they had already agreed to a tour by the Welsh Football Association and that "one tour by a British team at the same time is enough."

DOMINION OF CANADA
FOOTBALL ASSOCIATION
INCORPORATED 1923

Patrons:
DUKE OF CONNAUGHT
LORD WILLINGDON
W. R. MILTON, Esq.
Lt.-Col. T. HERBERT LENNOX, K.C.
The HON. W. C. NICHOL.

Secretary-Treasurer
SAMUEL DAVIDSON
290 INKSTER BOULEVARD
Winnipeg, Man.

Telegraphic Address: "SOCCER WINNIPEG"

OFFICERS for SEASON
1928-29

Hon. President:
DAVID FORSYTH

President:
JOHN RUSSELL
Vancouver

Vice-Presidents:
THOS. HOLLAND
CHAS. M. SMAIL
FRED. R. DAVIES

Secy.-Treas.:
SAMUEL DAVIDSON
290 Inkster Boulevard
Winnipeg

Council:
QUEBEC............J. Somerville
ONTARIO...........T. G. Elliott
NEW ONT..........H. H. Willcox
MANITOBA....H. W. Serymgeour
SASK.................J. Snowden
ALBERTA......F. Crumblehulme
B.C....................J. Adam

February 26th 1929

Mr. A. Buchanan,
Secy. Ayr United F.C.,
Somerset Park,
Hawkhill, Ayr,
Scotland.

Dear Sir:-

I have to acknowledge receipt of your favor of the 11th instant in which you state that your Club has been invited to tour Canada and the United States and ask our permission to enable you to undertake the proposed tour.

I very much regret to inform you that we are unable to grant permission to tour Canada as we have already arranged for a tour by the Welsh Football Association and my Council are of the opinion that one tour by a British team at the same time is enough.

I note that you say Mr. Peto is arranging the tour, but we took this matter up with Mr. Peto after seeing the Press reports that you were contemplating a tour and he assured us that no negotiations had been entered into for a tour of Canada and none were contemplated.

Again assuring you that we very much regret being unable to grant your request.

Yours very truly,

cc - Scottish F. A.
Mr. L. A. Peto.

Sam Davidson
Secretary-Treasurer

Letter from Canadian F.A.

President ARMSTRONG PATTERSON Hotel Fort Wayne Detroit, Mich. *First Vice-President* ELMER A. SCHROEDER 1211 Chestnut Street Philadelphia, Pa. *Second Vice-President* WILLIAM T. ANGUS 2702 East 128th Street Cleveland, Ohio	**United States Football Association, Inc.** INSTITUTED *at* NEW YORK CITY APRIL 5, 1913 *and* ORGANIZED PURSUANT *to the* MEMBERSHIP CORPORATION LAW STATE *of* NEW YORK, MAY 30, 1914 ~ *Affiliated with the Federation Internationale de Football Association*	*Third Vice-President* WINTON E. BARKER 306 Holland Building St. Louis, Mo. *Treasurer* WILFRED R. CUMMINGS 13 West 115th Street Chicago, Ill. *Secretary* THOMAS W. CAHILL Cornish Arms Hotel 311-323 West 23rd Street New York City *Telephone* Watkins 8577 *Cable* "Soccer" New York

New York, February 23, 1929.

Mr. A. Buchanan, Secy.,
Ayr United F. C.,
Somerset Park,
Ayr, Scotland.

My dear Sir:

   Your letter of February 2nd, concerning an invitation issued to your club by Mr. L. A. Peto for a series of games in the United States and Canada during the closed season of 1929, is hereby acknowledged.

   This was referred to Col. G. Randolph Manning, Chairman of the National and International Games and Foreign Relations Committee, who requested me to inform you that his committee, at the present time, is negotiating for the visit of a foreign team to these shores this Summer but the specific club has not been determined as yet. When a final decision is reached we will advise you.

          Yours very truly,

          T.W. Cahill
TWC/S   Secretary.

Letter from United States F.A. Inc.

Foreign teams at Somerset Park

16th February, 1946: Ayr United 1 Polish Army XI 6. The Ayr team contained three trialists playing under the names 'Newman', 'A. N. Other' and 'Freshman'. 'Newman' was the Ayr scorer.

19th October, 1946: Ayr United 1 Silesian XI 2. The opposition was a Polish touring team. Malky Morrison got the Ayr goal.

15th March, 1972: Ayr United 0 Gwardia 2. It was popularly thought that Gwardia was the first foreign team to play at Somerset Park. They were not even the first Polish visitors. The goals were scored by Szymckac (19 and 89). It was a very methodical performance by the Poles.

12th March, 1975: Ayr United 4 Aarhus 1. This was the John Murphy testimonial match. Goals: Rikki Fleming 1-0; Torben Mikkelson 1-1; Alex Ingram 2-1; Johnny Graham 3-1; John Dickson 4-1.

30th April, 1975: Ayr United 6 St. John's All Stars 0. Goals: Gerry Phillips 1-0 and 2-0; John Dickson 3-0; Hugh Cameron 4-0 and 5-0; Gerry Phillips 6-0. It was 5-0 at half-time.

30th July, 1975: Ayr United 3 Roda JC 3. Ayr goals: Johnny Graham, Gerry Phillips and Alex Ingram. Roda JC goals: Dick Nanninga, Toonira and Dick Advocaat. Dick Nanninga had the distinction of scoring for Holland in the 1978 World Cup final. Paul Pogba is the only other scorer of a World Cup final goal to have played at Somerset Park. Dick Advocaat's equaliser at Ayr came in the last minute. He was destined to return to Scotland as manager of Rangers.

15th July, 2009: Ayr United 1 Unirea Urziceni 2. Goals: Raul Rubescu 0-1; Mark Roberts 1-1; Andy Aitken own goal 1-2. This was a very accomplished performance against the Romanian champions. Their manager was Dan Petrescu who renewed the acquaintanceship of Ryan Stevenson. They were at Chelsea at the same time.

29th July, 2013: Ayr United 0 AEL Limassol 2. Goals: Orlando Sa 0-1; Tiago Targino 0-2. The visiting club was from Cyprus but the scorers were both Portuguese. This was a friendly in name only. Robbie Crawford was put on at half-time then get sent off for a tackle on Tiago Targino. He had been on the field for six minutes. In contrast Aderito Carvalho was treated with leniency when he put in a crude tackle on Gordon Pope later in the match.

Foreign teams - Other matches against

This section covers matches against foreign clubs in matches played neither abroad nor at Somerset Park.

5th July, 2013: Otetul Galati 2 Ayr United 0. Although listed here it was a closed-doors match against the Romanian club. The venue was Leigh Sports Village, located in Greater Manchester.

7th July, 2013: Dinamo Bucharest 1 Ayr United 1. This too was a match played at a sports centre with no paying public. The venue was Woodlesford, near Leeds. Craig Malcolm opened the scoring.

Foreign travel 1928/29 – The season of English rejection

You have already read about Ayr United's rejected attempt to play in the United States and Canada. Dispiriting correspondence in February 1929 was ample clarification that there was no scope for discussion. The board was similarly rebuffed when attempting to arrange friendlies in England during the 1928/29 season. Three invitations met three refusals with the consequence that thus far in the club's history our only match in England had been at Workington.

The letter *(page 180)* dated 7th March, 1929, rejected Ayr United's request for a match against Burnley at Turf Moor on 23rd March. The reason given is: "So many cases of ongoing sickness that we are taking the opportunity of resting our players." There is a hint of diplomacy in the closing sentence: "Otherwise we would have welcomed playing you here."

After the collapse of the Burnley plan Archie Buchanan, the Ayr United secretary-manager, contacted Leeds United in the hope of arranging a friendly at Elland Road on the same date suggested to Burnley, 23rd March. As you can see from the reply *(page 181)* they had already arranged to host Hearts on that day. Why was 23rd March a free Saturday? Why was there such short notice? Why did it have to be an away game? Questions one and two have the same answer. The Scottish Cup quarter-final results on 2nd March compelled the club to have a blank Saturday on the date of the semi-finals three weeks later. Neither was Somerset Park free on the 23rd due to an Alliance League fixture between Ayr United reserves and Montrose (the Montrose first team competed at this level).

Burnley and Leeds United had been given a short period of notice but the situation was different when Mr Buchanan wrote to Newcastle United requesting them to play Ayr United at St. James Park. The proposed date was Easter Monday 1929 and his letter

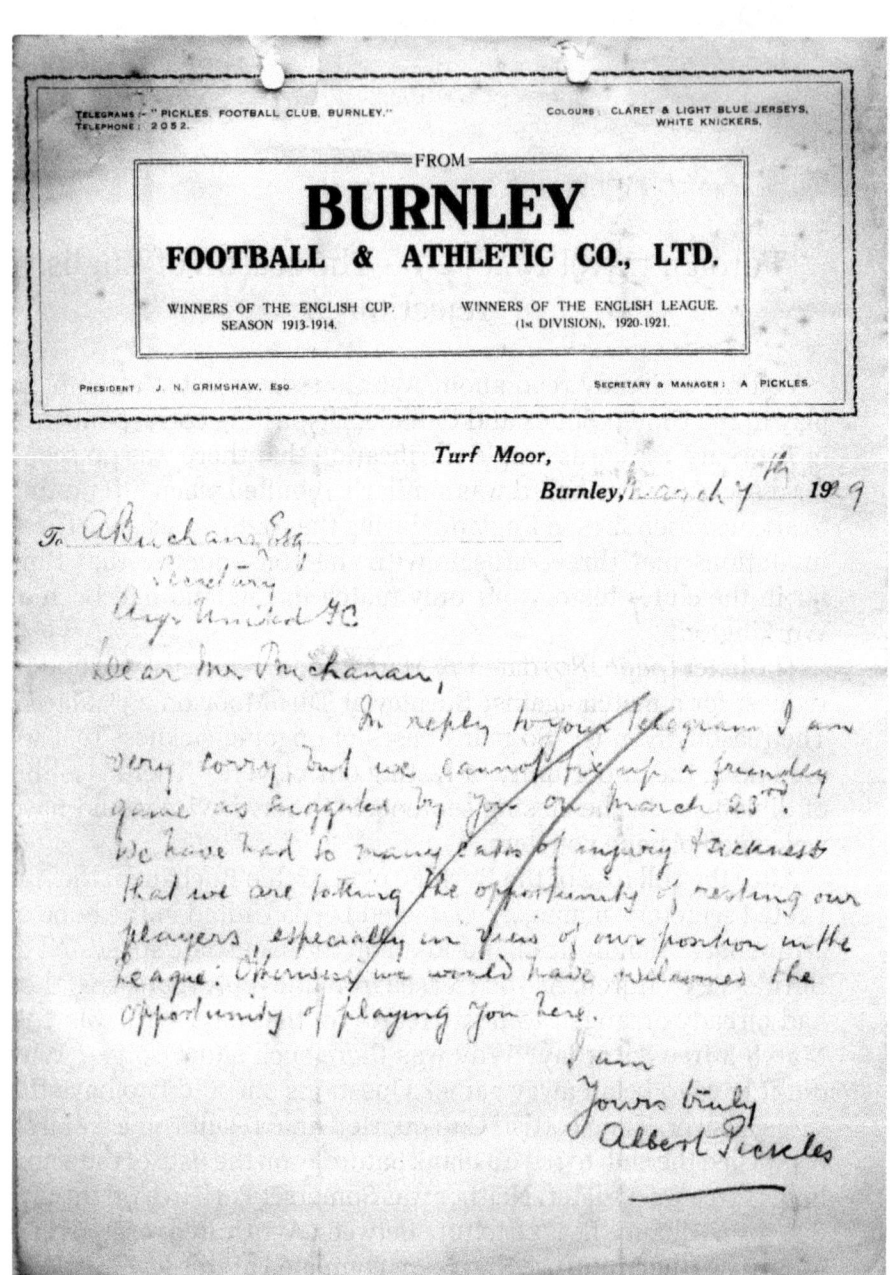

Rejection letter from Burnley F. & A.C..

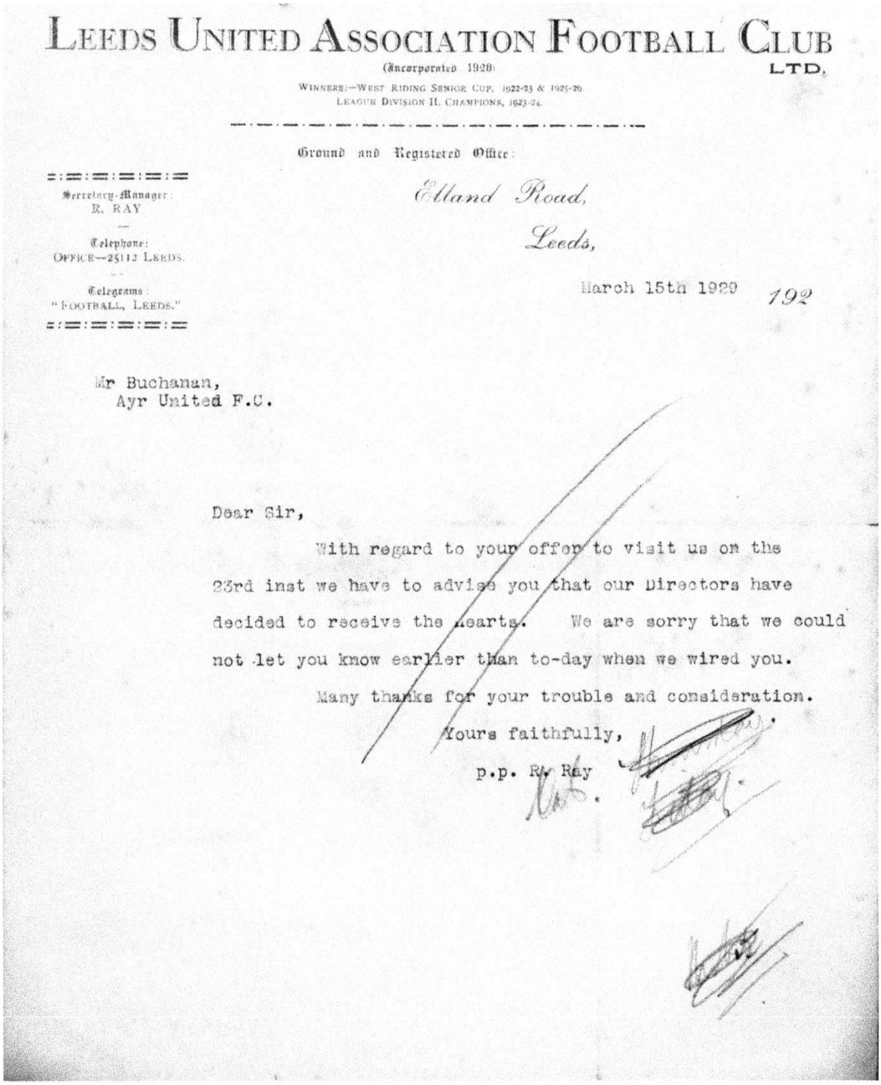

LEEDS UNITED ASSOCIATION FOOTBALL CLUB LTD.

(Incorporated 1920)

WINNERS:—WEST RIDING SENIOR CUP, 1922-23 & 1925-26
LEAGUE DIVISION II. CHAMPIONS, 1923-24

Ground and Registered Office:

Elland Road,

Leeds,

Secretary-Manager:
R. RAY

Telephone:
OFFICE—25112 LEEDS.

Telegrams:
"FOOTBALL, LEEDS."

March 15th 1929

192

Mr Buchanan,
Ayr United F.C.

Dear Sir,

With regard to your offer to visit us on the 23rd inst we have to advise you that our Directors have decided to receive the Hearts. We are sorry that we could not let you know earlier than to-day when we wired you. Many thanks for your trouble and consideration.

Yours faithfully,

p.p. R. Ray

Rejection letter from Leeds United A.F.C.

TELEPHONE,
CENTRAL Nº 477.

TELEGRAMS,
"FOOTBALL, NEWCASTLE"

NEWCASTLE UNITED FOOTBALL CO. LTD.

WINNERS, ENGLISH CUP, 1909-10. 1923-24.
LEAGUE CHAMPIONS, 1904-5. 1906-7. 1908-9. 1926-27.
ENGLISH CUP FINALISTS, 1904-5. 1905-6. 1907-8. 1910-11.

FRANK G. WATT,
SECRETARY

Registered Office,
ST. JAMES PARK,
NEWCASTLE-ON-TYNE.

10th. Oct. 1928

Mr. A. Buchanan,
Ayr United F.C.

Dear Sir,

    In reply to your letter of 3rd. inst. I regret my Directors cannot see their way to offer you a fixture at Newcastle on Easter Monday. We have a very heavy programme of matches over the Easter Holidays, and as the Gosforth Park Race Meeting is on that day, it is not profitable to arrange a game for this day.

                                Yours faithfully,
                                    Frank G. Watt.

Rejection letter from Newcastle United.

was dated 3rd October, 1928. A reply *(page 182)* was posted on 10th October and, as you can see, there was concern about fixture congestion in addition to the counter attraction of a race meeting.

Ayr United's first match -- Workington 4 Ayr United 2 -- against an English club was on 10th March, 1928

Illustrated are the programme cover (below) and centre pages (overleaf). The score detail including the scorers has already been obligingly completed by the original purchaser.

Workington Association Football Club,
Limited.
LONSDALE PARK GROUND.

Visit of SCOTTISH 2nd Div. LEADERS.

WORKINGTON
VERSUS
AYR UNITED
Saturday, March 10th, 1928.
KICK-OFF 3-15.

Official Programme = 1d.

BANG ON TIME!!!
Your Morning Paper — You **must** have it in time each day. A dependable service is part of our organisation; put it to the test. Our stock of publications is the most comprehensive in town. **Lending Library.**

———*O*———

Messenger's Bookshop,
Opposite Free Library.

Printed by The Workington Star Ltd., Oxford Street.

BYERS' CLOTHING STORES. WE SUPPLY **Bukta** AND **St. Margaret Football Clothing.** 8 & 10 **Pow St.,** WORKINGTON.	The Most Popular Shops for HIGH- TOBACCOS and **G. TOGNAREL** We can Supply **ICES** of the Highest Qual etc. at the most popular prices. RIGHT WOR M 2 HUDDART 4 WALTON 7 8 Mc.ILROY THOMPSON W 12 13 KILPATRICK BRAE 17 TURNBULL Mc.C 20 FLEMING HI LEFT AYR U **A H ME FRO** **Viaduc** Opposite LOW STATION, Wor

ASS CHOCOLATES, CONFECTIONERY,
FRESHMENTS.

46, Pow Street AND
Cafe-de-Luxe Bridge St.

to Dances, Parties, Picnics, Cafes, Cinemas
T DRINKS OUR WINTER SPECIALITY.

NGTON LEFT *4*

LEN
        3
     PATTISON
  5   6
NES   ROBINSON
  9   10   11
LLEY   WARD / STRAUGHTON

DOUBTFULL

        15   16
ITH // TOLLAND   NISBIT
  8   19
LGAN   ROBERTSON
             21
         ~~PURDON~~
            PRICE   *2*
BURN
ITED.   RIGHT

HOME.

Hotel,
gton.   T. MURRAY, Proprietor.

BYERS'
CLOTHING
STORES.

Gent's & Boys'
OUTFITTERS.

AGENTS FOR THE
NOTED
SWEET-ORR TUG-
OF-WAR TROUSERS
& OVERALLS.

**8 & 10
Pow St.,**
WORKINGTON.

AYR UNITED SUPPORTERS' CLUB.

Ayr, 23rd Nov. 1928.

Dear Mr Buchanan,

We have resumed operations and propose offering the team a bonus of £1 in the event of a win against Rangers. I hope this will meet with the approval of the Directorate.

Will you please enquire of them as to whether they will be good enough to grant us permission to have a Sandwich man at that game to announce a meeting of the Club.

Yours faithfully,

R.A. Ashly.
Secretary

Letter from the Supporters' Club requesting permission to pay a £1 bonus to each player in the event of beating Rangers in the forthcoming home match on 1st December, 1928. The treasurer was not troubled. The match was lost 3-1.

BEN POPPLEWELL & SONS

Proprietors:
GAIETY THEATRE,
AYR.

Lessees:
PAVILION THEATRE,
AYR.

Phones—Private Office, 1010 Ayr.
Box Office, 156 Ayr.
Telegrams—"Gaiety, Ayr."

Phone—466 Ayr.
Telegrams—
"Pavilion, Ayr."

PLEASE ADDRESS REPLY TO   Gaiety   THEATRE, AYR, SCOTLAND.

11th July, 1929.

Ben Popplewell and Sons thank the Directors of the Ayr United Football Club for Complimentary Season Tickets, and wish to extend to the Players and Staff an invitation to attend the Gaiety Theatre each Friday evening First House as usual, during the Season.

A. Buchanan, Esq.,
Secretary,
Ayr United Football Club,
Somerset Park,
A Y R.

A more cheerful letter - confirmation of a reciprocal arrangement with the Gaiety Theatre in 1929.

Goals

The top ten highest scorers of all time

	League Cup	Scottish Cup	League Cup	Challenge Cup	Total
Peter Price	173	9	31	---	213
Sam McMillan	104	7	16	---	127
Terry McGibbons	118	7	---	---	125
Alex Ingram	82	11	24	---	118
	(Total including one in the Anglo Scottish Cup)				
Jimmy Richardson	109	1	---	---	110
Billy Brae	104	3	---	---	107
Alec Beattie	87	2	14	---	103
Jimmy Smith	97	3	---	---	100
Malky Morrison	67	1	25	---	93
Michael Moffat	74	3	9	1	91
	(Total including four in the play-offs)				

Note: The League Cup did not appear until 1946 therefore four players on the list did not appear in the competition. Michael Moffat is the only listed player to have appeared in the Challenge Cup. The bulk of Jimmy Richardson's Ayr United career spanned the World War One years when the Scottish Cup competition was suspended. He was also away on active service for more than two years. The list is valid as at the close of season 2018/19.

Quickest goals

29th July, 2017, (League Cup): Ross Docherty versus Annan Athletic away: fifteen seconds.

5th February, 2000, (First Division): Neil Tarrant versus Morton at home: twenty seconds.

18th August, 1998, (League Cup): Glynn Hurst versus Motherwell away: twenty-two seconds.

Neil Tarrant

10th April, 1982, (First Division): Alan McInally versus Falkirk at home: twenty-three seconds.

14th August, 1954, (League Cup): Gordon Finnie versus Dundee United away: twenty-five seconds. (The *Ayr Advertiser* stated 25 seconds and the *Ayrshire Post* stated 20 seconds. Reports of the build-up indicate that the *Advertiser* was more likely to be correct).

3rd October, 2015, (League One): Jordan Preston versus Cowdenbeath at home: 28 seconds.

14th January, 1922, (First Division): John Quinn versus Hamilton Accies at home: "less than half a minute".

7th October, 1911, (Second Division): Hilly Goodwin versus East Stirling at home: thirty seconds.

10th March, 1934, (First Division): Fally Rodger versus Partick Thistle away: thirty seconds.

21st August, 1948, ('B' Division): Jock Wallace versus Kilmarnock away: thirty seconds.

19th March, 1949, ('B' Division): Malky Morrison versus Dundee United at home: thirty seconds.

17th September, 1955, ('B' Division): Bobby Stevenson versus Montrose at home: thirty seconds.

18th November, 2017, (Scottish Cup): Lawrence Shankland versus Banks O'Dee away: thirty-two seconds.

7th December, 1974, (First Division): Alex Ingram versus Dundee at home: thirty-five seconds.

20th March, 2004, (First Division): Lee Hardy versus Inverness Caledonian Thistle at home: thirty-five seconds.

2nd April, 1991, (First Division): Ally Graham versus Clyde away: thirty-nine seconds.

The precise times of early goals was not always recorded in older match reports. For example Charlie Phillips scored for Ayr United in the first minute of a league fixture against St.Johnstone at Recreation Park, Perth, on 4th January, 1913, and the *Ayrshire Post* report mentioned that it came in an attack initiated straight from the kick-off and that the ball hit the net before any opposition player had touched it. No national nor local report (*Ayr Advertiser/Ayrshire Post/Perthshire Advertiser*) gave the time in seconds therefore a possible contender is omitted from the above list. Ross Docherty's goal as listed is the earliest *recorded* time for an Ayr United goal in a competitive fixture.

Quickest debut goals

10th November, 1962, (Second Division): Sandy Jones versus Hamilton Accies away: "little more than thirty seconds".

15th August, 1964, (League Cup): Bert Whittington versus Dumbarton at home: "first minute".

26th August, 2000, (First Division): Paddy Connolly versus Falkirk at home: seventy-seven seconds.

14th October, 1995, (Second Division): Willie Wilson versus Stenhousemuir at home: "second minute".

23rd August, 1997, (First Division): Ian Ferguson versus Partick Thistle at home: "second minute".

Quickest goals conceded

10th May, 2014, (Championship play-offs): Greg Stewart (Cowdenbeath away): nine seconds.

20th October, 1956, (First Division): George Mulhall (Aberdeen at home): ten seconds.

16th December, 1972, (First Division): Alex Cropley (Hibs away): eleven seconds.

19th November, 1988, (First Division): Gerry McCoy (Partick Thistle at home): twelve seconds.

25th January, 1994, (First Division): David Elliot (St.Mirren away): nineteen seconds.

6th May, 1989, (First Division): Ian McPhee (Airdrie at home): twenty-eight seconds.

Statistic arising from Ayr United versus Morton on 5th February, 2000

This was a First Division fixture which Ayr United won 3-0. The goal times were 1, 45 and 90. This meant that they were scored at the beginning, the middle and at the end.

Milestone league goals

Number 1,000: Danny Tolland at home to Arthurlie on 31st December, 1927.

Number 2,000: Alec Beattie at home to St.Johnstone on 4th January, 1947.

Alex Bone – scorer of the 5,000th league goal.

Number 3,000: Willie McIntyre at home to Brechin City on 16th December, 1961.
Number 4,000: Ally Love away to Falkirk on 4th October, 1980.
Number 5,000: Alex Bone away to St.Mirren on 7th August, 1999.
Number 6,000: Lawrence Shankland away to Alloa Athletic on 22nd September, 2018.

Milestone Scottish Cup goals

Number 100: Albert Smith at home to East Stirling on 22nd January, 1938.
Number 200: Alex Ingram at home to Stirling Albion on 24th February, 1973.
Number 300: James Grady away to Deveronvale on 5th January, 2002.

Milestone League Cup goals

Number 100: Jim Fraser at home to Dumbarton on 13th August, 1952.
Number 200: Peter Price at home to Montrose on 13th August, 1958.
Number 300: Sam McMillan away to Third Lanark on 6th September, 1965.
Number 400: Rikki Fleming away to Dunfermline Athletic on 9th August, 1975.
Number 500: Darren Henderson away to Rangers on 4th September, 1996.

Scoring bursts

16th September, 1911, (Scottish Qualifying Cup): Ayr United 10 Whithorn 0. It was 8-0 at half-time.
10th September, 1927, (Second Division): Ayr United 5 Albion Rovers 3. Four of Jimmy Smith's five first half goals were scored in the space of fifteen minutes.
10th November, 1928, (First Division): Partick Thistle 4 Ayr United 8: It was 4-2 for Partick Thistle at half-time. This is a club record for away goals in a league fixture.
31st December, 1927, (Second Division): Ayr United 6 Arthurlie 1: Three Ayr goals in three minutes.
17th January, 1931, (Scottish Cup): Ayr United 11 Clackmannan 2: It was 8-1 at half-time.

9th January, 1932, (First Division): Ayr United 6 Leith Athletic 1: Alex Merrie hat-trick in eight minutes.

19th August, 1933, (First Division): Ayr United 4 Hearts 3: Three Ayr goals between the fifth and eleventh minute.

27th March, 1937, (Second Division): Ayr United 5 King's Park 0: Three Ayr goals in four minutes.

25th August, 1937, (First Division): Ayr United 4 Kilmarnock 2: Ayr went 4-0 up with goals timed at 2, 12, 13 and 17. The Kilmarnock captain had won the toss then chose to play facing the sun in the first half.

8th October, 1949, ('B' Division): Ayr United 4 St.Johnstone 0: Four Ayr goals in eleven minutes.

13th August, 1952, (League Cup): Ayr United 11 Dumbarton 1: Six Ayr goals in the second half.

8th November, 1952, ('B' Division): Alloa Athletic 3 Ayr United 6: Four Ayr goals in six minutes.

24th January, 1953, ('B' Division): Albion Rovers 5 Ayr United 6: Four Ayr goals in ten minutes.

17th October, 1953, ('B' Division): Ayr United 3 St.Johnstone 4: Ayr goals timed at 52, 54 and 56 to pull back the three-goal deficit at that stage.

19th October, 1957, (Second Division): Berwick Rangers 0 Ayr United 6: Four Ayr goals in eleven minutes.

23rd November, 1957, (Second Division): Ayr United 4 Stenhousemuir 3: Peter Price's goals were timed at 40, 42 and 47. Albeit that it was a 7-minute hat-trick this feat was bridged by half-time.

21st December, 1957, (Second Division): Cowdenbeath 6 Ayr United 5. Four of the Ayr goals were time at 53, 55, 56 and 58.

29th March, 1958, (Second Division): Hamilton Accies 4 Ayr United 5. The deficit was 4-1 then Peter Price scored in 72, 73, 78 and 80.

13th August, 1958, (League Cup): Ayr United 7 Montrose 1. Four of the Ayr goals were timed at 80, 81, 88 and 89. Peter Price scored those in 80, 81 and 89. Six Ayr goals were scored in the second half.

9th September, 1967, (Second Division): St.Mirren 3 Ayr United 3. This game produced three goals in less than three minutes. Adamson (7, penalty) then Kane (90 seconds later) made it

2-0 for St.Mirren then within a minute of the second goal Alex Ingram narrowed the deficit to 2-1.

12th December, 1970, (Reserve League): Ayr United reserves 12 Cowdenbeath reserves 2. It was 2-1 to Ayr reserves at half-time.

15th January, 1983, (league): Ayr United 4 Falkirk 0. The last three goals were timed at 83, 87 and 88.

12th September, 1987, (Second Division): Cowdenbeath 1 Ayr United 6: Four of the Ayr goals were timed at 60, 69, 70 and 71.

7th November, 1987, (Second Division): Montrose 2 Ayr United 4: The Ayr goals were timed at 61, 63, 64 and 74. This amounted to three goals in three minutes and four goals in thirteen minutes.

19th March, 1988, (Second Division): Ayr United 6 Albion Rovers 2. The first three goals were scored in a three-minute burst timed at 6, 8 and 9. This made it 2-1 to Ayr on account of the second goal being an own goal.

14th March, 1992, (First Division): Raith Rovers 2 Ayr United 4: Three Ayr goals in six minutes.

6th March, 2001, (First Division): Ayr United 6 Falkirk 0: Five Ayr goals in fifteen minutes.

8th January, 2005, (Scottish Cup): Ayr United 3 Stranraer 3: Four of the goals were timed at 43 (Stranraer), 45 (Ayr), 45 (Stranraer) and 46 (Ayr).

4th August, 2012, (League Cup): Ayr United 6 Clyde 1: It was 0-0 at half-time.

4 November, 2017 (League One): Arbroath 1 Ayr United 4: Three Ayr goals in five minutes.

Players scoring five or more in a league fixture

10th September, 1927: Jimmy Smith scored five at home to Albion Rovers.

14th January, 1928: Jimmy Smith scored five at home to Bathgate.

10th November, 1928: Jimmy Smith scored five away to Partick Thistle.

22nd August, 1933: Terry McGibbons scored six away to Third Lanark.

5th January, 1946: Malky Morrison scored six at home to Stenhousemuir.

Ayr United versus Berwick Rangers on 22nd August, 1964. Eddie Moore scoring one of his three headed goals in this League Cup tie

28th March, 1953: Andy Torrance scored five at home to Forfar Athletic.
26th November, 1955: Peter Price scored five at home to East Stirling.
2nd January, 2001: Glynn Hurst scored five away to Morton.

Players scoring at least a hat trick in a Scottish Cup tie

1st February, 1922: Archie Muir scored three away to Lochgelly United.
19th January, 1929: Alex Sharp scored three away to Berwick Rangers.
17th January, 1931: Charlie McGillivray scored four at home to Clackmannan.
17th January, 1931: Danny Tolland scored three at home to Clackmannan.
10th February, 1951: Jimmy Baker scored three away to Queen's Park.
4th February, 1956: Bobby Stevenson scored four at home to Berwick Rangers.
27th February, 1960: Peter Price scored three at home to Airdrie.
16th February, 1974: Davy McCulloch scored three away to Stranraer.
16th February 1974,: George McLean scored three away to Stranraer.
24th January 1998: Ian Ferguson scored three away to Alloa Athletic.

Hat-trick by a full-back

The only instance of an Ayr United full-back scoring a hat-trick in a competitive game occurred in a league fixture on 19th October, 1968. In a 7-1 win at home to Stenhousemuir, Dick Malone was fielded at right-back when he achieved the feat. Only the second of his three goals was from a penalty kick.

Hat-trick of headers:

27th October, 1956: First Division: Ayr United 4 Airdrie 1: Peter Price.
22nd August, 1964: League Cup: Ayr United 6 Berwick Rangers 0: Eddie Moore.

12th September, 1964: Second Division: Queen of the South 4 Ayr United 3: Eddie Moore.

13th April, 1985: First Division: Ayr United 5 Airdrie 1: Ian McAllister.

Connoisseur's hat-trick (left foot, right foot and header)

4th January, 1936: league: Ayr United 4 Albion Rovers 1. Terry McGibbons scored all four – two with his right foot, one with his left foot and one with a header.

24th July, 2018: League Cup: Ayr United 5 Stenhousemuir 0. Lawrence Shankland scored a hat-trick then got substituted in the 52nd minute. His goals comprised one with each foot and one with a header.

Most goals in a calendar year:

In the calendar year 1928 Jimmy Smith scored 53 (51 league, 2 Scottish Cup).

In the calendar year 1958 Peter Price scored 52 (40 league, 1 Scottish Cup, 11 League Cup).

Own goals in the league

Up to the 2019 close season, Ayr United had the benefit of eighty league goals which had been put in the net by opposition players. The clubs responsible for these gifts are Arbroath (6), Dumbarton (6), Queen's Park (6), Kilmarnock (5), Stirling Albion (5), Alloa Athletic (4), Morton (4), Albion Rovers (3), Clyde (3), Cowdenbeath (3), St.Mirren (3), Aberdeen (2), East Fife (2), Falkirk (2), Forfar Athletic (2), Motherwell (2), Raith Rovers (2), Stenhousemuir (2), St.Johnstone (2), Stranraer (2), Abercorn (1), Airdrie United (1), Berwick Rangers (1), Brechin City (1), Dundee United (1), Dunfermline Athletic (1), East Stirling (1), Hamilton Accies (1), Hearts (1), Hibs (1), Leith Athletic (1), Montrose (1), Queen of the South (1), Ross County (1).

Own goals in the Scottish Cup

The Scottish Cup own goal count up to the close of season 2018/19 totals five.

McDougall (Airdrie) 1926/27.

Allan (Queen of the South) 1934/35.

Wells (Peebles Rovers) 1959/60.

McChesney (Queen of the South) 1975/76.
MacPherson (Dunfermline Athletic) 2001/02.

Own goals in the League Cup

To the close of season 2018/19 the League Cup own goal count totals eight.

Ross (Dundee United) 1945/46.
Montgomery (St.Johnstone) 1955/56.
Rae (Falkirk), 1961/62.
Robinson (Hearts) 1980/81.
Carson (Motherwell) 1981/82.
Thomson (St.Mirren) 1982/83,
Teale (Motherwell) 1998/99.
Dowie (Dumbarton) 2017/18.

Own goal miscellany

On 18th December, 1965, Ian Stirling of Arbroath headed an own goal in a Second Division fixture at Ayr. On 23rd December, 1967, he again headed an own goal while playing for Arbroath in a Second Division fixture at Ayr.

In a Second Division fixture at Stranraer on 23rd November, 1968, home centre-half Jim Hannah scored an own goal against Ayr United from forty yards.

On 27th September, 1975, Ayr United reserves lost 8-1 at home to Aberdeen reserves. Ayr United reserves conceded three own goals.

The greatest number of own goals in the club's favour in any one season is four. This happened in 1968/69 (all league) and again in season 2012/13 (all league).

Scoring for both teams

Ayr United 2 Rangers 1 – First Division – 21st November, 1970 – Cutty Young scored for both teams.
Ayr United 2 St.Mirren 1 – League Cup – 14th August, 1976 – Davy Wells scored for both teams.
Ayr United 3 Airdrie 2 after extra time – Irn Bru Cup – 4th September, 2016 – Conrad Balatoni (on his Ayr United debut) scored for both teams.

The milestone own goals in the league

Number One: Cochrane (Abercorn) 15th October, 1910. Away.
Number Ten: Richardson (Leith Athletic) 8th August, 1936. Home.
Number Twenty: Ralph Collins (Kilmarnock) 1st January, 1954. Away.
Number Thirty: Willie Toner (Kilmarnock) 24th September, 1960. Home.
Number Forty: Jim Hannah (Stranraer) 23rd November, 1968. Away.
Number Fifty: Davie Hayes (Morton) 14th September, 1983. Away.
Number Sixty: Norrie McCathie (Dunfermline Athletic) 25th February, 1995. Home.
Number Seventy: Paul Maxwell (Dumbarton) 21st August, 2010. Home.
Number Eighty: Leo Fasan (Falkirk) 15th September, 2018. Home.

Goals in consecutive league games (individual)

The club record is nine. This was achieved by Peter Price in 1955/56 and Henry Templeton in 1987/88. Even when Jimmy Smith scored sixty-six league goals in 1927/28 his best run for scoring in consecutive league games was seven. The record for scoring in consecutive league games starting from a debut is four. This was achieved by Lawrence Shankland in 2017/18.

Goals in consecutive games (team)

Between 30th December, 2017, and 4th August, 2018, Ayr United scored in twenty-five consecutive games in all competitions. This is a club record. The next best is twenty-two which happened between 5th September, 1936, and 23rd January, 1937.

Goals in consecutive home games (team)

13th August, 1958 – 9th March, 1960 = 40 matches. Time span 1 year 209 days.
20th August, 1910 – 13th April, 1912 = 33 matches. Time span 1 year 236 days.

14th July, 2017 – 10th November, 2018 = 31 matches. Time span = 1 year 119 days.

Illustrated above are the three best runs but it should be noted that only competitive matches are included. In particular there is a large number of exclusions from the 1910 – 1912 statistics comprising the Ayrshire League, Ayrshire Cup, Ayr Charity Cup and friendlies.

Greatest number of goals in a season (team)

The club record is 139 in 1958/59, comprising 115 in the league, four in the Scottish Cup and twenty in the League Cup. Taking into account the league only, the team record is 122 in 1936/37.

Least number of goals in a season

The 1966/67 season concluded with twenty league goals, ten in the League Cup and none in the Scottish Cup.

Greatest number of goals conceded in a season

The highest number conceded in a season dates to 1934/35 when 112 were leaked in the league and nine in the Scottish Cup.

A century of goals in a season

Ayr United have beaten the century barrier seven times. For the purpose of these statistics all competitions have been included with the exception of minor tournaments such as the Ayrshire Cup, the Ayr Charity Cup and the Kilmarnock Charity Cup. The team of 1968/69 had a near miss with ninety-nine.

1958/59: Second Division 115: League Cup 20: Scottish Cup 4: Total 139 in 46 games.
2017/18: League One 92: Challenge Cup 6: League Cup 15: Scottish Cup 11: Total 124 in 46 games.
1936/37: Second Division 122. Total 122 in 35 games.
1927/28: Second Division 117: Scottish Cup 4: Total 121 in 40 games.
1955/56: 'B' Division 103: League Cup 10: Scottish Cup: 5: Total 118 in 44 games.
1957/58: Second Division 98: League Cup 14: Scottish Cup 2: Total 114 in 44 games.

1987/88: Second Division 95: League Cup 3: Scottish Cup 6: Total 104 in 44 games. .

Games in which both teams have scored at the death

27th December, 1958 (Second Division): Ayr United 4 Stranraer 4: Ayr United went 4-3 ahead in the closing minute.

10th December, 1960 (First Division): Ayr United 1 Raith Rovers 1: Raith Rovers took the lead in the last minute.

29th April, 2006, (Second Division): Peterhead 1 Ayr United 2: Peterhead equalised in stoppage time.

13th March, 2010, (First Division): Airdrie United 1 Ayr United 1: Ayr United took the lead in stoppage time.

26 March, 2011, (Second Division): Stenhousemuir 2 Ayr United 1: Ayr United equalised in stoppage time. The goal was timed at 90+1. A goal was then conceded in 90+3.

Historically no goal time was shown as later than 89. The concept then evolved of using 90+ to denote stoppage time.

Comebacks

29th March, 1930 (First Division): Ayr United 3 Hamilton Accies 3: Ayr United scored twice in the last three minutes.

21st December, 1957 (Second Division): Cowdenbeath 6 Ayr United 5. Ayr United attained a 5-4 lead after being 4-0 down, albeit that the match was ultimately lost.

29th March, 1958 (Second Division): Hamilton Accies 4 Ayr United 5: The home team had a 4-1 lead with eighteen minutes left.

9th October, 1971 (First Division): Airdrie 3 Ayr United 4: It was 3-1 for Airdrie with less than half an hour to go.

5th April, 1980 (First Division): Ayr United 2 St. Johnstone 2: St. Johnstone had a 2-0 lead with four minutes left.

28th September, 1991 (First Division): Morton 3 Ayr United 4: With twelve minutes left it was 3-1 for Morton.

20th September, 1986 (Second Division): Ayr United 2 East Stirling 1: Ayr United came from behind with two goals inside the last five minutes.

17th August, 1999 (League Cup): Ayr United 2 Hamilton Accies 1: With five minutes remaining it was 1-0 for Hamilton.

1st March, 2003 (First Divison): Arbroath 1 Ayr United 2: There was no historical precedent for Ayr United winning a match in which the team was losing after 89 minutes. Stewart Kean's goals were timed at 89 and 90. This was before the trend whereby goal times were shown as 90+ when scored in stoppage time. The latest conceivable recorded goal time was therefore 90.

18th February, 2017 (Championship): Dumbarton 2 Ayr United 2: It was 2-0 for Dumbarton entering stoppage time and Ayr United had been down to ten men since the 27th minute. The Ayr goals were timed at 90+1 and 90+3. To this point of the game Ayr United had been outplayed and, with the prospect of a comeback seeming so unlikely, the majority of the visiting supported departed at 2-0 down.

Consecutive games without scoring

Ayr United did not score in the final two league matches of 1922/23 nor in the first three league matches of 1923/24.

Between September and October 1977 no goals were scored in five straight games comprising a League Cup tie and four league matches. (The League Cup tie included a successful shootout against Queen's Park but these goals cannot be included for record purposes).

No goals were scored in the last four league games of 1989/90 plus the first game of 1990/91 which was a League Cup tie.

In October 1994 a barren run spanned four league fixtures and a B & Q Cup tie.

Between November and December 1917 no goals were scored in four consecutive home league games. This was equalled between October and December 1999. That barren run at home from October to December 1999 was preceded by a scoreless League Cup tie at home (13th October) to make the actual total five.

Although not valid for record purposes, Ayr United played five pre-season friendlies in the summer of 1997 and failed to score in either of them (with the exception of shootouts in the Livingston Tournament).

Hugh Sproat.

Long range goals

2nd December, 1939: Ayr United 7 Partick Thistle 0 (league): Jimmy Craik scored the final goal from the halfway line.

17th February, 1951: Ayr United 2 Stirling Albion 0 (league): Norrie McNeil scored the only goal of the first half. It came from a free-kick just inside the centre circle in his own half.

22nd July, 1978: Girvan Amateurs 1 Ayr United 12 (twelve): Goalkeeper Hugh Sproat scored with a long kick from his goal area. However this match was only a friendly.

8th December, 1997: Goalkeeper Kevin McKeown scored at Stranraer with a long kick from his goal area but it was only a reserve match.

14th December, 2013: Ayr United 2 Dunfermline Athletic 4: Brian Gilmour scored from his own half to put Ayr 1-0 ahead.

Long range goals conceded

1st January, 1948: Kilmarnock 4 Ayr United 4. Kilmarnock's Frank Mennie put his team 3-2 ahead from his own half.

3rd January, 1981: Ayr United 3 East Stirling 3. Seven minutes from the end goalkeeper Charlie Kelly put East Stirling 3-2 ahead when kicking from hand in his penalty area.

Last day escapes

29th April, 1931: First Division: Ayr United 1 Kilmarnock 0.

Team: Hepburn, Robertson, Fleming, Yorke, McLeod, McCall, Tolland, Armory, Merrie Brae and Ferguson.

Kilmarnock: Clemie, Leslie, Nibloe, Morton, Smith, McEwan, Connell, Muir, Maxwell, Napier and Aitken.

Goal: Danny Tolland

East Fife were already fated to relegation and with one game left Ayr United occupied the second spot which was also a relegation place. Third bottom Hibs had finished their campaign with twenty-five points. Ayr United also had twenty-five points but with an inferior goal average. The issue was simple. One point in the final match would ensure safety and relegate Hibs. Home advantage was vital since this was an Ayr team without an away league win all season. However the opponents just happened to be Kilmarnock so there was no hope of being granted any favours. It was a beautiful evening with a crowd estimated at 14,000 to 15,000. In the 76th minute Danny Tolland scored with a header from a Pearson Ferguson cross. It is on record that: "The crowd yelled themselves hoarse." Hibs went down but Leith Athletic survived in the First Division. It was a fact that Hibs were not even the best team in Leith. When the result at Ayr became known Hibs held a meeting at which it was discussed whether it was viable for the club to continue.

27th April, 1935: First Division: Airdrie 3 Ayr United 2.

Team: Hepburn, Bourhill, Strain, Taylor, Clark, Holland, McGibbons, McCall, Fleming, Fitzgerald and Rodger.

Airdrie: Hawthorn, Calder, Shaw, Thompson, Crosbie, McAllister, Ross, Watson, Hogg, Law and Mooney.

Goals: Jimmy Fleming 0-1; Watson 1-1; Terry McGibbons 1-2; McAllister 2-2; Robert Hogg 3-2.

On the final league Saturday the question had to be resolved as to which club would be going down with the already doomed Falkirk. The contenders were Ayr United and St.Mirren. Entering the last game we had two points more but with an inferior goal average. The pertinent fixtures were Celtic versus St.Mirren and Airdrie versus Ayr United. One point at Broomfield Park would guarantee safety irrespective of the result at Celtic Park. Only a St.Mirren win and an Ayr defeat would bring Second Division football to Somerset Park. The travelling support was vast. Two special trains left Ayr in addition to the convoy of cars and buses. At half-time it was 2-0 to Celtic and 2-1 to Ayr. Airdrie's 65th minute equaliser and 88th minute winner meant that St.Mirren's failure to win had to be relied upon. A rumour swept the ground that St.Mirren had won 3-2. It was nonsense. Celtic won 2-1. St.Mirren's relegation was ungraciously celebrated by Ayr fans when later passing through Paisley by train.

30th April, 1938: First Division: Ayr United 0 Dundee 0.

Team: Hall, Dyer, Strain, Taylor, Currie, Mays, McGibbons, Dimmer, Yardley, Gemmell and Thow.

Dundee: Lynch, Rennie, Richards, Cowie, Morgan, Smith, Boyd, McMenemy, Coats, Baxter and Roberts.

Morton were already guaranteed to be relegated. The question of which club would be joining them seemed straightforward. Queen of the South were considered to be virtual certainties to accompany them in making the drop. They needed to beat Rangers at Ibrox on the final day. Not even a draw would save them. The likelihood of them winning there was not even considered. At Somerset Park the half-time scoreboard showed 0-3 corresponding to letter A in the alphabetical key in the match programme. That match was Rangers versus Queen of the South. People laughed in the belief that the score had been inserted the wrong way round. Frighteningly it was true. This meant that in the event of a Queen of the South win (they won 3-2) Ayr United needed to draw to survive while opponents Dundee had to win. At 0-0 the situation was rendered doubly dangerous by facing the other team in peril, a scenario that would recur in 1998. Supporters turned up in the expectation of watching a stress free end-of-season match only for the second half to be fraught with tension. Dundee could muster no potency in attack and, with the match remaining scoreless, they went down.

Dundee Join Morton in Second Division

From the Glasgow Herald on the Monday

3rd May, 1976: Premier Division: Ayr United 2 Motherwell 1.

Team: Sproat, Filippi, Murphy, Fleming, Tait, Hyslop, Phillips, McSherry, Ingram, McCulloch and Robertson; substitutes – McDonald and Kelly.

Motherwell: Rennie, McLaren, Wark, Watson, McVie, Stevens, Marinello, Gardner, Graham, Davidson and McAdam; substitutes – Millar and Kennedy.

Goals: Pat Gardner 0-1; Davy McCulloch 1-1; Gerry Phillips 2-1.

St. Johnstone had long since been stranded at the foot of the table. In order that Ayr United would not go down with them the expectation was that a draw would probably be enough in this Monday evening fixture. This was on the assumption that Dundee United would lose against Rangers at Ibrox on the next night. A win would guarantee safety regardless. It transpired that

Craig Buchanan – he performed heroically in the last day escape at Dumbarton.

Dundee United got a draw so anything less than an Ayr win against Motherwell would have resulted in relegation. A goal down at half-time, the outlook was bleak. Malky Robertson struck a penalty wide in the 62nd minute. Depression! Davy McCulloch equalised in the 75th minute and five minutes later Gerry Phillips put the ball in the net. Referee Alistair McKenzie pointed for a corner-kick in the belief that the ball had already crossed the line by the time Davy McCulloch had cut it back. Mr McKenzie then had a confab with his linesman. Goal! There were echoes of 1938 because an unexpected result at Ibrox relegated Dundee. Defeat there would have put Dundee United down.

14th May, 1983: First Division: Clyde 3 Ayr United 2.

Team: Rennie, Shanks, McGee, Armour (Speir), McAllister, Morris, McInally, Connor, Frye, Ward and Christie (McNaughton).

Clyde: Young, McVeigh, Rae, Dempsey, Flexney, Evans, Reilly, Sinclair, Masterton, O'Neill and Nevin; substitutes – Brogan and Doherty.

Goals: Danny Masterton (1-0); Pat Nevin 2-0; Derek Frye 2-1; Jim Doherty 3-1; Derek Frye 3-2.

As with previous last day escapes the scenario involved a club already fated to relegation, in this case Queen's Park, and the question remaining as to which club would occupy the other relegation spot. Entering the last day the two candidates were Ayr United and Dunfermline Athletic. We had a one point lead and a much better goal difference. A Dunfermline win away to St.Johnstone would mean that we would require a draw at Shawfield, bearing in mind that it was two points for a win at this time. St.Johnstone were high on incentive. They had a one point lead at the top and an inferior goal difference to Hearts in second place. On the assumption that Hearts would win their last match (they did) St.Johnstone would need to beat Dunfermline to claim the title. They achieved this by a 1-0 margin which was most fortuitous since the Ayr team stuttered to defeat. Safety was achieved not through our own efforts but those of St.Johnstone.

Jimmy Brown – ironically his best Ayr United performance was his last. That was on the occasion of the last day escape at Dumbarton on 12th May, 1984.

12th May, 1984: First Division: Dumbarton 0 Ayr United 3.

Team: Brown, Hume, McGee, Buchanan, McAllister, Collins, Shanks, Connor, McInally, Sloan (Evans), and Murphy; unused substitute – Christie.

Dumbarton: Carson, Montgomerie, Martin McGowan, Pat McGowan, McNeil, Clougherty, Ashwood, Craig, Moore, Tommy Coyle and Joe Coyle; substitutes – Walsh and Burnett.

Goals: Gerry Collins 0-1 and 0-2; Alan McInally 0-3.

By the last day Alloa Athletic were already consigned to the Second Division. It was now down to whether they would be joined by Ayr United or Raith Rovers. We had a one point lead with an inferior goal difference yet the odds heavily favoured our Kirkcaldy counterparts. The pertinent fixtures were Meadowbank Thistle versus Raith Rovers and Dumbarton versus Ayr United. Second-placed Dumbarton were already assured of promotion to the Premier Division but they stood to be champions in the event of Morton losing at home to Kilmarnock combined with a home win at Boghead Park. Morton went on to win 3-2 but Dumbarton set about Ayr United with an intensity that implied a belief that they could be champions. Raith Rovers had easily the least daunting fixture and, surely enough, they beat Meadowbank Thistle 3-1. The consequence was that an Ayr win was required against a team with home advantage and high on incentive. Gerry Collins scored with two headers in quick succession near the interval. The travelling support was manic. Lawrie McGee got sent off with twenty minutes to go but goalkeeper Jimmy Brown was playing the game of his life. In a counter attack Alan McInally scored a fantastic solo goal in the closing minutes. Cue bedlam!

12th May, 1998: First Division: Partick Thistle 1 Ayr United 3.

Team: Castilla, Shepherd, Miller, Millen, Traynor, Anderson, Donowa (D'jaffo), Davies, Ferguson, Findlay and Henderson; unused substitutes – Duthie and McKeown.

Lawrie McGee

Partick Thistle: Hamilton, Boyle, Archibald, Watson, MacDonald, Stirling (Martin), Lauchlan, Henderson, Lawrence, Evans and Lyons; unused substitutes – Nicolson and McKenzie.

Goals: Ian Ferguson 0-1; Gareth Evans 1-1; Laurent D'jaffo 1-2; Billy Findlay 1-3.

Ayr United or Partick Thistle? By the last day it was down to which one of these clubs would be accompanying Stirling Albion in taking the drop. It had not been anticipated that it would come down to this. On the previous Saturday Partick Thistle had beaten Dundee 3-0 at Dens Park. This result could not have been foreseen. Dundee had already clinched the title so it could only have been attributable to a lack of incentive. With Falkirk winning 3-1 at Ayr on the same day it meant that we were one point ahead of Partick Thistle but with an inferior goal difference. Not that goal difference mattered in this situation. For survival we required a minimum of a draw at Firhill while the home team had to win. As in 1938 the last day quest for survival was against the other club in peril. Ian Ferguson's coolly taken 22nd minute goal eased the nerves to some degree. The Partick Thistle support in the 8,424 crowd erupted when Gareth Evans made it 1-1 in first half stoppage time. Fears of them gathering momentum in the second half got dispelled with the introduction of Laurent D'jaffo in the 51st minute. He was a revelation and he scored five minutes after going on. Billy Findlay put the seal on victory with an impeccable strike in stoppage time.

Hugh Sproat in opposition to Ayr United for Motherwell on 9th August, 1980.

League - all time record

Played	Won	Drawn	Lost	Goals for	Goals against
3,732	1,437	847	1,448	6,039	6,184

Included is the Regional League of 1939/40 and also the five games played at the start of that season before the league programme got abandoned. These statistics are valid up until the close of season 2018/19. Unfinished matches are excluded with the exception of Ayr United versus Airdrie on 27th April, 2002. This remains our only abandoned match in which the score stood. Shootouts are also excluded as are play-off matches in general. Also excluded is the Ayr United versus Falkirk result on 9th March, 1935 (see 'Corruption' section). The result was declared void and a replay was ordered. The replay result is included. Another exclusion is the Ayr United versus Peterhead result on 15th November, 2014, which was also declared void (Peterhead fielded an ineligible player) but the replay is included for record purposes. Both voided matches were lost 3-2 at home. The respective replays ended Ayr United 3 Falkirk 1 and Ayr United 3 Peterhead 3.

The highest league placing of fourth was achieved in 1915/16. The lowest has been second from the foot of the old style Second Division in 1964/65. 1958/59 witnessed the highest number of league wins with twenty eight. The lowest is one, dating to 1966/67.

Ian Cashmore senior looks on while Eric Morris makes his jump.

League - opening games

Played	Won	Drawn	Lost	Goals for	Goals against
104	40	26	38	161	162

This is the club's accumulative opening day league record up to and including 2018/19. The abandoned league programme of 1939/40 has been included but not the resultant Regional League.

Record winning margin in an opening league game (two-way tie)

17th **August, 1921:** First Division: Queen's Park 1 Ayr United 6.

Team: Nisbet, Smith, McCloy, Hogg, McBain, Gibson, McDougall, Cunningham, Quinn, Slade and Low.

Queen's Park: Newton, Sneddon, Currie, Pirie, Gillespie, Calderwood, Scott, Gossman, Fyfe, McAlpine and Condie.

Goals: John Quinn 0-1 and 0-2; Andy Fyfe 1-2; Donald Slade 1-3; Robert McDougall 1-4; Donald Slade 1-5; Harry Cunningham 1-6.

This match is covered in the section dealing with the club's biggest away wins in the top tier. Please refer to page 39.

9th **August, 1980:** First Division: Ayr United 5 Motherwell 0.

Team: Rennie, Shanks, Nicol, McSherry, McAllister, Fleeting, Frye, Love, Morris, Connor and Christie; substitutes – Cashmore and Hendry.

Ayr United versus East Stirling on 17th October, 1981. Left to right: Gerry Christie, Stevie Nicol (in his last game before signing for Liverpool), Billy Hendry (head only, in background) and Derek Frye.

Motherwell: Sproat, O'Rourke, Chic McLelland, MacLeod, Carson, Kidd, Clinging, Larnach, Steve McLelland, McLaughlin and Gahagan; substitutes – Irvine and McKeever.

Goals: Derek Frye 1-0; Stevie Nicol 2-0; Jim Fleeting 3-0; Ian Cashmore 4-0; Joe Carson own goal 5-0.

The Motherwell team contained former Ayr United players Hugh Sproat, Steve McLelland and Brian McLaughlin (Sproat and McLaughlin would eventually return). Future Ayr United players in their squad were Mike Larnach, who was in the starting line-up, and Willie Irvine, who was listed as a substitute. Their manager was Ally MacLeod and, almost in the nature of a job swap, the Ayr boss was ex-Motherwell manager Willie McLean. Stewart Rennie and Mark Shanks were ex-Motherwell players in the Ayr team. The result was repayment in full for Motherwell's 5-0 win at Ayr on 23rd February, 1980.

Record losing margin in an opening league game

12th August, 1933: First Division: Aberdeen 8 Ayr United 0.

Team: Hepburn, Robertson, Ure, Reid, Currie, McCall, McGibbons, McGrath, Merrie, Brae and Rodger.

Aberdeen: Smith, Cooper, McGill, O'Reilly, Thomson, Fraser, Beynon, Beattie, Armstrong, Mills and Gall.

Goals: Matt Armstrong with five; Jackie Beynon with two; Willie Mills.

The directors claimed that the memory of Matt Armstrong scoring five would soon be wiped out. This became a classic case of being careful what you wish for. The next league match took place at Ibrox just three days later (on a Tuesday evening). It ended Rangers 9 Ayr United 1 and Jimmy Smith scored six (not to be confused with the identically named player who had joined Ayr United from Rangers in 1927). Seventeen goals conceded in the first two games looked ominous but there was a revival in which the team finished eighth in the twenty-club league.

David Reid – an inside-forward signed from Craigview Athletic in the summer of 1931.

Record consecutive opening league game wins

The club record is six. This occurred when the opening league fixtures from 1967 until 1972 inclusive were all won.

Longest run without an opening league game win

The run of eight winless opening league games from 1992 until 1999 inclusive is a club record. In the 1990s there was just one opening game league victory from the ten played. Out of those ten there were six 1-1 draws.

Opening league game halcyon years

From 1960 until 1977 inclusive there was one opening day league defeat out of eighteen, the exception being in 1964.

Scoreless league openers at home

The three entries in this section occurred in 1924, 1966 and 2008. The gap in each case was forty-two years (see 'Coincidental Happenings' section).

Stewart Rennie

League Cup

Up until the conclusion of 2018/19 the club had scored 592 goals in the competition with Peter Price (thirty-one) being the chief contributor. Not included in the total is the goal scored in the abandoned game against Hearts in 1979. The shootout goals against Queen's Park in 1977/78, Dumbarton in 2000/01, Kilmarnock in 2001/02, Dunfermline Athletic in 2006/07 and Hearts in 2011/12 are also excluded.

The club's first League Cup goal was scored by Bert Harper at Dumbarton on 23rd February, 1946.

Ian Crawford, with thirteen, has the most in a single season (1950/51).

The highest team total in a single season was twenty-four in 1950/51.

The semi-finals have been reached in 1950/51, 1969/70, 1980/81 and 2011/12. The final was reached in 2001/02.

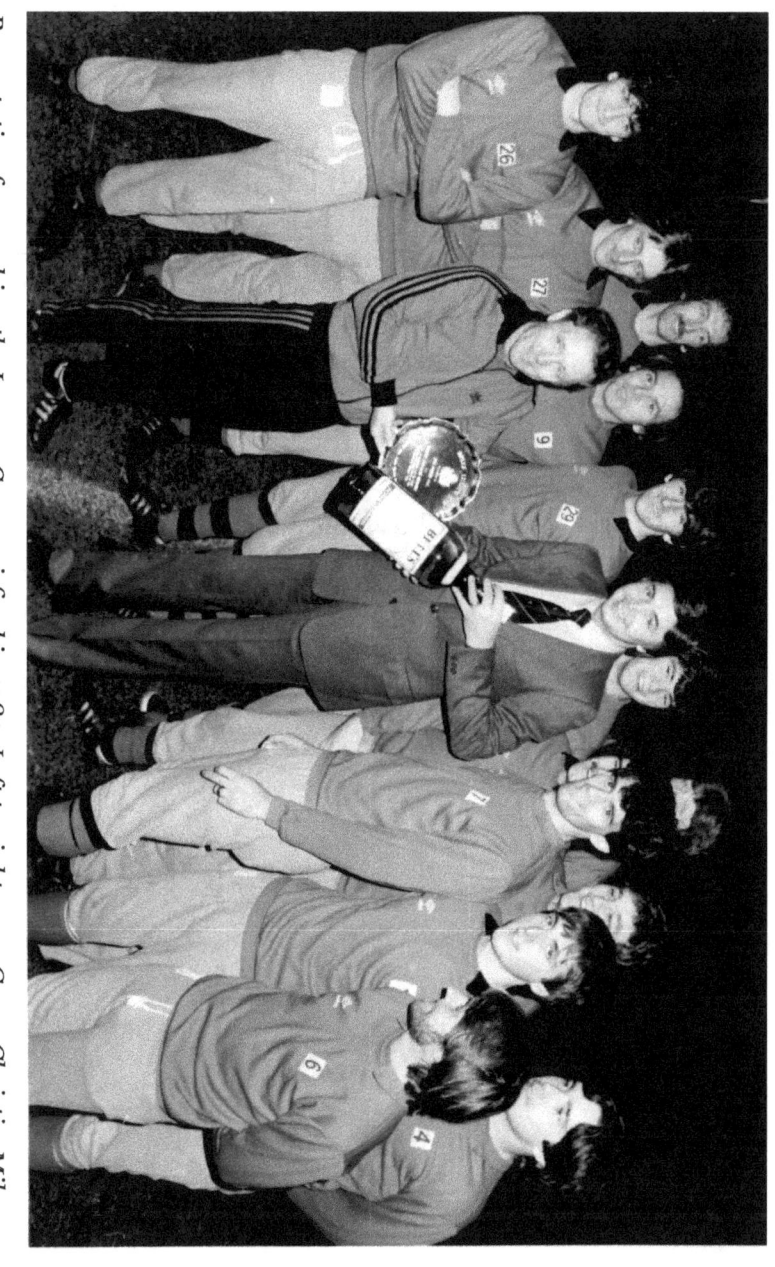

Presentation for reaching the League Cup semi-final in 1980. Left to right rear: Gerry Christie, Mike Larnach, Eric Morris, Jim McSherry, Robert Connor, Billy Hendry, Mark Shanks, Stevie Nicol (top of head only), Derek Frye and Billy McColl. Left to right front: Willie McLean, Bell's representative, Jim Fleeting, Ian Cashmore and Ally Love.

League competitions: Texaco Cup / Anglo-Scottish Cup

Ayr United competed in this competition between 1972/73 and 1977/78 inclusive, scoring thirteen goals in total. The breakdown is: Davy McCulloch 3, Gerry Phillips 3, Walker McCall 2, Brian Bell 1, Rikki Fleming 1, Johnny Graham 1, Alex Ingram 1 and Malky Robertson 1.

Davy McCulloch – the club's joint top scorer in the Texaco Cup/Anglo Scottish Cup.

League competitions: Centenary Cup/ B & Q Cup / League Challenge Cup / Alba Challenge Cup / Ramsdens Cup/Petrofac Training Cup / Irn Bru Cup

The competition was introduced in 1990 to commemorate the centenary of the Scottish Football League. Participation was restricted to league clubs outwith the Premier League. It was initially planned on a one-off basis. The success was instrumental in it being commuted to an annual competition. In the interim period 1998/99 remains the only season in which it was not held. Ayr United reached, but lost, the first two finals.

Up to and including 2018/19 the club had scored ninety-four goals in the competition, this total not including the shootout goals against East Stirling in 1994, Queen of the South in 2006, Montrose in 2017 and Queen's Park in 2018. At the top of the charts for these goals are Ally Graham and Tommy Walker (both with five), Hugh Burns and Alex Williams (both with four) and Sam McGivern, Mike Smith and Alan Forrest (each with three). Tommy Walker's goal against Brechin City at Somerset Park on 2nd October, 1990, was the first goal by any club in this cup.

Club record win in the competition – Ross County 0 Ayr United 4 on 10th August, 1996, and East Stirling 1 Ayr United 5 on 16th August, 2017.

Club record defeat in the competition – Ayr United 0 St.Johnstone 4 on 26th August, 1996.

Alex Stuart.

Managers

For record purposes periods of interim management are excluded except in cases where the interim management has preceded a full appointment.

Herbert Dainty	Close season 1914 until April 1915.
Lawrence Gemson	April 1915 until April 1918.
John Cameron	Close season 1918 until close season 1919.
James MacDonald	Close season 1919 until close season 1923.
Jimmy Richardson	Close season 1923 until close season 1924.
Jimmy Hay	Close season 1924 until January 1926.
Archie Buchanan	January 1926 until September 1931.
Alex Gibson	September 1931 until January 1935.
Frank Thompson	January 1935 until close season 1940.
Bob Ferrier	Close season 1940 until December 1948.
Archie Anderson	April 1949 until close season 1953.
Reuben Bennett	Close season 1953 until April 1955.
Neil McBain	April 1955 until close season 1956.
Jacky Cox	August 1956 until November 1961.
Bobby Flavell	November 1961 until December 1961 (17 days).
Gerry Mays	December 1961 until December 1962.
Neil McBain	December 1962 until October 1963.
Bobby Flavell	October 1963 until December 1964.
Tom McCreath	December 1964 until close season 1966.
Ally MacLeod	Close season 1966 until November 1975.
Alex Stuart	November 1975 until September 1978.
Ally MacLeod	September 1978 until December 1978.
Willie McLean	January 1979 until April 1983.
George Caldwell	Close season 1983 (after being interim manager) until October 1985.
Ally MacLeod	October 1985 until December 1990.

George Burley	January 1991 until December 1993.
Simon Stainrod	December 1993 until September 1995.
Gordon Dalziel	October 1995 (after being interim manager) until November 2002.
Campbell Money	November 2002 until August 2004.
Mark Shanks	August 2004 until March 2005.
Robert Connor	May 2005 until February 2007.
Neil Watt	March 2007 until October 2007.
Brian Reid	October 2007 until May 2012.
Mark Roberts	May 2012 until December 2014.
Ian McCall	January 2015.

Ayr United versus St.Mirren in a Scottish Cup tie on 16th February, 1985. The visiting goalkeeper in the photo is future Ayr manager Campbell Money.

Maternity

Peter Price

On 7th November, 1959, Ayr United beat Celtic 3-2 at Celtic Park in a First Division fixture. Peter Price played in this match despite having barely slept over a period of three days. This was because wife Christina was in hospital for the impending birth of daughter Jacqueline, who was safely delivered at 6lb 10oz. Although not scoring against Celtic his contribution was significant.

Paul Cairney

On 19th November, 2016, Falkirk won 1-0 at Ayr in a Championship fixture. The Ayr team took to the field with Paul Cairney wearing the captain's armband. This honour was bestowed on him because his wife had given birth a matter of hours earlier. After taking part in the toss-up the armband was passed to Nicky Devlin.

Michael Moffat

On 2nd February, 2019, Ayr United won 3-1 at Alloa in the Championship. Michael Moffat scored twice. This was an exceptional achievement considering he lacked sleep. His wife Megan had given birth to daughter Mila at 8.14 that morning. He showed no outward signs of tiredness so he played for the entire match.

Mark Shanks

Nicknames and soubriquets

Beer Barrel: Tony Carroll: 1940.
Big shyness: David Craig: 1998–2004.
Cally: Ian McAllister: 1977–1991.
Casper: Eric Morris: 1979–1985 *and* Mark Duthie 1998–1999.
Chic: Jim Charnley: 1983–1984.
Cutty: Quintin Young: 1969–1971.
Dally: John Duncan: 1948–1950.
Dandy: Jim McLean: 1958–1962 *and* George McLean 1970–1975.
Danny Kaye: Jacky Robertson: 1952–1955.
Dibble: Campbell Money: 1999–2002 (coach) and 2002–2004 (manager).
Dixie: Alex Ingram 1966–1969 and 1970–1977.
Do *(pronounced dough)*: Donald Murray: 1929–1931.
Doc: Ross Docherty: 2015–
Dun: Jimmy Hay: 1915–1918 (player) and 1924–1926 (manager).
Elkie: Jacky Clark: 1939–1940.
Fally: Charlie Rodger: 1931–1935 and 1939–1940.
Fermer: Jock Smith: 1919–1926.
Freddy: Derek Frye: 1979–1983.
Goofy: Ian McGiffen: 1974–1978. *(The nickname arose from the connotations within the surname. He bore positively no resemblance to the Disney character!).*
Henry: James Hall: 1937–1940.
Hep: Bob Hepburn: 1926–1937.
Hilly: Alex Goodwin: 1911–1915.
The Kaiser: Jim Fleeting: 1979–1983.
The Man in Black: Davy Stewart: 1967–1973.

Mark Duthie

Brian Ahern

The Moff:	Michael Moffat: 2011–2014 and 2017–
Manuel:	Brian Ahern: 1981–1983.
Marko:	Mark Roberts: 2009–2014 (player) and 2012–2014 (manager).
The Mighty Quinn:	Stan Quinn: 1966–1973.
Nile:	John Tyson: 1946–1947.
The Patna Flyer:	Tommy Robertson: 1929–1934 and 1939–1940.
Peanut:	Paul Sheerin: 2001–2003.
Peerie:	Harry Cunningham: 1920–1925.
Pundy:	Andy Aitken: 1968–1971.
The Provost:	Sam Leckie: 1949–1957.
Puck:	William Ure: 1932–1935.
Puskas:	Willie Hendry : 1957 - 1959.
Roger:	Robert Connor: 1977–1984 and 1996–1997.
Rossco:	Ross Scott: 1978–1979 and 1987–1991.
Sanny:	Alex McAnespie: 1964–1978.
Shay:	Stephen Grindlay: 2008–2010.
Snakey:	John Traynor: 1991: 2000.
Sprigger:	Robert White: 1912–1917.
Spud :	John Murphy: 1963: 1978.
Susie:	Arthur Paterson: 1964–1967. *(The nickname could be interpreted as being detrimental but it arose from his flamboyant playing style).*
Switcher:	Jimmy McLaughlan: 1910–1920.
Tottie:	Jim McGhee: 1958–1962.
Tucker:	Tommy Sloan: 1984–1986.
Viva:	Bobby Rough: 1968–1973.
Warhorse:	Willie Robertson: 1927–1929.
Yogi:	John Hughes: 2000–2002.

Penalty kicks

Switcher McLaughlan holds the club record for scoring the most penalty kicks. Between seasons 1910/11 and 1919/20 he netted forty league goals, twenty-five of which were from penalties. In the same period he got one in each of the Scottish Cup and the Scottish Qualifying Cup for a grand total of twenty-seven.

18th November, 1911: Scottish Qualifying Cup: Dumbarton 4 Ayr United 1. Speedie scored a hat-trick of penalties for the home team.

15th October, 1927: Second Division: Morton 0 Ayr United 2. Bob Hepburn saved both of Morton's penalties.

17th January, 1931: Scottish Cup: Ayr United 11 Clackmannan 2. Goalkeeper Bob Hepburn exercised his right as captain to take the penalty from which he made it 6-1.

2nd September, 1931: First Division: Dundee 2 Ayr United 2. Four penalties were awarded, three of which were scored with. Tommy Robertson scored with the two Ayr United penalties. Dundee's Gilmour scored with his first penalty and had his second one saved.

23rd January, 1937: Second Division: Brechin City 2 Ayr United 3. Four penalties were awarded. Each team missed their first and scored with their second.

13th August, 1955: League Cup: St.Johnstone 5 Ayr United 1. Ayr goalkeeper Willie Travers saved three penalties although the third was netted on the rebound.

8th March, 1958: Second Division: Ayr United 3 Arbroath 3. Of the three penalties awarded, none were scored with. Ayr goalkeeper

Joe Mackin saved two and team mate Jimmy Whittle struck his too high.

13th December, 1969: Reserve League: Ayr United reserves 1 Hibs reserves 2. Jim McFadzean hit an Ayr penalty wide. The referee ordered a retake for encroachment. Alex McCall hit the retake over the top. Another retake was awarded since goalkeeper Thompson Allan had moved too early. Andy Aitken took the third attempt and the ball was touched out for a corner-kick.

18th September, 2010: Second Division: East Fife 2 Ayr United 3: Mark Roberts created a club record by scoring a hat-trick of penalties in this match including a stoppage time winner. In what little that was left he was sent off. One of the East Fife goals was also from a penalty.

16th October, 2010: Second Division: Forfar Athletic 4 Ayr United 1: Forfar were awarded four penalties by two referees. Owing to traffic problems the appointed referee arrived late and took over for the second half. In the first half the only goal was a Ross Campbell penalty for Forfar. In the second half, with the score at 2-0, Forfar got three penalties. Neither of these awards was a retake. David Crawford saved from Ross Campbell then Scott Allan within ninety seconds. Martyn Fotheringham made the score 3-0 with Forfar's fourth penalty.

The following outfield players have saved a penalty while playing in goal in an emergency (all league): Jimmy McLeod, Alloa Athletic away, 9th February; 1926: Fally Rodger, Celtic away, 13th January 1940: John Robertson, Dundee away, 18th April, 1998.

In season 2010/11, thirty-five penalties were awarded in all Ayr United games i.e. League, Scottish Cup, League Cup, Challenge Cup and Play-offs. Nineteen were in Ayr United's favour and sixteen were conceded. Of the nineteen given, seventeen were scored with (Mark Roberts 14, Andy Rodgers 2 and Alan Trouten 1). The two unsuccessful penalties were taken by Mark Roberts and saved by the same East Fife goalkeeper (Michael Brown) in consecutive games. Of the sixteen conceded, fourteen were scored with and two saved (by David Crawford in the same match at Forfar).

18th September, 1976: Premier League: Ayr United 1 Dundee United 4. Visiting goalkeeper Hamish McAlpine missed two penalties. Hugh Sproat saved the first one. The next one went over the crossbar.

10th April, 1982: First Division: Ayr United 1 Falkirk 0. Apart from Forfar (2011) and Dunfermline (2016) this is the only other historical precedent for the opposition failing with two penalties inside two minutes but they were missed rather than saved by Jimmy Brown.

30th October, 2004: Second Division. Peter Cherrie saved a penalty on his debut, a 1-0 away win over Morton. On 6th November, 2004 (Second Division) he saved a penalty in his second match for Ayr United, a 4-3 win at home to Alloa Athletic.

15th May, 2016: Championship play-off final, 2nd leg. This was decided by a shootout at home to Stranraer. Greg Fleming saved the first three. Technically these were not penalties because a penalty can only be awarded when an offence has been committed.

3rd December, 2016: Championship: Dunfermline Athletic 1 Ayr United 1: Greg Fleming saved a penalty from Kallum Higginbotham in the 83rd minute. Less than ninety seconds later he saved another penalty from the same player.

Greg Fleming saved the first five penalties he faced in season 2016/17. These were against St.Mirren (19th July), Dundee United (20th August), Falkirk (7th October) and two against Dunfermline Athletic (3rd December). The sixth one he faced was struck wide by St.Mirren's Lawrence Shankland (17th December). The seventh was also saved. That was against Falkirk (14th January). To this point of his Ayr United career (signed 1st June, 2015) he had faced ten penalties and only been beaten once. His first penalty save for the club was against Stenhousemuir on 24th October, 2015. At Peterhead on 23rd April, 2016, Rory McAllister struck the post from the spot. At Dunfermline on 13th February, 2016, former Ayr United player Michael Moffat did succeed in beating him with a penalty. After the save at Falkirk he faced one other penalty in his Ayr United career. That was away to Hibs in the Scottish Cup on 4th March, 2017, and Jason Cummings scored from it. Shootouts are technically not penalties because no offence has been committed but, as previously mentioned, in the shootout against Stranraer on 15th May, 2016, (play-off final) he saved three and, in addition, in the shootout away to Queen's Park (Scottish Cup) on 24th January, 2017, he saved two.

Points

Club record at two points for a win: sixty-one in 1987/88.

Club record at three points for a win: seventy-seven in 1996/97.

Club record lowest: nine in 1966/67.

Postponements

On 14th January, 1939, an Ayr United versus Queen's Park fixture was publicised as being the first major postponement at Somerset Park. The story was wrong. As far back as 8th February, 1902, the pitch was declared unplayable for a Second Division fixture between Ayr FC and East Stirling. Seven inches of snow landed on the town between 11 o'clock on the Friday night and daybreak. It was reported that snow in Ayr had not lain to such a depth in more than forty years. One week later the ground remained unplayable for what would have been a league visit from Abercorn.

On 29th January, 1910, the ground was unplayable for a Second Division match between Ayr FC and Dumbarton and the same situation occurred on 20th November, 1915 in connection with a First Division fixture between Ayr United and Clyde. In earlier years the ground was deemed playable in conditions which would have compelled a postponement in the modern age. Pedantically it could be argued that there was a grain of truth in that January 1939 match being reported as the first major postponement at Somerset Park. The argument is based on the fact that prior to season 1924/25 the pitch ran on a different alignment (north-east to south-west rather than the east to west alignment it was converted to).

On 8th December, 1962, Stranraer played a Second Division game at Ayr. The club's next home league match took place on 2nd March, 1963. Between those dates Somerset Park hosted a Scottish Cup tie with Dundee United. Between playing at Forfar on 22nd December, 1962, and East Fife at Methil on 23rd February, 1963, that Scottish Cup tie was the only game Ayr United took part in.

The winter of 2009/10 was comparable to that of 1962/63. On 5th December, 2009, Dunfermline Athletic played a First Division game at Ayr. The club's next home league match took place on 6th March, 2010. Between those dates Somerset Park hosted a Scottish Cup tie with Brechin City.

After playing at Dumbarton on 13th November, 2010, Ayr United's next league match was at home to Dumbarton on 2nd January, 2011. The only match between those dates was a Scottish Cup tie at home to Sunnybank on 20th November, 2010.

In January 1979 Ayr United had six postponements and the club took part in an Ayrshire Cup tie only that month.

From 12th December, 1981, until 23rd January, 1982, Ayr United had seven postponements and an abandonment.

The following matches (all league) were postponed because the opposition clubs claimed that they could not field a strong enough team: Celtic (home) 6th March, 1976; Celtic (home) 10th March, 1976; Motherwell (home) 13th March 1976; Partick Thistle (home) 3rd March, 1984.

In season 1998/99 a Clydebank versus Ayr United league fixture was postponed ten times before going ahead at Boghead Park, Dumbarton, on the evening of 27th April, 1999. The original scheduled date was 9th January.

An unusual postponement took place on 8th February, 1958. Somerset Park was playable but bad weather conditions prevented the Berwick Rangers party from travelling.

The earliest point of the season at which an Ayr United game has been postponed due to ground conditions was on 10th August, 2004. This was for a League Cup tie away to Hamilton Accies. The ground was waterlogged despite it being an artificial surface. The next earliest match to be postponed for ground conditions was Montrose (away) in the league on 21st September, 1985.

The following matches were postponed when the pitch was playable but it was considered that the wind was too strong. Ayr

United versus Dundee (Scottish Cup) on 8th February, 2000; Ayr United versus Raith Rovers (league) on 11th November, 2005; Ayr United versus Stenhousemuir (league) on 30th January, 2016; Ayr United versus Inverness Caledonian Thistle (league) on 7th December, 2018.

John Duncan

Tommy Sloan

Quotations

"What's the use of there being a Second League at all if there's to be no automatic promotion? The Second League might as well be a separate and distinct body. The whole thing is a farce."
Ayrshire Post dated 18th April, 1913, after Ayr United had retained the Second Division title but were left to sweat on a vote for promotion.

"The time was when Christmastide was associated with merriment. Even the most casual glance around sufficed to dispel any idea that Christmas Day itself was anything else than a tragedy."
On Christmas Day 1915, Ayr United beat Kilmarnock 2-0 in a First Division fixture at home. It being during the Great War not even this did much, if anything, to lighten the mood. This piece of social commentary from the Ayrshire Post succeeded in passionately capturing the local sentiment.

"The management seem to have lost all power of judgement."
A 2-1 defeat at home to Third Lanark on 30th September, 1922, left an Ayrshire Post reporter in no doubt about where to lay the blame.

"The manner of our defeat in the Scottish Cup will remain an unhappy memory."
At the annual general meeting in 1924 chairman Lawrence Gemson voiced justifiable bitterness at being denied a semi-final place due to an outrageous refereeing decision.

It is to be hoped that Ayr supporters will now have learned the value of properly selected oratory."
After a 2-1 win at home to Kilmarnock on 2nd January, 1935, the Ayrshire Post had a dig at the habit of barracking.

Neil McBain in the comfort of his office on 15th January, 1963.

Neil McBain on 15th January, 1963 – little prospect of a thaw before the scheduled visit of Albion Rovers on Saturday 19th January.

"When Carroll, Ayr's new outside-right from Luton Town, wears off some of his superfluous fat, he will be an attraction at Somerset Park."

Ayr Advertiser reporting on Tony Carroll's debut on 2nd March, 1940. The fans nicknamed him Beer Barrel Carroll.

"Football next year is in the lap of the Gods."

Chairman Andrew Wright at an annual general meeting lasting five minutes on 30th May, 1940. At the same meeting it was decided to close the club down for the duration of the war.

"The day the Somerset roar was born."

Ayr Advertiser reporting on victory over Rangers on 12th January, 1957.

"There were no queues to get into Somerset Park on Saturday. There were as many drafts blowing through the Stand as paying customers."

Ayr Advertiser reporting on a 5-3 defeat by Arbroath on 24th March, 1962.

"Play football? You could skate on it."

Manager Neil McBain when Ayr United versus Albion Rovers was postponed on 19th January, 1963."

"The length of time the club will be able to carry on depends upon the support it receives from the public of Ayr and district through the turnstiles and the Development Club."

Board statement issued on 24th November, 1964.

"If he parted with the ball a little sooner he wouldn't be in my team. He would be in the Scotland team."

Ally MacLeod talking about Ian Hawkshaw on Scotsport on the evening of 23rd April, 1966, promotion having been won with a draw at Arbroath that afternoon. Note the confident reference to 'my team'. He wasn't the manager at this time.

"Ayr United still without a league victory."

David Coleman throughout most of season 1966/67 when the results were coming through on the BBC teleprinter.

"I feel sure that I have had enough playing experience to have a shot at being manager."
> Alex Ferguson on accepting the managerial post at East Stirling after his release by Ayr United.

"Why should a Premier League side like ourselves be over the moon at beating Rangers?"
> Alex Ingram in his Ayrshire Post column reflecting on a 3-0 win at home to Rangers on 11th October, 1975.

"The world and his whippet have written off Ayr United as relegation fodder."
> Ayrshire Post reporting on a 1-0 home defeat against St.Mirren in the Premier League on 18th March, 1978.

"This is a very intimidating place to come."
> St. Mirren manager Jimmy Bone after a 3-3 draw at Ayr on 8th May, 1993.

"I well remember coming to Somerset Park as a boy. The first game I saw was against Queen of the South in 1965 and I was in the record crowd when Ayr beat Rangers four years later."
> Campbell Money upon his appointment as Ayr United manager on 20th November, 2002.

"In twenty-three years in the game the day when we won promotion at Brechin was the best I've ever had. I won leagues, cups, played in the Premier League and in Europe but Brechin, with its three pitch invasions, was my highlight. I will have that memory until I die."
> Mark Roberts after being relieved of his managerial duties on 15th December, 2014.

"If you support Barcelona you want to play for them, and with me it's no different with Ayr."
> Ryan Stevenson on rejoining Ayr United from Partick Thistle on 21st January, 2016.

"I supported Ayr United when I was young."
> The first words spoken by legendary Liverpool goalkeeper Tommy Lawrence in a documentary film about his career.

Campbell Money.

"It's over". (In a loud voice).
> *The West Sound broadcast on 28th April, 2018, confirming that Raith Rovers had failed to beat Alloa Athletic and Ayr United were the League One champions.*

"People are giving me credit for some kind of masterful team talk but the reality is our fans were different class and played a huge part in getting us back into that game. At times it felt like the Somerset Road end was pulling the ball into the net."
> *Ian McCall commenting to the Ayrshire Post after a 2-0 half-time deficit against Falkirk had been transformed into a 3-2 win on 15th September, 2018.*

"You know if you lose a goal here the atmosphere can change."
> *Inverness Caledonian Thistle manager John Robertson in tribute to the intensity of the Ayr fans on 29th January, 2019.*

What Ayr United have given me is my drive and all my ambition back."
> *Ian McCall on 11th May, 2019.*

Ally Fraser – two Scottish Cup goals for Ayr United including a last minute winner in a replay at Hamilton on 27th February, 1991. It prompted a Roger Milla-style celebration.

Scottish Cup

Up until the conclusion of 2018/19 the club had scored 380 goals in the competition. For record purposes shootouts have been ignored. The semi-finals have been reached in 1973, 2000 and 2002.

Scottish Cup scorers - The complete list

11 Alex Ingram.
10 Danny Tolland.
9   Peter Price.
8   George McLean.
7   Davy McCulloch, Terry McGibbons, Sam McMillan, Jacky Robertson.
6   Jimmy Baker, Harry Cunningham, Murdoch McKenzie, Mark Roberts.
5   Ian Ferguson, Declan McDaid, Own goals (McDougall /Airdrie/1926-27, Allan/Queen of the South/1934-35, Wells/Peebles Rovers/1959-60, McChesney/Queen of the South/1975-76, MacPherson/Dunfermline Athletic/2001-02).
4   Hyam Dimmer, Willie Japp, Andy McCall, Charlie McGillivray, Brian McLaughlin, Alex Merrie, Craig Moore, Eddie Moore, Arthur Paterson, Lawrence Shankland, John Sludden, Bobby Stevenson, Jock Taylor, Henry Templeton, Jimmy Yardley.
3   John Anderson, Eddie Annand, Billy Brae, Scott Crabbe, Kenny Cunningham, James Grady, Johnny Graham, Johnny Kilgannon, Michael Moffat, Archie Muir, Jim Nisbet, Tommy Robertson, Alex Sharp, Donald Slade, Jimmy Smith, Neil Tarrant, Gary Teale, Alan Trouten, Andy Walker, Gareth Wardlaw, Alex Williams.
2   Alec Beattie, Tommy Bryce, Robert Connor, Craig Conway, John Doyle, Neil Duffy, Andrew Ferguson, Pearson Ferguson, Gordon Finnie, Leslie Fitzgerald, Jimmy Fleming, Rikki Fleming,

Jim Dick

Ally Fraser, Billy Fulton, Andy Geggan, Ally Graham, Darren Henderson, Dougie McCracken, Pat McGinlay, Alastair McIntyre, John McLean, Willie Neil, Bryan Prunty, John Quinn, Chris Robertson, John Robertson, Malky Robertson, Andy Rodgers, Paul Sheerin, Ryan Stevenson, Tommy Walker, Jock Wallace.

1   Jock Aitken, Davy Armour, Conrad Balatoni, Stuart Bannigan, Aaron Black, Jimmy Brannan, Stevie Bryce, Paul Cairney, Bobby Cairns, Mark Campbell, Gerry Christie, Gerry Collins, David Craig, Gordon Cramond, Ian Crawford, Jimmy Crichton, Billy Crosbie, Jim Dick, Ross Docherty, Michael Donald, Ryan Donnelly, David Dunn, Alex Ferguson, Bud Fisher, Alan Forrest, Willie Fraser, David Gemmell, Duncan George, David Gormley, Alec Gray, Robert Hart, Billy Hendry, Bob Hepburn, Tony Hepburn, Willie Irvine, Sandy Jones, Dean Keenan, Tommy Kilpatrick, Mike Larnach, Alan Lithgow, Allan Livingstone, Willie Lyle, Andy Lyons, Gordon Mair, Craig Malcolm, John Malcolm, Dick Malone, Anthony Marenghi, Danny Masterton, Ian McAllister, Alex McAnespie, Walker McCall, Dan McColgan, Dougie McCracken, Robert McDougall, Jim McGhee, Michael McGowan, Neil McGowan, Craig McGuffie, Tommy McGuigan, Switcher McLaughlan, Steve McLelland, Tam McManus, Norrie McNeil, Mattha Morgan, Dougie Mitchell, Eric Morris, Malky Morrison, Jimmy Murphy, Andy O'Connell, Gerry Phillips, Tommy Ramsay, Thomas Reid, Jimmy Richardson, Willie Robertson, Bobby Rough, David Sinclair, Albert Smith, John Steele, John Tyson, William Ure, Jerome Vareille, Jacky Walters, Michael Wardrope, Peter Weir, Jimmy Whittle, Kenny Wilson, Marvyn Wilson.

Scottish Cup wins against clubs from a higher league

21st January, 1928: First round: Ayr United 2 Bo'ness 0

Team: Hepburn, Purdon, Fleming, Robertson, McColgan, Turnbull, Nisbet, Tolland, Smith, Brae and Kilpatrick.

Bo'ness: Dempster, Hume, Ramsay, Middleton, Walker, Thomson, Lynas, Martin, Cochrane, Cottingham and Oswald.

Goals: Jimmy Smith 1-0 and 2-0.

A cup win against a club from a higher league would ordinarily be defined as a shock but this particular result might have been

Paul Agnew – the man in possession when the final whistle blew on the 2-0 Scottish Cup win over Kilmarnock.

expected. It was a contest between the Second Division's leading club and a club fighting to avoid relegation from the First Division. Jimmy Smith killed the tie with a goal in the third minute and another in the sixth minute.

15th February, 1964: Third round: Aberdeen 1 Ayr United 2

Team: Gallacher, Murphy, Maxwell, Frew, Toner, Lindsay, Hubbard, McMillan, Kilgannon, Grant and Cunningham.

Aberdeen: Ogston, Shewan, Hogg, Burns, Coutts, Smith, Kerrigan, Cooke, Graham, Winchester and Hume.

Goals: Billy Graham 1-0; Kenny Cunningham 1-1; Johnny Kilgannon 1-2.

In terms of league placings this match was entered as the fourth lowest club in Scotland. Not even the wildest of optimists would have entertained even a glimmer of hope. When Billy Graham scored ten minutes into the second half it was expected. It was further expected that those metaphorical floodgates would then open. In the 77th minute John 'Tubby' Ogston dropped a Johnny Hubbard cross. Sam McMillan got to the loose ball then squared it for Kenny Cunningham to fire an equaliser. At 1-1 it was a sensation. In the 87th minute a long kick from goalkeeper John Gallacher hit Doug Coutts on the shoulder then fell for Johnny Kilgannon. He got past Coutts in an instant then, faced by the advancing Ogston, got a shot away. The ball rose over Ogston then dipped into the net. Your writer will never forget the thrill of seeing Aberdeen 1 Ayr United 2 spelling itself out on the BBC teleprinter.

14th February, 1998: Fourth round: Ayr United 2 Kilmarnock 0.

Team: Finnbogason, Robertson, Hogg (D'jaffo 64), Millen, Burns, Anderson, Dick, Traynor, Ferguson, Agnew and Bowman; unused substitutes – Bonar and Castilla.

Kenny Wilson

Peter Weir

Roddy Grant.

Kilmarnock: Marshall, MacPherson, Baker, Lauchlan, McGowne, Reilly, Mitchell (Bagan 84), Holt, Wright, Roberts (Henry 85) and Vareille (McIntyre 70).

Goals: Jim Dick 1-0; Ian Ferguson 2-0.

In the build-up to this tie the Kilmarnock fans were in buoyant mood. They were the Scottish Cup holders and there was a strong feeling of nigh invincibility in their faction of the 9,286 crowd. Kristjan Finnbogason could not be beaten in the Ayr goal. As the second half progressed there was even a hope that a home win was possible. After Gordon Dalziel sent on an attacker for a defender (Laurent D'jaffo for Keith Hogg) in the 64th minute the balance swung in our favour. Jim Dick scored with a ferocious header from an Ian Ferguson cross for 1-0. Seven minutes to go! Two minutes later Laurent D'jaffo dispossessed Kevin McGowne to set up Ian Ferguson who turned quickly then struck a shot into the far corner of the net. The jubilation had not yet died down from the first goal.

23rd January, 1999: Third round: Ayr United 3 Kilmarnock 0.

Team: Castilla, Robertson, Winnie, Millen, Traynor, Craig, Hurst, Davies, Walker, Teale and Lyons (Reynolds 85); unused substitutes – Welsh and Ferguson.

Kilmarnock: Marshall, MacPherson, Montgomerie, McGowne, Baker, Reilly, Holt (Mahood 74), Durrant, Roberts, McCoist and Mitchell; unused substitutes – Henry and Lauchlan.

Goals: Andy Lyons 1-0; Andy Walker 2-0 and 3-0 (penalties).

This was supposedly the day on which Kilmarnock were returning to Ayr to extract a much desired revenge only to suffer a defeat of even more catastrophic proportions. In the 29th minute a John Davies shot rebounded off Andy Walker then landed for Andy Lyons to score with a drive from eighteen yards. In the 81st minute Ray Montgomerie got sent off for pulling Glynn Hurst back by the shirt. Andy Walker scored from the resultant penalty. Two minutes later there was a strong feeling of déjà vu. Martin Baker

Andy Lyons – opening scorer in the 3-0 Scottish Cup rout of Kilmarnock on 23rd January, 1999.

David Winnie – a defensive stalwart in the 3-0 Scottish Cup win over Kilmarnock.

Gary Teale.

pulled down Gary Teale for a second penalty at a time when the commotion had not yet died down from the previous one. Andy Walker made it 3-0 with the cheekiest of penalty kicks. He simply sent a gentle dink down the middle.

15th February, 2000: Third round replay: Ayr United 1 Dundee 1 after extra time. Ayr won 7-6 in the shootout.

Team: Nelson, McMillan (Grant 101), Robertson, Scally (Crilly 85), Craig, Duffy, Teale, Wilson, Hurst, Tarrant (Reynolds 70) and Shepherd.

Dundee: Langfield, Smith, McSkimming (Sharp 119), Robertson, Tweed, Raeside, Boyack (Banger 62), Rae, Bayne (Grady 79), Wilkie and Falconer.

Goals: Gavin Rae 0-1; Neil Duffy 1-1.
Shootout: James Grady 0-1; Neil Duffy 1-1; Willie Falconer 1-2; David Craig 2-2; Lee Sharp 2-3; Glynn Hurst 3-3; Lee Wilkie 3-4; Marvyn Wilson 4-4; Robbie Raeside 4-5; Gary Teale 5-5; Barry Smith 5-6; Paul Shepherd 6-6; John Robertson 7-6.

It was a tense night. In the shootout Marvyn Wilson, Gary Teale and Paul Shepherd all had to score to keep Ayr United in the tie. It was the club's first shootout at Somerset Park with the exception of youth matches. There was a possibility that the tie might have been abandoned at the end of ninety minutes. The snow was particularly bad and the lines had to be swept clear.

26th February, 2000: Fourth round: Motherwell 3 Ayr United 4.

Team: Nelson, McMillan, Shepherd, Craig, Robertson, Duffy, Wilson, Tarrant (Crilly 70), Reynolds, Teale and Hurst; unused substitutes – Grant and Campbell.

Motherwell: Goram, Doesburg, McGowan, Denham (Davies 82), McMillan, Townsley (Nevin 60), Brannan, Valakari, Twaddle (Nicholas 72), Goodman and McCulloch.

Paul Shepherd.

Goals: Gary Teale 0-1; Lee McCulloch 1-1; Don Goodman 2-1; Gary Teale 2-2 (penalty); Ged Brannan 3-2 (penalty); Neil Tarrant 3-3 and 3-4.

What a match! It was 3-3 at half-time. Adding to the drama was Craig Nelson going off for treatment and full-back John Robertson having to play in goal for seven minutes. Mickey Reynolds was sent off in the 63rd minute following a tackle on Pat Nevin. By then it was 4-3 to Ayr but the cause was handicapped by having to play a man short for such a prolonged period. Television pictures proved that Lee McCulloch's goal should not have stood since it did not cross the line.

26th January, 2002: Fourth round: Ayr United 3 Dunfermline Athletic 0.

Team: Nelson, Robertson, Lovering, Duffy, Hughes, Craig, Wilson, McGinlay, Crabbe (Annand 84), Grady and Sheerin (Scally 75); unused substitutes – McEwan, Sharp and Dodds.

Dunfermline Athletic: Scott Y Thomson, Skinner (Panopoulas, half-time), Skerla, Scott M Thomson, Nicholson, Ferguson (Hampshire 67), Crawford, Petrie (Kilgannon 61), Mason, MacPherson and Bullen; unused substitutes – Nicholls and Harrower.

Goals: James Grady 1-0; Gus MacPherson own goal 2-0; John Robertson 3-0.

On the half-hour mark an inswinging corner-kick from Scott Crabbe appeared to be going straight in but James Grady got his head on it to make absolutely sure. Nine minutes later Gus MacPherson slammed a John Robertson cross into his own net while trying to put it out for a corner. In the 58th minute John Robertson was sent clear by Scott Crabbe and his initial shot stuck in the mud. He then reacted quickly to poke it into the net. Late in the match Barry Nicholson and Scott M Thomson both hit the Ayr crossbar.

Marvyn Wilson

Ayr United versus Hibs in the Scottish Cup on 18th January, 2011. Celebrating the tie's only goal are (left to right) Jonathan Tiffoney, Mark Roberts (the scorer) and Stuart Bannigan.

6th March, 2002: Quarter-final replay: Ayr United 2 Dundee United 0.

Team: Nelson, Robertson, Lovering, Duffy (McEwan 57), Hughes, Craig, Wilson, McGinlay, Crabbe (Kean 77), Grady (Sharp 90) and Sheerin.

Dundee United: Gallacher, Hannah (Aljofree 80), Lauchlan, Easton, Miller, Lilley (Winters 66), McCunnie, Griffin, Venetis (Carson 53), Thompson and McCracken.

Goals: Scott Crabbe (penalty) 1-0; Paul Sheerin (2-0).

In the 11th minute Anastasios Venetis brought down Paul Lovering at the cost of a penalty kick which Scott Crabbe converted. It was so nearly 2-0 in the 52nd minute when a John Robertson cross was met by Neil Duffy whose header struck a post. Yet that scoreline became a reality in the 79th minute. Paul Sheerin intercepted a wayward pass then advanced to within twenty yards of goal from where he scored with a left-foot curling shot.

18th January, 2011: Fourth round replay: Ayr United 1 Hibs 0.

Team: Crawford, Tiffoney, Smith, Malone, Campbell, McCann, Bannigan, McLaughlin, Rodgers, Roberts (Robertson 90) and Easton; unused substitutes – Woodburn, Kelly, Moore and McWilliams.

Hibs: Smith, Hart (Wotherspoon 67), Murray, Dickoh, Hanlon (Booth 80), Rankin, Miller, McBride, Nish, Riordan and Duffy (Zemmama 64); unused substitutes – Galbraith and Stack.

Goal: Mark Roberts.

There was ample historical precedent for eliminating a club from a higher league from the Scottish Cup but this was the first Ayr United team to achieve the feat against a club from two leagues higher. The match was won by a 19th minute goal of quite brilliant individual quality. An Andy Rodgers cross spun off a defender then

Paul Lovering

got brought under control by Mark Roberts who wrong-footed an entire line of defenders to create enough space to find the net with a clinical left-foot shot.

Scottish Cup defeats against clubs from a lower league/non league

28th February, 1920: Third round replay: Ayr United 0 Armadale 1.

Team: Kerr, Semple, McCloy, Hogg, Gillespie, McLaughlan, Smith, Crosbie, Richardson, McBain and Gray.

Armadale: Robb, Dick, Kiernan, Gardner, Kirkbride, Scoullar, Speirs, Gordon, Poole, Anderson and Smith.

Goal: Gordon.

This was First Division versus Central League. The tie might even have been lost on the Saturday before when it took a 75th minute penalty to salvage a draw. Johnny Crosbie and Jimmy Hogg missed the first game because they were in Cardiff on Scotland duty. For the replay the team was at full strength in addition to home advantage and meticulous preparation. The killer goal came in the 36th minute.

14th February, 1931: Third round: Bo'ness 1 Ayr United 0.

Team: Hepburn, Willis, McCall, Yorke, McLeod, Turnbull, Nisbet, Tolland, McGillivray, Young and Brae.

Bo'ness: Fraser, Clark, Gray, W. Aitken, Fagan, McLaren, Lumsden, J. Aitken, Taylor, McDonald and Pratt.

The embarrassment of losing to a Second Division club was accentuated by that club sitting bottom of their league. There was a break-in during the second half when the home team had a penalty claim rejected. The anger of these fans turned to joy in when McDonald scored with a header ten minutes from the end.

20th January, 1932: First round replay: St.Johnstone 2 Ayr United 0.

Team: Hepburn, Robertson, Fleming, Taylor, McLeod, McCall, Tolland, Smith, Merrie, Brae and McLean.

St.Johnstone: McLaren, Welsh, Wilson, Ferguson, Ireland, McBain, Ritchie, Benzie, Benson, Nicol and Nicholson.

Goals: Jimmy Benson 1-0 and 2-0.

This Wednesday afternoon replay followed a draw at Ayr on the Saturday when St.Johnstone made it 3-3 in hotly contested circumstances in the final minute. There were claims of a handball in the build-up. Both linesmen were consulted before the goal stood. In this season St.Johnstone won promotion from the Second Division as runners-up on goal average. With Ayr United striving to avoid relegation from the First Division there was little difference in status. At Muirton Park home advantage was asserted. Jimmy Benson's goals came in the 11th minute then in the 33rd minute.

19th February, 1935: Second round third replay: Ayr United 1 King's Park 2.

Team: Wilson, Taylor, Ure, McCall, Currie, Holland, Fisher, Landsborough, McGibbons, Brannan and Rodger.

King's Park: Milton, Temple, Soutar, Brown, Baird, Hillan, Andrew, Young, Bryce, Laird and Lang.

Goals: Terry McGibbons 1-0; Andrew 1-1; Andrew 1-2.

Airdrie had to wait patiently to find out which club they would be playing in the third round. Draws at Ayr, Stirling and neutral Firhill could not separate First Division Ayr United from Second Division King's Park, even with extra time in both replays. The third replay took place at Hampden on a Tuesday afternoon, despite the Firhill match having taken place on the previous afternoon. Of the 14,300 Hampden crowd 6,490 passed through the unemployed gate. Terry

McGibbons scored in the 18th minute "quite in accordance with the run of play." At 1-0 to Ayr, King's Park missed two first half penalties. Andrew (57 and 62) won the match for King's Park.

25th January, 1936: First round: Ayr United 2 St.Mirren 3.

Team: Hepburn, Bourhill, Strain, Baigrie, Currie, Holland, Pope, McGibbons, Fleming, Steele and Torbet.

St.Mirren: McCloy, Baird, Ancell, Cunningham, Wilson, Miller, Latimer, Knox, MacGregor, McCarron and Gall.

Goals: Jimmy Knox 0-1; Terry McGibbons 1-1; Cunningham 1-2; Terry McGibbons 2-2; Cunningham 2-3.

By the end of the season Ayr United would be bottom of the First Division and St.Mirren would be promoted as runners-up in the Second Division. It may have been a defeat against a club from a lower league but it could not have been defined as a shock. It was 2-2 at half-time then Cunningham struck the deciding goal in the 75th minute. The crowd was 17,241. King George V had died five days before this tie but the weekend football went ahead as scheduled. Newspapers reporting this match carried details of the impending funeral.

21st January, 1939: First round: Alloa Athletic 2 Ayr United 1.

Team: Hall, Dyer, Strain, Ross, Currie, Mays, McConnell, McKenzie, Yardley, Gemmell and Thow.

Alloa Athletic: D. McFarlane, Hamilton, Bulloch, McDonald, H. McFarlane, Ferguson, Moore, Gallacher, Gillespie, Smith and Fitzsimmons.

Goals: David Gemmell 0-1; Moore 1-1; Gillespie 2-1.

As in 1936 this defeat was against a club on course to finish as runners-up in the Second Division. David Gemmell scored for Ayr in the 11th minute. There was a great chance to enhance that lead from the penalty spot ten minutes into the second half. Hugh McConnell had his effort saved. Suitably encouraged Moore scored for Alloa within a minute. As if to continue the momentum the home team immediately got possession from the recentre and advanced upfield whereupon Gillespie struck the post then netted the rebound. What might have been a 2-0 lead became a 2-1 deficit within several minutes.

13th February, 1954: Second round: Berwick Rangers 5 Ayr United 1.

Team: Round, Fraser, Leckie, Jeffrey, McNeil, Nesbit, Japp, Munro, Tracy, Finnie and Beattie.

Berwick Rangers: Devanney, Hogg, McColl, Taggart, Cassidy, Mitchell, Younger, Muir, Kingsmore, McGovern and Blaikie.

Goals: Kingsmore 1-0; Muir 2-0; Kingsmore 3-0; Blaikie 4-0; Willie Japp 4-1; Kingsmore 5-1.

At this time Berwick Rangers played in 'C' Division. On the Saturday before the tie the injured Norrie McNeil travelled to spy on them in their league game at home to Aberdeen reserves. This in itself was an indication of just how low a level they were playing at. This was the same level as Ayr United reserves, albeit that Berwick played in the North and East region of that league as opposed to the South and West region. Manager Reuben Bennett ordered his players to "go all out from start to finish." Brian Kingsmore, an Irish divinity student, destroyed Ayr United with a hat-trick. It could be said that we were left without a prayer! It was a contrast to our 9-3 win in the Scottish Cup at Berwick in 1929. This demise in 1954 prompted talk of a boycott.

9th February, 1955: Fifth round replay: Ayr United 2 Inverness Caledonian 4 after extra time.

Team: Round, Govan, Leckie, Traynor, McNeil, Gallagher, Japp, Robertson, Kelly, Lindsay and Beattie.

Inverness Caledonian: Bruce, Anderson, Fraser, Bolt, Farmer, McIntosh, MacFarlane, Baillie, Brown, Mackenzie and Main.

Goals: Baillie 0-1; Jacky Robertson 1-1; Alec Beattie 2-1; Brown 2-2; MacFarlane 2-3; Mackenzie 2-4.

It had taken an 81st minute equaliser from Alec Beattie in a 1-1 draw to keep Ayr United in the Scottish Cup when the clubs had met at Telford Street on the Saturday. However the embarrassment of losing to Highland League opposition was deferred merely to the Wednesday afternoon. It may seem that the attendance of 4,217 was a good one considering the inconvenient kick-off time. Not so! In 1955 it was thought to be worryingly low for a Scottish Cup tie. It was 2-2 after ninety minutes then, in the first half of extra time, Caley scored twice and squandered a penalty. At 2-1 to Ayr Jock Govan retired from the tie with a facial injury.

1st February, 1967: First round: Elgin City 2 Ayr United 0.

Team: Millar, Malone, Murphy, Oliphant, Quinn, McAnespie, Black, Mitchell, Ingram, Hawkshaw and Paterson.

Elgin City: Connell, Gerrard, Laing, Sanderson, D. Grant, Smith, Fraser, Graham, W. Grant, Gilbert and Middleton.

Goals: Willie Grant 1-0 and 2-0.

This tie took place on a Wednesday evening after being postponed due to ground conditions on the Saturday. If the match had taken place on the appointed Saturday there could have been no better day to bury bad news since the major focus was on Rangers losing at Berwick. First Division Ayr United losing on a Highland League ground was a footballing disaster. An historical precedent was Dundee losing at Fraserburgh in 1959. The crowd at Elgin was reported as being 13,500. The true figure, still impressive, was 9,579. In the final seconds of the first half Dick Malone got sent off for a tackle on Willie Grant. The ground being waterlogged it was probably a harsh decision by referee Bert Crockett. Willie Grant scored twice in the second half (70 and 75).

25th January, 1975: Third round: Ayr United 1 Queen's Park 2.

Team: McGiffen, Filippi, Murphy, McDonald, Fleming, Tait, Doyle, Graham, Ingram, Phillips and McVake; substitutes – McAnespie and McCulloch.

Queen's Park: Cameron, McGowan, Currie, Bowie, Campbell, Donnelly, McGill, Thomson, Paton, McWilliams and McKay; substitutes – Colgan and Rennie.

Goals: Hugh McGill 0-1; Alex Ingram 1-1; Jimmy Paton 1-2.

Even after going a goal down in the 31st minute there was a confidence that a team laced with club legends would eventually overcome our Second Division opponents. Such confidence was justified when Alex Ingram scored with a flying header eight minutes into the second half. A deep feeling of unease then enveloped the ground when Queen's Park took the lead again twelve minutes later. The fightback was frantic. With quarter of an hour left Johnny Doyle was downed. Penalty! Johnny Graham struck the post from the spot. In the closing minutes Gerry Phillips and Alex Ingram both shot high from close range.

18th February, 1976: Fourth round replay: Queen of the South 5 Ayr United 4 after extra time.

Team: Sproat, McDonald, Murphy, McAnespie, Fleming, McSherry, Doyle, Graham, Ingram, McCulloch and Robertson; substitutes – Dickson and Phillips.

Queen of the South: McLean, McChesney, Miller, Clark, Boyd, McLaren, Dempster, Peter Dickson, Reid, O'Hara and George Dickson; substitutes – Hutton and Donald.

Goals: Iain McChesney own goal 0-1; Nobby Clark 1-1; Davy McCulloch 1-2; Ian Reid 2-2; Malky Robertson 2-3; George Dickson 3-3; Peter Dickson 4-3; Alex Ingram 4-4; Peter Dickson 5-4.

Derek Frye

In later years reflection on this tie invariably gave mention to exaggerated attendance figures. The true figure was 7,880. In the first tie on the Saturday Ayr United had squandered a 2-0 lead then, at 2-2, Johnny Graham's 84th minute penalty kick was saved by Alan Ball. A spectator at the Palmertson replay was an eleven-year-old Dumfries boy called Ian McCall, an Ayr United manager of the future. 3-3 at half-time, 4-4 after ninety minutes – the match was enthralling. Peter Dickson's winner came in the 116th minute. First Division Queen of the South had conquered Premier League Ayr United. It was John Doyle's last game for the club prior to moving to Celtic.

30th January, 1982: Third round: Alloa Athletic 2 Ayr United 1.

Team: Rennie, Shanks, Ahern, Hume, McAllister, Fleeting, Frye, Kean, Morris, Connor and Christie; substitutes – Larnach and Ward.

Alloa Athletic: Hunter, Ballantyne, McKenzie, Purdie, Stewart, Holt, Paterson, Oliver, McComb, Smith and Grant; substitutes – Murray and Haggart.

Goals: Drew Paterson 1-0; Robert Connor 1-1; Alan Holt 2-1.

Ayr United boss Willie McLean and his assistant George Caldwell were both ex-Alloa players. The result prompted Mr McLean to comment: "This is the biggest disappointment I have ever suffered in football." A goal down at half-time, there was a hope of a revival when Robert Connor equalised in the 58th minute. At 1-1 Derek Frye struck the crossbar. Alan Holt's winner came in the 68th minute. There was plenty time left to get back level yet as the tie progressed the home team looked more likely to increase their lead. The defeat was more comprehensive than the result suggested.

29th January, 1983: Third round: Ayr United 1 Albion Rovers 2.

Team: MacKay, Shanks, Connor, Morris, McAllister, Fleeting, Frye, McInally, Larnach, Ahern and Christie; substitutes – Hendry and McNaughton.

Albion Rovers: Balavage, Allan, Grant, Leishman, Burgess, Collins, Dow, Gray, Evans, Livingstone and Conn; substitutes – Gibson and McQueen.

Goals: Alec Livingstone 0-1 and 0-2; Mike Larnach 1-2.

The signs of impending doom were there virtually from the start. Robert Dow had a goal disallowed after four minutes. Then we had the sight of Scott MacKay having to make a series of impressive saves to keep our Second Division opponents at bay. Alec Livingstone (69 and 73) created a 2-0 deficit which sent a gloom over the ground. Mike Larnach scored nine minutes from time. Jim Robb was forthright with his comments in the *Ayr Advertiser*: "Thousands of fans have already had enough. Many more will follow them away from the terracing unless something is done quickly." The Albion Rovers manager was Martin Ferguson, brother of the more illustrious Alex.

6th January, 1996: Second round: Ayr United 0 Ross County 2.

Team: Duncan, Clarke, Traynor, George, Jamieson, Sharples, Smith, Steel, Dalziel, Balfour (Byrne 77) and Kinnaird (Wilson 77); unused substitute – Barnstaple.

Ross County: Hutchison, Herd, MacKay, Robertson, Bellshaw, Furphy (Williamson 82), Ferries, Grant (MacLeod 85), MacPherson (Milne 71), Connelly and Golabek.

Goals: Cammy Robertson 0-1; John Sharples own goal 0-2.

This was Ross County's second season at league level having ascended from the Highland League. The contest was Second Division versus Third Division. Captaining Ross County was former Ayr United player Willie Furphy whom the club had recently tried to sign once more. In the 68th minute Cammy Robertson scored with a speculative shot, Cammy Duncan having been distracted by the presence of Brian Grant. Five minutes later John Sharples sliced a Willie Furphy cross into his own goal. The goals came against the run of play although this did not mask the clear fact that it was a bad display. Anger at the outcome was vocal.

Willie Furphy

19th January, 2019: Fourth round: Auchinleck Talbot 1 Ayr United 0.

Team: Doohan, Geggan (Smith 36), Rose, Higgins, Harvie, McDaid, Murdoch (McGuffie 75), Docherty, Crawford, Moffat and Moore (Bell 84); unused substitutes – Ferguson, Hilton, McCowan and Hare-Reid.

Auchinleck Talbot: Leishman, Lyle, McPherson, McCracken, Pope, White, Stephen Wilson (McIlroy 70), Armstrong, Hyslop, Glasgow (Shankland 76) and Graham Wilson (Samson 76); unused substitutes – Kemp, Waite and Hewitt.

Goal: Craig McCracken.

Ex-Ayr United players in the home squad were Willie Lyle, Craig McCracken, Gordon Pope, Gareth Armstrong, Mark Shankland and David Waite. Even their boss Tommy Sloan was a former Ayr United player. There was a peculiar irony that a contender for the worst result in the club's history should happen at a time when the team was three points off the top of the Championship with a game in hand and a superior goal difference. In fact six days later top place was reached. In the 78th minute a Mark Shankland free-kick was delivered into the penalty area where Craig McCracken rose unchallenged to score with a header.

Scottish Internationalists

The players listed here are those to have played for Scotland at full international level while still attached to Ayr United. Johnny Crosbie made one more international appearance while at Birmingham City but that has been disregarded for the purpose of this list. The matches in 1919 were deemed to be unofficial Victory internationals yet are justifiably recorded here as full internationals.

Johnny Crosbie

Ireland 0 Scotland 0: 19th April, 1919: Windsor Park.
Wales 1 Scotland 1: 26th February, 1920: Ninian Park.

Jimmy Richardson

Ireland 0 Scotland 0: 19th April, 1919: Windsor Park.
England 2 Scotland 2: 26th April, 1919: Goodison Park.

Jimmy Hogg

Scotland 2 Ireland 1: 4th March, 1922: Celtic Park.

Jock Smith

England 1 Scotland 1: 12th April, 1924: Wembley.

Phil McCloy

England 1 Scotland 1: 12th April, 1924: Wembley.
Scotland 2 England 0: 4th April, 1925: Hampden Park.

Jim Nisbet

Norway 3 Scotland 7: 26th May, 1929: Brann Stadion, Bergen.
Germany 1 Scotland 1: 1st June, 1929: Deutsches Stadion, Berlin.
Holland 0 Scotland 2: 4th June, 1929: Olympisch Stadion, Amsterdam.

Jimmy Hogg played for Scotland on 4th March, 1922. This photo shows him in 1956.

SCOTTISH FOOTBALL ASSOCIATION LIMITED

GEORGE G. GRAHAM,
Secretary.

Telegrams, "Executive, Glasgow."

Telephones { 581 South.
{ 582 "

48 CARLTON PLACE,

Glasgow, 25th April, 1929.
C.5.

Mr. A. Buchanan,
    Ayr United F.C.

Dear Sir,

<u>CONTINENTAL TOUR.</u>

    J. Nisbet is invited to take part in tour arranged by this Association, embracing the following matches:-

        26th May at Bergen   (Norway)
        28th "   "   Oslo   (do)
        2nd.June "   Berlin   (Germany)
        4th "   "   Amsterdam(Holland)

    Party will leave Glasgow on Tuesday 21st. May and return to Glasgow on Wednesday 5th June.

    I will be pleased to know not later than Tuesday first, 30th April, if the player accepts the invitation, in which case, he will be required to sign the enclosed agreement.

    In event of player accepting invitation, please furnish me with the following information for Insurance purposes;- Full name of player, private address, age; also please send me two small unmounted photographs for passport purposes.

    The player shall bring his boots, shin-guards and all necessary equipment other than jerseys, knickers and stockings.

                              Yours truly,

                                  G.G. Graham.
                                     SECY.

Jim Nisbet played for Scotland in the continental tour in 1929. This letter is the Scottish Football Association's invitation to take part.

Bob Hepburn

Scotland 3 Ireland 1: 19th September, 1931: Ibrox Park.

John Doyle

Scotland 1 Romania 1: 17th December, 1975: Hampden Park.

Wilf Armory. He was an inside-forward signed from Spennymoor United in June 1930. After Ayr United his clubs were Aldershot, Nuneaton Borough and Folkestone. He died on 21st December, 1996, thus ending a 62-year association with Folkestone FC as a player, then as manager then as the club president. Even into old age he had a daily swim in the English Channel.

Sequences

Winning sequences

The greatest number of consecutive wins is twelve. These were all Second Division fixtures and the date span was 24th October, 1936, until 2nd January, 1937.

In 1968/69 Ayr United won eleven consecutive Second Division fixtures. Within the date span there was a win and a defeat in the Scottish Cup. Taking straight wins into account the total was ten. This comprised nine Second Division fixtures and one Scottish Cup tie. The date span comprised 23rd November, 1968, until 1st February, 1969.

The third best run of straight wins is nine in 2017/18. This occurred between 21st October, 2017, and 16th December, 2017. These matches comprised eight in League One and one in the Scottish Cup.

Ayr United had nine straight Second Division wins from the start of season 1911/12. The last three Second Division fixtures of 1910/11 were won with the consequence that twelve consecutive league wins could be claimed. However cup involvement meant that the club did not actually achieve twelve straight wins overall.

The club record for consecutive away league wins is seven. This happened in 1958/59.

The second best run of away league wins is six. This dates to season 1998/99.

Losing sequences

Between 17th December, 1966, and 11th February, 1967, ten consecutive First Division matches were lost. During that spell there was a Scottish Cup defeat at Elgin therefore the club record for consecutive defeats is eleven. The run was broken with a draw at home to Motherwell then the next four league matches were lost. It meant that one point was taken from a run of fifteen league fixtures.

The largest number of consecutive league defeats from the start of a season is five. It happened in 1964/65.

Winless sequences

The club's worst run of consecutive games without a win is thirty-one. It happened in 1966/67. These games comprised the first twenty-eight First Division games of the season and within that run there were two winless League Cup ties and a winless Scottish Cup tie.

Ayr United won a First Division fixture away to Morton on 12th April, 1930. The club's next away league win came in a First Division fixture at Hamilton on Boxing Day 1931. This remains a club record run for consecutive away league fixtures without a win. The total, in common with the previous statistic, was thirty-one.

The second worst run of winless away league fixtures also happened after winning away to Morton. That win occurred on 16th April, 1994. The club's next away league win happened at Montrose on 23rd September, 1995. That run of consecutive away league matches without a win amounted to twenty-two.

The next worst run of winless away league fixtures is eighteen. This comprised all seventeen in 1966/67 plus the first one in 1967/68.

The longest winless run after being appointed Ayr United manager relates to John Cameron who failed to win in the first eight fixtures between 17th August, 1918, and 5th October, 1918.

The sequence was broken on 12th October with a 3-2 win over Hearts at Tynecastle. There were extenuating circumstances. Earlier in 1918 Cameron had been repatriated after being held captive in Germany since shortly after the outbreak of war in 1914. He had not fully recovered from his ordeal.

On 1st September, 2015, Ayr United beat Stenhousemuir 5-2 at home in a league fixture. It was the club's first midweek win since a 2-1 victory in a league match at Livingston on 6th March, 2012. A 3-3 draw at home to Peterhead on 3rd March, 2015, ended a run of thirteen consecutive midweek defeats. In that game we had an 88th minute equaliser and it was a reprieve match. Up to the win over Stenhousemuir the club endured a sequence of twenty midweek matches comprising eighteen defeats, a draw at Airdrie in a play-off and the draw with Peterhead referred to above. Ignored for statistical purposes are midweek matches with an afternoon kick-off (technically holiday matches and all lost), a Friday evening match with Dunfermline (not really midweek but still lost) and friendlies. The Stenhousemuir result was the first midweek win at home since a 2-1 Scottish Cup victory over Falkirk on 15th February, 2012, and the first midweek league win at home since beating Partick Thistle 1-0 on 10th March, 2010.

Unbeaten Sequences

The club best for consecutive unbeaten league games is seventeen dating to 1958/59. There were no cup games during that run.

In 1979/80 the club had sixteen consecutive unbeaten league games. There were two League Cup defeats during that run.

On 21st January, 1950, Cowdenbeath won 2-1 at Ayr. The next home league defeat came on 13th September, 1952, when Stenhousemuir won 4-2 at Somerset Park. Within that time Ayr United were unbeaten in thirty-three consecutive home league games. It remains a club record.

On 14th February, 1987, Ayr United lost 2-0 at Arbroath. The next away defeat (in any competition) was at Perth on 27th February, 1988. This unbeaten away run amounted to twenty-two. The breakdown was eighteen in the league, three Scottish Cup ties and one League Cup tie.

Abercorn won a Second Division fixture at Ayr on 26th November, 1910. Ayr United's next home league defeat did not happen until 17th August, 1912, when Abercorn were also the opponents.

Ayr United have completed the following league campaigns unbeaten at home: 1911/12 (champions Second Division), 1936/37 (champions Second Division), 1950/51 (third 'B' Division), 1951/52 (third 'B' Division) and 2008/09 (runners-up new style Second Division).

No visiting team has ever won a league fixture at Somerset Park on Burns Day. This record goes right back to Ayr FC and the inception of league football at Somerset Park in season 1897/98. An interesting aside is that when Beresford Park existed his statue faced straight into that ground.

Shutouts

From 16th November, 1912, to 1st January, 1913, Ayr United played eight consecutive matches without losing a goal. All of these matches were league fixtures and the goalkeeper in all cases was Robert 'Sprigger' White. This remains the club record for consecutive shutouts. In his first ten games for the club (all league) he conceded just one goal and that was from a penalty kick in his second game. The ten games referred to are the first two plus the eight shutouts.

From 21st July, 2018, to 18th August, 2018, Ayr United played seven consecutive games without losing a goal. This run comprised four League Cup ties, two league fixtures and an Irn Bru Cup tie. In each of these games the goalkeeper was Ross Doohan.

From 28th December, 1968, to 1st February, 1969, Ayr United played six consecutive games without losing a goal. This run comprised five league games plus one in the Scottish Cup. In each of these games the goalkeeper was Davie Stewart.

The club's highest number of league shutouts in a season is eighteen dating to 1968/69. The ratio was one in two from the thirty-six league fixtures and the goalkeeper for all eighteen was Davie Stewart. For season 1912/13 the ratio of league shutouts was also one in two and this involved thirteen shutouts from twenty-six fixtures.

Taking all competitive matches into account the club record for the greatest number of shutouts in a season is twenty-one. Again this dates to season 1969/69 and again the goalkeeper in all twenty-one matches was Davie Stewart. In addition to the eighteen league shutouts there were two in the League Cup and one in the Scottish Cup.

The next greatest number of shutouts in a season is twenty. This occurred in season 2018/19 and the goalkeeper in all twenty matches was Ross Doohan. The breakdown was fourteen in the league, four in the League Cup, one in the Irn Bru Cup and one in the Scottish Cup.

Special titles

The professor

Bert Whittington was an 18-year-old centre-forward (who could also play on the wing) when he signed for Ayr United from Lochend in July 1964. At that time he was a student at Strathclyde University. He achieved a first class honours BSc in electrical engineering and a PhD. After working as a research officer he became a lecturer at Edinburgh University and in 1994 he was promoted to a personal chair in electrical power engineering. Professor Bert Whittington's professional career was outstanding. His professional football career did not bear comparison but he did score in the first minute of his Ayr United debut. That was in a 2-1 win at home to Dumbarton in a League Cup sectional tie on 15th August, 1964. His captain was Ally MacLeod. In that 1964/65 season he made two League Cup appearances plus twelve in the league. He scored two goals. These were the debut goal referred to and one in a 3-0 home league win over Dumbarton on 19th September. At the age of fifty-six he died in a road accident.

The knighthood

On Monday, 3rd September, 1973, Ayr United signed Alex Ferguson, the released Falkirk striker. He went on to make eighteen starting appearances in the league (plus eight substitute listings), four starting appearances in the Scottish Cup and two in the Texaco Cup. In the process he scored ten goals, comprising nine in the league and one in the Scottish Cup. He was released at the end of the season then went into management with East Stirling. His managerial career then progressed with St.Mirren, Aberdeen and Manchester United. He remains the longest serving Manchester United manager of all time and during his tenure the club won thirty-eight trophies. The Queen's Birthday Honours list in 1999 confirmed that he was to become Sir Alex Ferguson. The other Manchester United manager to have received a knighthood was Matt Busby. On 14th February, 1945, he was released as a player by Liverpool. On the same day it was announced that he had agreed to manage Ayr United. The Ayr United board issued a denial.

The Member of the British Empire

Johnny Hubbard signed for Ayr United in the summer of 1962. He was a 31-year-old left winger who was acquired after his release from Bury whom he had joined in 1959 after a decade at Rangers. Johnny was born in South Africa but he was a winger in the style beloved of Scottish fans. His pace and skill made him a troublesome prospect for defenders in his path. He remained at the club for two seasons. These were inauspicious seasons for the club despite the high level of his individual performances. He made sixty-five appearances comprising fifty-one in the league, three in the Scottish Cup and eleven in the League Cup. Eight goals were scored. These comprised five in the league and three in the League Cup. The expression 'all round sportsman' could have been made for him. He was exceptional at cricket and tennis. In 1998 he was awarded an MBE for services to sport. These services were exceptional since he put in a power of work to help sport flourish in Ayr and Prestwick. At the age of eighty-seven he passed away on 21st June, 2018.

Substitutes

In season 1966/67 the concept of substitutes was introduced to Scottish Football, albeit that it was deferred until 1967/68 for the Scottish Cup. At that time only one substitute was allowed and the expression 'twelfth man' was used. In earlier phases of history Ayr United had used substitutes in testimonial matches and friendlies only. The first Ayr United player to go on as a substitute in a competitive fixture was Stan Quinn. This was during a League Cup tie at home to Cowdenbeath on 20th August, 1966. He went on for Dougie Mitchell.

In season 2016/17 a new ruling permitted a fourth substitute (rather than the regular three) to be used in the Scottish Cup provided that the tie was in extra time. On 24th January, 2017, Michael Rose went on for Nicky Devlin in stoppage time in extra time in our replay away to Queen's Park. Ayr United therefore became the first club to implement this ruling.

Tallest players

In February 1974 Ayr United signed goalkeeper Louden Muir from Blantyre Celtic. He was 6'7"; he did not make a first team appearance.

In March 2009 the club signed central defender Kevin James on loan from St.Johnstone. He too was 6'7".

Testimonials

Bobby Cunningham

15th August, 1911: Ayr United 1 Rangers XI 4.

Team: Massey, Armour, Gardiner, Dickson, Connell, McLaughlan, A.H. Goodwin, Logan, Phillips, Simpson and Goodwin.

Rangers XI: Cameron, Ormond, Richmond, R. Brown, Waddell, Bodan, Paterson, J.L. Goodwin, Dunne, Gibson and A.H. Brown.

Goals: Hilly (Alex Hill) Goodwin 1-0; A. Brown 1-1; Jacky Goodwin 1-2; Gibson 1-3; A. Brown 1-4.

Bobby Cunningham had been a forward with Ayr FC back in the Springvale Park days. In August 1901 he was appointed as trainer of Ayr FC, a position he held through to the amalgamation in 1910. The brothers Hilly and Jacky Goodwin scored for their respective teams.

Bert Tickle

21st August, 1912: Ayr United 1 Queen's Park 2.

Team: Massey, Fletcher, Thomson, Connell, Tickle, McLaughlan, H.J. Miles, Page, Phillips, Simpson and Campbell.

Queen's Park: Kerr, Yeudal, Russell, Walker, Wilson, Alexander, Anderson, Keith, Young, Forsyth and Hill.

Goals: Bob Young 0-1; Harry Simpson 1-1; James Anderson 1-2.

Bert Tickle was a centre-half who had formerly played for Preston North End and Parkhouse. He was the Ayr United captain on the occasion of the club's inaugural league fixture. It was reported that: "With tickets sold and not represented at the match Tickle should reap a good sum from his benefit." In December 1912 he was transferred to St.Bernard's but by February 1913 he was at St.Johnstone.

Switcher McLaughlan

20th August, 1919: Ayr United 2 Celtic 2.

Team: Kerr, Agnew, McCloy, Hogg, Gillespie, McLaughlan, Billy Crosbie, Johnny Crosbie, Richardson, McBain and Kennedy.

Celtic: Shaw, Shea, Kelly, McLean, Gilchrist, Cassidy, McAtee, Mackay, Burns, Craig and Pratt.

Goals: Jimmy Richardson 1-0 and 2-0; Joe Cassidy 2-1; Tully Craig 2-2.

Switcher's actual name was Jimmy but he was seldom referred to by anything other than his nickname. He played in the original Ayr United team back in 1910 and he was immediately a favourite of the supporters. From his half-back role he displayed fearsome shooting and he developed a reputation as an expert at converting penalties. His testimonial proceeds amounted to £226: 18s: 5d. This equated almost exactly to the monthly wage bill for the entire playing staff at this time.

Jimmy Richardson

4th January, 1921: Ayr United 3 League Select 3.

Team: Lindsay, Hunter, Smith, Hogg, Gillespie, McLaughlan, Scott, Stevenson, Richardson, Slade and Cowan.

League Select: Gould (Queen's Park), Struthers (Queen's Park), Woodburn (Ayr United), Cumming (Cumnock Juniors), Porter (Hearts), Newton (Clyde), Mackay (Celtic), Gourlay (Morton), McKenzie (Ayr United), Cassidy (Celtic) and McPhail (Kilmarnock).

Donald Slade 1-0; Newton 1-1; Jimmy Richardson 2-1; Murdoch McKenzie 2-2; Jimmy Gourlay 2-3; Cowan 3-3.

£112 was taken at the gate but this figure did not take account of the tickets which were sold and not used. The linesmen were regular goalkeeper George Nisbet and regular left-back Phil McCloy. Jimmy Richardson remains the club's third highest scorer of league goals despite missing more than two seasons due to active service.

George Nisbet

30th August, 1922: Ayr United 2 Celtic 2.

Team: Nisbet, Smith, McCloy, Walls, McLeod, Gibson, Kilpatrick, Cunningham, Quinn, McKenzie and McLean.

Celtic: Connelly, Glasgow, Jim Murphy, Gilchrist, McStay, McMaster, Jackson, Thomson, McFarlane, Murphy and Connolly.

Goals: Murdoch McKenzie 1-0; Harry Cunningham 2-0; Murphy 2-1; Jean McFarlane 2-2.

George Nisbet was a fearless goalkeeper who would instinctively put his head into the midst of flailing boots. He guarded the Ayr United goal from February 1917 until February 1926 but he started more games than he finished. Almost predictably he was carried off with a head injury at Alloa in his last match. Note Jean McFarlane scoring. This actually was his name. It was derived from the French for John. The gate money amounted to about £100 but this figure had yet to be supplemented by the proceeds from ticket sales.

Jimmy Hogg

3rd January, 1924: Ayr United 3 Third Lanark 2.

Team: Nisbet, Mathieson, Soden, Hogg, Gillespie, McLaughlan, Boyd, Anderson, Richardson, Slade and McAdam.

Third Lanark: Muir, Jackson, Robertson, Caldwell, Wilson, McGregor, Jamieson, Devlin, Houston, Anderson and McGoldrick.

Ayr United goals: John Anderson, Donald Slade and McAdam. Third Lanark goals: McGoldrick and Soden own goal.

Former Ayr United players in the team were Switcher McLaughlan, Alex Gillespie, who was now the club trainer, and Jimmy Richardson who was now the club manager. The small crowd of around 1,000 was attributable to the glut of matches. First Division fixtures had been played on each of the preceding days and another was looming two days later. Jimmy Hogg was a half-back who had a liking for heavy tackling.

Phil McCloy

28th April, 1924: Ayr United 0 Rangers 1.

Team: "Lindsay", Woodburn, McCloy, Murphy, McLeod, Stewart, "Gibson", Cunningham, "Newman", McKenzie and Kilpatrick.

Rangers: Robb, Reid, McCandless, Ireland, Nicholson, Walls, Kilpatrick, Craig, Kirkwood, Macdonald and Morton.

Goal: Tully Craig.

Tully Craig scored for Celtic in Switcher McLaughlan's testimonial in 1919 and here in 1924 he scored for Rangers in the Phil McCloy testimonial. The punctuation in the Ayr team listing denotes the three trialists with concealed names. This match took place two weeks and two days after McCloy had played for Scotland in a 1-1 draw in the first international to be staged at Wembley. On that occasion his full-back partner was Ayr United team mate Jock Smith.

Sam Aitken

24th May, 1924: Ayr Select 1 R.S. McColl's XI 3.

Ayr Select: Massey (Ayr United), Miller (Parkhouse), Aitken (Ayr FC), White (Ayr FC), Gillespie (Ayr United), McLaughlan (Ayr United), Hamilton (Ayr FC), Massie (Ayr FC), Phillips (Ayr United), Cameron (Parkhouse) and Lindsay (Ayr FC). Substitutions: Galbraith (Parkhouse) for Phillips and Montgomery (Ayr FC) for Hamilton.

R.S. McColl's XI: R.S. McColl (Queen's Park), Henry (Manchester City), Garden (Queen's Park), Bowie (Rangers), Campbell (Rangers),

Roberts (Queen's Park), Jarvis (Stoke City), John McMenemy (Celtic), Raitt (Third Lanark), Jimmy McMenemy (Celtic) and T.N. McColl (Queen's Park).

Ayr Select goal: Montgomery.

R.S. McColl's XI goals: William Raitt and Jimmy McMenemy. The scorer of the other goal was unreported.

This match was played at Beresford Park and it truly was played between two teams of veterans. Most of these players made their mark in the Edwardian era and some were playing in an age when Queen Victoria was on the throne. The game was not long underway when Charlie Phillips decided to walk off. Gladstone Hamilton, at the age of forty-five, broke his leg when accidentally kicking the ground. This match was in aid of Sam Aitken who had formerly played at centre-half for Ayr FC, Middlesbrough, Raith Rovers and Ayr United. Here in 1924 he was virtually blind, this condition having been caused in battle during the Great War.

Jock Smith

17th September, 1924: Ayr United 1 Kilmarnock 1.

Team: Cochran, Woodburn, Smith, Hannah, Stewart, Turnbull, Thomson, John McLean, Anderson, Brae and James McLean.

Kilmarnock: Morton, Hood, Gibson, Brown, Clark, McEwan, Walker, Smith, Gray, Wilson and Lindsay.

Goals: Wilson 0-1; Jock Smith 1-1.

Beresford Park was the venue. While trailing 1-0 a second half penalty was awarded. Naturally the taker could have been no one other than Jock Smith and he obliged by converting it. The *Ayrshire Post* report noted: "The penalty was negotiated in an unorthodox manner, completely deceiving Morton." Although playing at left-back on this occasion Smith's career flourished as a right-back

John Woodburn

26th April, 1926: Ayr United 1 Kilmarnock 1.

Team: Hepburn, Woodburn, Smith, Massie, McLeod, Stewart, Fleming, Paton, McCosh, Brae and Kilpatrick.

Kilmarnock: Clemie, Hood, Nibloe, Morton, Dunlop, McEwan, Wishart, Smith, Weir, Cunningham and Crump.

Goals: James Weir 0-1; John McCosh 1-1

The Beresford Park attendance was quoted as being "very poor". The *Ayrshire Post* report went so far as to comment that: "Friendly games as benefit functions are a proved failure." The reason given for this opinion was that: "Players' attitudes were lacking." In common with other players receiving a testimonial John Woodburn had rendered fine service to the club. As a full-back and captain he had inspirational qualities and was deserving of a better testimonial. He was an uncle of Winnie Ewing of SNP fame.

Tommy Kilpatrick

27th April, 1927: Ayr United 1 Rangers 4.

Team: Hepburn, Woodburn, Dean, Russell, Melville, Fleming, Nisbet, Tolland, Gourlay, Brae and Walters.

Rangers: Moyes, Weir, R. Hamilton, Osborne, Ireland, J. Hamilton, Hair, Chalmers, Marshall, Purdon and Smith.

Goals: Hair 0-1; Ireland 0-2; Chalmers 0-3; Weir own goal 1-3; Chalmers 1-4.

The crowd figure was quoted as "about 1,000". Tommy Kilpatrick had formed a reputation for being a pacey winger on either flank but, ironically for a player with natural fitness, he was not fit to play in his testimonial having fractured a bone in his leg in a home match against Queen of the South on 4th December, 1926. Purdon and Smith of Rangers were to become team mates at Ayr the following season. This was the legendary Jimmy Smith.

Billy Brae

29th August, 1928: Ayr United 4 Kilmarnock 1.

Team: Hepburn, Price, 'Trialist', Robertson, Watson, McMurtrie, Simpson, Neil, Wardrope, Sharp and Brae.

Kilmarnock: Gould, Leslie, Nibloe, Inglis, Stewart, Ramsay, Clelland, Williamson, Weir, Mathieson and Gray.

Goals: Wardrope 1-0; Alex Sharp 2-0; Joe Nibloe 2-1; Wardrope 3-1 and 4-1.

The Ayr team had two trialists. One of them was a left-back with a concealed name. The other was centre-forward Wardrope who was then registered with Armadale. His hat-trick, albeit in a benefit match, was impressive enough for terms to be offered. The offer was accepted. Half-time entertainment comprised sprint races which were well received by the crowd.

Willie Fleming

23rd September, 1931: Ayr United 2 Celtic 2.

Team: Hepburn, Willis, McCall, Yorke, Scobbie, Gemmell, McGillivray, Tolland, Merrie, Fleming and Rodger.

Celtic: Coen, Hogg, Miller, Morrison, Gallacher, Scarff, McGhee, Smith, O'Donnell, Solis and Kavanagh.

Goals: Danny Tolland 1-0; Charlie McGillivray 2-0; Jock Morrison 2-1; Peter Kavanagh 2-2.

The *Ayr Advertiser* columns opined: "There was a very poor attendance considering the faithful service Fleming has rendered the club." The choice of opposition was most fitting, the player having signed from Celtic. He got a hat-trick on his Ayr debut at home to Arbroath on 22nd August, 1925. This made him the second of four players to have got a hat-trick on a competitive debut for Ayr United. In his benefit match a 2-0 half-time lead was wiped out by a penalty and a goal in the last minute.

Bob Hepburn

19th September, 1934: Ayr United 1 Manchester City 4.

Team: Hepburn, Taylor, Ure, Andy McCall, Currie, Holland, Mair, Brae, McGibbons, Fisher and Tommy McCall.

Manchester City: Swift, Dale, Barkas, Busby, Percival, Bray, Toseland, Marshall, Heale, Herd and McLuckie.

Goals: Bobby Marshall 0-1; Jimmy Heale 0-2 and 0-3; Jimmy McLuckie 0-4; Terry McGibbons 1-4.

Goalkeeper Bob Hepburn was most fortunate in having such prestigious opponents for his testimonial. Manchester City were the FA Cup holders. With an estimated 8,000 inside Somerset Park there was no repetition of the testimonial apathy that had previously afflicted these occasions. The match marked a return to Ayr for Alec Bell, a native of the town. He had formerly played for Parkhouse and Manchester United and was now the Manchester City trainer.

Jock Taylor

26th April, 1939: Ayr United 1 Barnsley 2.

Team: Hall, Dyer, Strain, Taylor, Currie, Smith, Hope, Dimmer, Craig, Gemmell and Thow.

Barnsley: Binnes, Williams, Everest, Brunskill, Harper, Bokas, Bullock, Steele, Calder, Asquith and McGarry.

Goals: Lewis Thow 1-0; George Bullock 1-1; Danny McGarry 1-2.

This match was arranged as part of the deal that involved John Steele being sold to Barnsley in the summer of 1938. They came to Ayr having recently won the Third Division North. Jock Taylor entered the match in the knowledge that he had been freed. He was a wing-half signed from Hibs on 7th August, 1931.

Davy Currie

Talks regarding a testimonial match for Davy Currie got halted by the war therefore his proposed benefit match did not happen.

Norrie McNeil

13th September, 1950: Ayr United 5 Hibs 5.

Team: Round, Duncan, Perrie, Thyne, McNeil, Nesbit, Henderson, Gallagher, Crawford, Goldie and Beattie.

Hibs: Younger, Govan, Cairns, Howie, Paterson, Combe, Gunning, Johnstone, Reilly, Turnbull and Ormond.

Goals: Bob Thyne 1-0; Hugh Goldie 2-0; Lawrie Reilly 2-1; Alec Beattie 3-1, Hugh Goldie 4-1; Eddie Turnbull 4-2; Willie Ormond 4-3; Bobby Johnstone 4-4; Andy Nesbit 5-4; Lawrie Reilly 5-5.

In the season already underway Hibs were to become the runaway champions of Scotland. Bob Thyne, a friend of Norrie McNeil, guested and scored for the Ayr team. McNeil was the Ayr United captain and a solid centre-half but it was always going to be a busy night against a team containing four of the legendary 'Famous Five'. An injury to Tommy Younger meant that reserve left-half John Ogilvie played in goal for Hibs in the second half. His performance was outstanding.

Andy Nesbit

19th September, 1951: Ayr United 2 Queen of the South 3.

Team: Round, Thomson, Cryle, Bainbridge, McNeil, Nesbit, Japp, Fraser, McCulloch, Hutton and Beattie.

Queen of the South: Henderson, Sharp, Binning, Brackenridge, Waldie, Greenock, Oakes, Patterson, Inglis, Brown and Cruickshank.

Goals: Jacky Oakes 0-1; Willie McCulloch 1-1; Jimmy Inglis 1-2; Jim Patterson 1-3; Alec Beattie 2-3.

Willie McCulloch, then of Airdrie, guested and scored but at 3-1 down he hit a penalty over the crossbar. Former Ayr United players

David Purdie.

Cryle and Bainbridge also made guest appearances. Unfortunately George Cryle was considerably off the pace. In reference to Alec Beattie's goal a few minutes before the end, the *Ayrshire Post* report observed: "Henderson would have needed a policeman's torch to see it in the fast gathering gloom."

Alec Beattie

21st September, 1955: Ayr United 3 Rangers 0.

Team: Round, Leckie, Thomson, Traynor, Gallagher, Haugh, Tracy, McMillan, Price, Stevenson and Beattie.

Rangers: Ritchie, Elliot, Pryde, Miller, Lawrie, Smith, Paton, McMillan, Murray, Queen and Waddell.

Goals: Peter Price 1-0; Sam McMillan 2-0; Sam Leckie 3-0.

This match should have taken place in September 1953 but in that month the clubs were drawn against each other in the two-legged League Cup quarter-finals (4-2 defeat at Ibrox, 3-2 win at Ayr). Nonetheless Rangers honoured their commitment in 1955. Outside-left Beattie had joined from Rangers in August 1946. This match was organised by the Ayr United Supporters' Association. A committee member phoned Blackpool to request the services of Stanley Matthews in the Ayr team. Joe Smith, their manager, refused.

On 30th July, 1957, while still registered with Ayr United, Alec Beattie died after being in a coma for twenty-three days. The cause was a road accident in the east end of Glasgow.

John Duncan

Ayr United sold John Duncan to Newcastle United in November 1949. In the closing weeks of 1951/52 he suffered a knee injury bad enough to enforce his retirement from football. Talks took place about a testimonial match but there were persistent problems. Eventually it was agreed that Newcastle United would play at Ayr on 5th August, 1961. Then the Scottish Football Association intervened to ban the match. The reason was: "It cannot be played before the official start of the season." Bureaucracy prevailed and the John Duncan testimonial match never happened.

Sam McMillan

1st April, 1966: Ayr United 1 Kilmarnock 0.

Team: Millar, Malone, McAnespie, Oliphant, Monan, Thomson, Grant, McMillan, Balfour, Hawkshaw and Paterson.

Kilmarnock: Dick, King, McFadzean, Murray, Beattie, O'Connor, McLean, McInally, Bertelsen, Queen and McIlroy.

Goal: Sam McMillan

This match was played on a Friday night and it doubled up as the first leg of the Ayrshire Cup final (the second leg was lost 3-0). Earlier that day the England squad (soon to be World Cup winners) had trained on Somerset Park in preparation for their match against Scotland at Hampden the next day. Kilmarnock were beaten by a Sam McMillan header in the 31st minute. His eventual benefit cheque amounted to £750. In season 1952/53 he had played for Ayr United in a league fixture on a one-off basis. The summer of 1955 brought about his transfer from Irvine Meadow and he continued playing for the club until the end of season 1967/68.

John Murphy

12th March, 1975: Ayr United 4 Aarhus 1.

Team: Sproat, Taylor, Murphy, McAnespie, Fleming, Filippi, Doyle, Graham, Ingram, McCulloch and Gibson; substitutes – Dickson, McLean and Train.

Goals: Rikki Fleming 1-0; Torben Mikkelson 1-1; Alex Ingram 2-1; Johnny Graham 3-1; John Dickson 4-1.

Blackpool had agreed to play in the John Murphy testimonial on 7th August, 1974, then withdrew. An attempt was made to fix up Greek club Olympiakos to take part but the fighting in Cyprus caused their players to be conscripted into the Forces. Birmingham City then agreed provided that the clubs were not drawn together in the Texaco Cup. They were! Aarhus, from Denmark, duly obliged. Celtic took a bundle of tickets for this match, sold them all, and sent

Clydebank versus Ayr United at Kilbowie Park on 3rd March, 1990. The goalkeeper is David Purdie. Stevie McIntyre is facing the camera.

Gordon Cramond

Ayr United a cheque for £212. John Murphy's playing career at the club extended from 1963 until 1978.

Alex McAnespie

8th May, 1978: Ayr United/Kilmarnock Select 4 Old Firm Select 6

Ayr United/Kilmarnock Select: Stewart (Kilmarnock), Wells (Ayr), Cramond (Ayr), Fleming (Ayr), McDicken (Kilmarnock), McAnespie (Ayr), Provan (Kilmarnock), McCulloch (recently transferred from Kilmarnock to Notts County), McLelland (Ayr), McCulloch (Ayr) and McSherry (Ayr); substitute – Malone (formerly Ayr but with Hartlepool United at this time).

Old Firm Select: McCloy (Rangers), Mackie (Celtic), Filippi (Celtic), Aitken (Celtic), Jackson (Rangers), Glavin (Celtic), Doyle (Celtic), McLean (Rangers), Wilson (Celtic), Smith (Rangers) and Cooper (Rangers); substitute – Jardine (Kilmarnock – no Old Firm connection).

Ayr United/Kilmarnock Select goals: Gordon Cramond, Steve McLelland, Gerry Phillips and Alex McAnespie (penalty).
Old Firm Select goals: Ronnie Glavin with two, Roy Aitken with two and an Iain McCulloch own goal.

Though lacking the intensity of a competitive match this was a worthwhile spectacle. Alex McAnespie scored with a penalty in his testimonial although goalkeeper Peter McCloy stood suspiciously far from the centre of goal! An Ayr United career which began in 1964 was now at an end. He was commonly known as 'Sanny' and, although capable of playing with a bit of style, his reputation was that of a hard man.

The late Gordon Cramond

15th May, 1989: Ayr United 2 Kilmarnock 0.

Team: Purdie, McCann, Hughes, Furphy, McAllister, Evans, Templeton, Wilson, Walker, Kennedy and Cowell; substitutes – Sludden and McIntyre.

Goals: Henry Templeton 1-0 (penalty) and 2-0.

Gordon Cramond died in January 1989 and this Ayrshire Cup final doubled up as a benefit match. He was aged just thirty-nine. Henry Templeton converted a 27th minute penalty after he had been downed then scored again two minutes from the end to ensure that the cup was retained. Cramond was bought from St.Johnstone in March 1976 and was sold to Kilmarnock on Hogmanay 1979. He was a creative and tenacious midfielder who played a major role in Ayr United's Premier League survival in 1976 and again in 1977.

Ian McAllister

11th December, 1990: Ayr United 1 Celtic 2.

Team: Purdie, McIntyre, Evans, McAllister, Gillespie, Smyth, Bryce, Johnston, Walker, Graham and Templeton; substitutes – Love, Hughes, Furphy and Cunningham.

Celtic: Murdoch, Morris, Wdowczyk (Grant, half-time), Galloway, Elliott (McNally 81) Whyte, Hayes (Hewitt, half-time), McStay, Nicholas (Dziekanowski 59), Walker and and Fulton; unused substitutes – Coyne and Creaney.

Goals: David Smyth own goal 0-1; Henry Templeton 1-1; David Smyth own goal 1-2.

Ian McAllister was called up from Ayr United Boys' Club in the summer of 1977. Recurring injuries prompted his decision to quit in December 1991. His Ayr United career span remains beaten by John Murphy only. In central defence Cally was a rock. His testimonial was originally scheduled for 6th March, 1990, but ground conditions compelled a postponement. When eventually played in December it was Ally MacLeod's last match in charge of Ayr United.

Ally MacLeod

28th July, 1993: Ayr United 0 Blackburn Rovers 1.

Team: Duncan (Spence 72), Burley, Robertson, McQuilter, Traynor (Howard 72), George, Kennedy, Sludden (Carse 68), McInally, Burns and Annand; unused substitutes – Fabiani and Sweeney.

David Smyth – a good solid player notwithstanding his own goal mishaps in the Ian McAllister testimonial.

John Sludden

Blackburn Rovers: Mimms, May, Le Saux, Sherwood, Marker, Andersson, Ripley, Atkins, Gallacher, Newell and Wilcox; substitutes – Dickins, Dobson, Makel and Berg.

Goal: Nicky Marker.

Ex-Ayr United players John Sludden and Alan McInally made an appearance. At this time McInally was still under contract to Bayern Munich. Losing to a 75th minute goal has to be put into context. Blackburn Rovers had finished as runners-up to Manchester United in the Premiership in the previous season, then went on to win it in the season soon to get underway. Ally MacLeod remains Ayr United's most successful manager of all time. At the time of his testimonial he was the commercial manager of Airdrie.

John Traynor

23rd March, 2001: Ayr United 1 Newcastle United 2.

Team: Rovde (Dodds, half-time), Burns, Lovering, Renwick, Traynor (Duncan 60), Craig, Crilly (Black 76), Grady (Stevenson, half-time), Bradford, McGinlay (Chaplain; half-time) and Reynolds (Kean 58).

Newcastle United: Karelse, Gavilan, Glass (Kendrick 15), McGuffie, Beharall (Brennan, half-time), Boyd, Coppinger, McClen, Lualua (Bonvin, half-time), McMenamin and Dimas.

Goals: Colin McMenamin 0-1; Mickey Reynolds 1-1; Mark Boyd 1-2.

John Traynor made his Ayr United debut in a 0-0 draw away to Raith Rovers on 9th November, 1991. His career at the club ended against the same opposition. On 10th August, 1999, he was stretchered off during a Challenge Cup tie at home to Raith Rovers. His elbow was dislocated. He played no more first team football and got released at the end of the season. He was just as adept as a full-back as he was in midfield. It was frustrating that his senior career was curtailed in this way. At the time when he donned an Ayr shirt to appear in his testimonial he was an Auchinleck Talbot player.

Nigel Howard.

David Harkness

28th July, 2008: Ayr United XI 1 Rangers XI 4

Team: Thomson (Stewart 71), Kinnaird, McGowan (Bagan 27), Forrest (Aitken, half-time), Henderson, McInnes (Nichol 60), Murphy (Ireland 64), Weaver, Anson (Crawford 64), Gormley and Agnew (Stevenson, half-time).

Rangers XI: Robinson (Gallacher 71), Lowing, McLachlan (Forbes 84), McMillan (Craig 62), Harvey, Emslie, Shinnie, Fleck, Loy, Lennon and Efrem (Stirling 77).

Goals: Steven Lennon 0-1 and 0-2; Rory Loy 0-3; David Gormley 1-3; Rory Loy 1-4.

At this time David Harkness had been the groundsman at Somerset Park for thirty years. Throughout that time the pitch was lovingly cared for and regularly drew favourable comments for its lushness. Despite the crowd figure for this match being around 1,200 it was all-ticket at the insistence of the police. The team contained four trialists. They were David Thomson, David Bagan, Lloyd Murphy and David Gormley.

Martyn Campbell

18th July, 2015: Ayr United 0 Coleraine 1.

Team: Fleming, Devlin (Muir 73), Boyle, Docherty (Wardrope 73), Martyn Campbell (McCracken 69), Mark Campbell (McLauchlan 6 then Woods for McLauchlan 80), Gilmour, Crawford, Caldwell (McKenzie 79), Kisuka (Nisbet 64) and Donald (Adams 64); unused substitute: Newman.

Coleraine: Brown, Higgins, Harkin, Morrow (McLaughlin), Doherty, Parkhill (McGonigle), Mullan, McCauley (Lyons), Ogilby, Falconer and Canning; unused substitute – Finlay.

Goal: Ruaidhri Higgins.

Martyn Campbell was rewarded with a testimonial for ten years of service. Unfortunately the attendance of 674 was modest even by the standards of pre-season. Martyn's brother Mark had also been a central defender with Ayr United but he moved in 2004 so the brothers Campbell did not appear in the same Ayr United team. Until now! At this time Mark was with Auchinleck Talbot and he played for the first six minutes. Ross Caldwell, Cristiana Kisuka and Jamie Adams all featured as trialists.

Trainers / Physiotherapists

As the role of the olden-day trainer evolved so too did the job title. The modern equivalent carries the title of physiotherapist, colloquially abbreviated to physio. Trainers of old were involved in the treatment of injuries as well as ensuring that players were put through their paces.

Alex Aitken	Close season 1910 until February 1920.
Jimmy Quaite	February 1920 until close season 1923.
Alex Gillespie	Close season 1923 until close season 1929.
Jimmy Dalziel	Close season 1929 until close season 1935.
Harry Rae	August 1935 until close season 1936.
Alex Aitken	Close season 1936 until February 1938.
Eddie Summers	February 1938 until January 1940.
Jimmy Dalziel	January 1940 until close season 1946 (club closed 1940 until 1945).
Davie Logan	Close season 1946 until close season 1948.
Eddie Summers	Close season 1948 until close season 1950.
Hugh Good	Close season 1950 until close season 1952.
Jimmy O'Neil	Close season 1952 until close season 1955.
Bob Cowie	Close season 1955 until November 1956.
Bobby Reid	November 1956 until November 1957.
Eddie Summers	November 1957 until close season 1962.
Jim Florence	Close season 1962 until close season 1963.
Bob Cowie	Close season 1963 until close season 1966.
Willie Wallace	August 1966 until close season 1983.
Hugh Hunter	Close season 1983 until October 1984.
Willie Wallace	October 1984 until January 1985.
John Hart	January 1985 until November 1985.
Bob Pender	November 1985 until October 1989.
Jim Martin	October 1989 until December 1989.
Martin McGowan	December 1989 until April 1991.

Ian Cardle	April 1991 until September 1992.
Andrew MacLeod	September 1992 until close season 1993.
Douglas Lauchlan	Close season 1993 until close season 1994.
Andrew MacLeod	Close season 1994 until close season 1995.
John Kerr	Close season 1995 until close season 2006.
Kevin MacLellan	Close season 2006 until February 2011.
Claire Bradley	February 2011 until close season 2012.
Kevin MacLellan	Close season 2012 until close season 2013.
Steven Maguire	Close season 2013 until December 2015.
Mark Duffy	January 2016 until close season 2016.
Steven Maguire	Close season 2016 until close season 2017.
Kevin MacLellan	Close season 2017 until February 2018.
Steven Maguire	February 2018.

Transfer fees

On 14th December, 2001, Gary Teale was sold to Wigan Athletic for £275,000. In time the deal exceeded £400,000 due to clauses about appearances and promotion. This made it the highest transfer fee received by the club.

On 21st October, 1981, Stevie Nicol was transferred to Liverpool for £300,000.

On 19th November, 1921, Neil McBain was sold to Manchester United for £4,600. At that time it was a club record fee for Manchester United.

On 5th May, 1920, Johnny Crosbie was sold to Birmingham City. The fee of £2,800 exceeded Newcastle United's offer of £2,500. In March 1921 Ayr United received a cheque for £2,854 : 5s : 3d, the adjustment being for lost interest due to late payment. In January 1920 Ayr United had agreed to buy Somerset Park from neighbours and landlords W.G. Walker. The price was £2,500. Crosbie's transfer fee therefore funded the purchase of the entire ground.

Turnover

The largest number of players to make a competitive appearance for Ayr United is forty-six in season 1997/98. It need hardly be stated that the transfer window had not yet been implemented. Gordon Dalziel was the manager responsible for this intense level of recruitment. He worked tirelessly in pursuit of improvement.

The second largest number of players to be engaged by Ayr United in competitive matches in a season is forty-five. Gordon Dalziel was also the manager responsible. The season was 1995/96. On 5th September, 1995, Simon Stainrod ceased to be the manager. Gordon Dalziel took interim charge and this developed into a permanent appointment on 31st October, 1995. His signing activity was consistent with his promise that: "I'm ready to pull this place apart."

The next largest number of players to experience competitive action for the club in a season is forty-four. This occurred in 1917/18. It being during the Great War there was great difficulty in the matter of players being available due to military demands and the demands of war work. Clubs were permitted to field players stationed in their area regardless of which club held their registration.

Weddings

Ayr United captain Willie McStay got married on 25th September, 1914. On the following day the team had a First Division fixture at home to St.Mirren. When the players emerged from the pavilion he had to run the gauntlet of showers of confetti.

The *Ayrshire Post* dated Friday 4th October, 2002, reported that Sandra Green and Tam Taylor were married in the Somerset Park centre circle.

The *Ayrshire Post* dated Friday 29 July, 2005, reported that Lee Martin and Craig Linden were married in the Somerset Park centre circle.

The *Ayrshire Post* dated Friday 2nd July, 2010, reported that Carolanne Hegarty and Gregor Cowan were married in the Somerset Park centre circle.

The *Ayrshire Post* dated 24th August, 2012, reported that Lyndsey Taylor and Douglas Kelly were married in the Somerset Park centre circle.

Index

A

Aarhus 176, 311
Abercorn 198, 200, 243, 293
Aberdeen 81, 82, 89, 108, 110, 111, 191, 198, 199, 220, 259, 277, 296
Adams (Arbroath 1937/38) 75
Adams, Jamie 151, 320, 321
Adams, Malky 134
Advocaat, Dick 176
AEL Limassol 177
Agnew, Paul, 258, 259
Agnew, Ralph 75
Agnew, Scott 148, 320
Agnew, Steven 148
Agnew, Willie 127, 301
Ahern, Brian 236, 237, 281
Ailsa Hospital 51
Airdrie 3, 4, 5, 9, 11, 31, 79, 83, 84, 91, 95, 97, 102, 114, 119, 126, 137, 168, 191, 197, 198, 199, 202, 206, 207, 216, 255, 275, 292, 308, 318
Airdrie United 11, 69, 156, 198, 202
Aitken, Alex 13, 79, 303, 322
Aitken, Andy (1968 – 1971) 162, 237, 239
Aitken, Andy (2009/10) 177
Aitken, Chris 86, 173, 320
Aitken, Jock 257
Aitken (Kilmarnock 1930/31) 206
Aitken, Roy 314
Aitken, Sam 91, 304
Aitken, Stephen 34
Aitken, W 274

Alba Challenge Cup 28, 227
Albion Rovers 2, 3, 48, 65, 75, 81, 82, 92, 122, 193, 194, 195, 198, 249, 250, 281, 282
Aldershot 41, 289
Alexander, Ian 31
Alexander (Queen's Park 1912/13) 300
Alexandria 1
Aliens Restriction Order 165
Aljofree, Hasney 272
Allan, Adam 198, 255
Allan, Peter 282
Allan, Ray 92
Allan, Scott 239
Allan, Thompson 7, 239
Allan, William 39
Alliance League 179
Alloa Athletic 13, 25, 28, 44, 65, 68, 111, 130, 144, 193, 194, 197, 198, 212, 232, 239, 240, 253, 276, 277, 281, 302
Almondvale Stadium 18
American All Stars 78
Anderson, Bobby 30
Anderson (Third Lanark 1915/16) 37
Arbroath 18, 74, 75, 81, 82, 91, 92, 101, 102, 118, 155, 195, 198, 199, 203, 238, 250, 292, 306
Arbuckle (Stenhousemuir 1945/46) 30
Armory, Wilf 206, 289
Armour (1911/12) 300
Armour, Davy 210, 257
Armour (Kilmarnock 1915/16) 73

Armstrong, Bill 107
Armstrong, Gareth (born 31st August, 1980) 102
Armstrong, Gareth (born 1st December, 1993) 163, 284
Armstrong (Kilmarnock 1915/16) 73
Armstrong, Matt 220
Arnott, Dougie 110
Arsenal 37, 73
Arthurlie 191, 193
Ashdown, Tracy 157
Ashwood, Kenny 212
Asquith, Beaumont 307
Aston Villa 79, 159
Atkins, Mark 318
Atkinson (Berwick Rangers 1928/29) 44
Atkinson, Jim 48
Auchinleck Talbot 284, 318, 321
Auld, Bertie 76, 77
Austria 173
Avci, Lyle 48
Ayr Academicals 160
Ayr Advertiser vii, 7, 95, 190, 250, 282, 306
Ayr Cattle Market 163
Ayr Charity Cup 201
Ayr FC 3, 13, 79, 83, 88, 91, 102, 156, 159, 164, 165, 243, 293, 300, 303, 304
Ayr Observer 164
Ayr Select 303, 304
Ayr Thistle 159
Ayr United Broadcast Group 54
Ayr United Media 51, 53, 54, 55, 157
Ayr United Supporters' Association viii, 50, 186, 310
Ayrshire and Galloway Hotel 84, 95
Ayrshire Cup 26, 122, 201, 244, 311, 315
Ayrshire League 127, 201
Ayrshire Medical Services 53

Ayrshire Post vii, 31, 49, 68, 75, 92, 96, 107, 164, 190, 247, 251, 253, 304, 305, 310, 326

B

'B' Division 2, 13, 30, 75, 91, 92, 101, 129, 130, 190, 194, 201, 293
Bagan, David 263, 320
Baigrie, Hugh 276
Baillie (Inverness Caledonian 1954/55) 278
Bain, Alan 134
Bainbridge (1951/52) 308, 310
Baird (King's Park 1934/35) 128, 275
Baird, Tommy 276
Baker, Jimmy 197, 255
Baker, Martin 263
Balatoni, Conrad 137, 199, 257
Balavage, John 282
Balfour, Evan 282
Balfour, John 76, 311
Ballantyne, Colin 281
Ballochmyle Thistle 13
Balunas, Matt 107
Banger, Nicky 267
Banks O'Dee 190
Bannigan, Stuart 257, 271, 272
Barbour, Willie 108
Barclay, J 2
Barclay, Willie 107
Bark, Jim 44
Barkas, Sam 307
Barnsley 307
Barnstaple, Kenny 99, 282
Barr, Darren 137
Barrowclough, Stewart 162
Bartle, Alan 31
Bathgate 74, 195
BBC 155, 157, 250, 259
BBC Alba 156
Beaton, David 34

Beaton, John 119
Beattie, Alec 75, 76, 86, 91, 92, 107, 108, 129, 130, 147, 188, 191, 255, 277, 278, 308, 310
Beattie, Frank 162, 311
Beattie, Jack 220
Becci, Attilio 75
Beharall, David 318
Bell, Alec 307
Bell, Bobby 76, 130
Bell, Brian 44, 226
Bell, John 37, 39, 73
Bell, Steven 56, 284
Bellshaw, Johnston 282
Benlaredj, Mohammed 167
Bennett, Reuben 229, 277
Bennie, Bob 105
Benson, Jimmy 275
Benzie (St.Johnstone 1931/32) 275
Beresford Park 84, 293, 304, 305
Berg, Henning 318
Bertelsen, Carl 311
Berwick Rangers 31, 40, 44, 63, 78, 84, 99, 101, 148, 194, 196, 197, 198, 244, 277
Beveridge (Stenhousemuir 1945/46) 30
Beynon, Jackie 220
Bickerstaff, Tommy 107
Biggart Hospital 51
Binnes (Barnsley 1938/39) 307
Binning, Jimmy 308
Birmingham City 285, 311, 324
Birrell, Thomas 39
Black & White Shop vii
Black, Aaron 257, 318
Black, Bertie 162, 278
Black, William 102, 127
Blackburn Rovers 89, 315, 318
Blacklands Boys' Club 148
Blackpool 31, 310, 311
Blaikie (Berwick Rangers 1953/54) 277

Blair, Danny 74
Blair, Tom 73
Blantyre Celtic 299
Blyth (Dundee 1932/33) 37
Blythe (Berwick Rangers 1928/29) 44
Bodan (Rangers 1911/12) 300
Boden, Alex 31, 76
Boghead Park 7, 21, 24, 89, 212, 244
Bohemians 165
Bokas, Frank 307
Bolt, Bobby 278
Bonar, Paul 259
Bone, Alex 77, 192, 193
Bone, Jimmy 251
Bo'ness 257, 274
Bonvin, Pablo 318
Booth, Callum 272
Borris, Ryan 86
Borthwick (Berwick Rangers 1928/29) 44
Bossy, Fabien 167
Botha, Ray 108, 110
Bourhill (1934/35 and 1935/36) 206, 276
Bowey, Steve 108
Bowie, Alistair 279
Bowie, Douglas 94
Bowie, James 303
Bowman, Gary 259
Boyack, Steven 267
Boyce, J 49
Boyd, Archie 39
Boyd (1923/24) 302
Boyd, Crawford 279
Boyd, Jimmy 207
Boyd, Mark 318
Boyd, Stuart 151
Boyle, Chris 118
Boyle, Jimmy 214
Boyle, Paddy 48, 56, 137, 320
Boyle, W G viii
Boyne (St.Bernard's 1927/28) 128

BP Youth Cup 147
B & Q Cup 119, 203, 227
Brackenridge, David 308
Bradford, John 34, 148, 318
Bradley, Claire 323
Bradley, Willie 31, 138, 142
Brae, Billy 37, 40, 74, 105, 106,
    128, 171, 188, 206, 220, 255, 257,
    274, 275, 304, 305, 306, 307
Brand (Arbroath 1937/38) 75
Brannan, Ged 267, 269
Brannan, Jack 48
Brannan, Jimmy 257, 275
Brann Stadion 285
Bray, Jacky 307
Brechin City 16, 26, 28, 63, 68, 69,
    72, 92, 118, 193, 198, 227, 238,
    244, 251
Bremner, H T 74
Brennan, Stephen 318
Brice, Gordon 76, 130
Bridgeton Waverley 101
Briggs, Jimmy 107
Brittany 171
Broadfield, Gary 34
Broadwood Stadium 81, 119
Brogan, John 210
Brolls, Norman 107
Broomfield Park 3, 79, 207
Brown, A H 300
Brown, Bob 31
Brown, George 105
Brown (Inverness Caledonian
    1954/55) 278
Brown, Jacky 308
Brown, Jimmy 211, 212, 240
Brown, Jimmy (Kilmarnock) 162
Brown (Kilmarnock 1924/25) 304
Brown (King's Park 1934/35) 275
Brown, Mark 137
Brown, Michael 239
Brown (Motherwell 1920/21) 73
Brown, R 300
Brown, Robbie 45

Brown, Rodney 320
Brown (St.Bernard's 1927/28) 128
Brown (Third Lanark 1915/16) 37
Brown, Tom 30
Browning (Dumbarton 1939/40) 129
Brownlie, Jimmy 37
Bruce (Inverness Caledonian
    1954/55) 278
Brunskill, Norman 307
Bryce (King's Park 1934/35) 128,
    275
Bryce, Stevie 110, 257
Bryce, Tommy 32, 255, 315
Bryson, Ian 122
B Sky B 156
BT Sports 157
Buchan, Willie 30, 31
Buchanan, Archie 20, 43, 179, 229
Buchanan, Craig 134, 209, 210, 212
Buchanan, Gordon 34
Buchanan, Gregor 137
Bullen, Lee 269
Bulloch, James 276
Bullock, George 307
Bulvitis, Nauris 108
Burgess, Robert 119
Burgess, Stuart 282
Burin Peninsula All Stars 171
Burke, Alex 163
Burke, James 1
Burley, George vii, 110, 122, 230, 315
Burn, Ramsay 134, 138
Burnett, Albert 212
Burnfoothill Primrose 147
Burnley 179, 180
Burns Day 11, 293
Burns, Gordon 318
Burns, Hugh 9, 110, 227, 315
Burns, Ian 259
Busby, Matt 297, 307
Burt, Willie viii
Bury 297
Byrne, David 282

C

'C' Division 277
Cafe Opera 173
Cain J 49
Cairney, Harry 34
Cairney, Paul 56, 137, 232, 257
Cairns, Bobby 45, 257
Cairns, Jimmy 308
Calder (Airdrie 1934/35) 207
Calder, Alex 30
Calder, Jock 307
Calderwood, W 40, 218
Caldow, Eric 45
Caldwell, George vii, 137, 229, 281
Caldwell, Ross 87, 320, 321
Caldwell (Third Lanark 1923/24) 302
Callaghan, Myles 7
Callaghan, Tom 86
Callaghan, Willie 86
Cambuslang Rangers 24
Cameron, Alex 156
Cameron, Bobby 279
Cameron, Duncan 303
Cameron, Hugh 49, 172, 176
Cameron, John (hospital radio) 51
Cameron, John (manager) 229, 291, 292
Cameron, Lachlan 157
Cameron (Rangers 1911/12) 300
Campbell, Alex 79
Campbell, Alistair 31
Campbell, Archie 79, 102, 127, 300
Campbell, Calum vii, 51, 54
Campbell, Ian 279
Campbell, Jacky 77
Campbell, Jim 44
Campbell, Mark 18, 34, 86, 148, 152, 257, 267, 320, 321
Campbell, Martyn 86, 108, 148, 163, 272, 320, 321
Campbell (Rangers 1923/24) 303
Campbell, Ross 239

Campbell (Stenhousemuir 1945/46) 30
Campbell, TK 74
Canada 167, 171, 172, 173, 174, 179
Canadian All Stars 172
Canning, Aaron 320
Cantwell, Jacky 75
Cappielow Park 26, 90
Cardiff City 73
Cardle, Ian 323
Carlin, Andy 34
Carrick Street Oval 160
Carroll, Tony 234, 250
Carse, Jimmy 315
Carson, Joe 122, 199, 220
Carson, Steve 272
Carson, Tom 212
Carvalho, Aderito 177
Cashmore, Ian (junior) 148
Cashmore, Ian (senior) 148, 153, 217, 218, 220, 225
Cassidy (Berwick Rangers 1953/54) 277
Cassidy, Joe 39, 301
Cassidy, John 162
Castilla, David 167, 212, 259, 263
Cathkin Park 81, 94
Cattanach, David 76
Cavin, Tommy 129
Celtic 22, 31, 58, 76, 93, 96, 97, 148, 154, 156, 207, 232, 239, 244, 281, 301, 302, 303, 304, 306, 311, 314, 315
Celtic Park 144, 154, 156, 207, 232, 285
Central League 274
Central Park 24
Challenge Cup 26, 28, 82, 188, 201, 227, 239, 318
Chalmers, Bill 78
Chalmers (Kilmarnock 1910/11) 127
Chalmers (Rangers 1926/27) 305
Chalmers, William 105

331

Chambers, BW 94
Chaplain, Scott 11, 20, 318
Charnley, Jim 122, 234
Chelsea 119, 177
Cherrie, Peter 240
Chisholm, Mark 45
Christie (Arbroath 1937/38) 75
Christie, Gerry 27, 210, 212, 218, 219, 225, 257, 281
Christmas Day 73, 74, 75, 76, 77, 92, 247
Church, Charlie 76
Ciardi, Marco 167
Clackmannan 40, 41, 193, 197, 238
Clark (Bo'ness 1930/31) 274
Clark, Frank 162
Clark, Jacky 129, 234
Clark, JJ 49
Clark (Kilmarnock 1924/25) 304
Clark, Nobby 279
Clark, Stewart 51
Clark, Willie 206
Clark, Willie (Albion Rovers 1954/55) 75
Clarke, John 282
Clarkson (Stenhousemuir 1945/46) 30
Clelland (Kilmarnock 1928/29) 306
Clemie, Sam 206, 305
Cliftonhill Park 2
Clinging, Ian 220
Clougherty, Mark 212
Clyde 32, 81, 92, 95, 190, 195, 198, 210, 243, 301
Clydebank 21, 24, 134, 137, 141, 244, 312
Coatbridge 2
Coats, Archie 207
Cochran, Andrew 304
Cochrane (Abercorn 1910/11) 200
Cochrane (Bo'ness 1927/28) 257
Coen, Joe 306
Coleman, David 250
Coleraine 320
Colgan, Gerry 279
Collins, Allan 129
Collins (Dumbarton 1939/40) 129
Collins, Gerry 134, 136, 137, 212, 257, 282
Collins, Ralph 200
Combe, Bobby 308
Comrie (Falkirk 1918/19) 127
Commonwealth Stadium 26, 28
Conacher (Clackmannan 1930/31) 40
Concarneau 172
Condie, H 40, 218
Condie, Tom 34
Conn, Sammy 282
Connell (1911/12) 49, 300
Connell (Elgin City 1966/67) 278
Connell, Willie 123, 206
Connolly, George 54
Connolly, Kenny 108
Connolly, Paddy 191
Connolly, Paddy (Celtic 1922/23) 302
Connor, Robert 210, 212, 218, 225, 230, 237, 255, 281
Conroy, Mike 134
Cook, Andy 86
Cooke, Charlie 259
Cooper, Davie 314
Cooper, Willie 108, 220
Coppinger, Jamie 318
Corbett, Alex 30
Cork Hibs 172
Corleton, Thomas 1
Corner Brook 172
Cottingham (Bo'ness 1927/28) 257
Coulston, Frank 77
County Hospital 50
Coupland, Joe 75
Court of Session 95
Coutts, Doug 259
Cowan (1920/21) 301
Cowan, Gregor 326
Cowdenbeath 24, 26, 28, 110, 111, 190, 191, 194, 195, 198, 202, 292, 298

Cowell, Jim 31, 34, 314
Cowie, Bob 322
Cowie (Dundee 1937/38) 207
Cox, David 119
Cox, Jacky 63, 129, 229
Coyle, Joe 212
Coyle, Tommy 212
Coyne, Tommy 315
Crabbe, Scott 45, 118, 255, 269, 272
Craggs, John 162, 163
Craig (1937–1939) 74, 307
Craig, Albert 212
Craig, David 10, 11, 45, 234, 257, 263, 267, 269, 272, 318
Craig, David (Newcastle United 1970/71) 162
Craig (Rangers 2008/09) 320
Craig, Tully 105, 301, 303
Craig, Willie vii, 157
Craigie (Deveronvale 2001/02) 45
Craigview Athletic 221
Craik, Jimmy 30, 129, 205
Cramond, Gordon 257, 313, 314, 315
Crampsey, Bob 156
Crampsey, Frank 76, 130
Crawford (2008/09) 320
Crawford, Andy 75
Crawford, David (goalkeeper) 16, 239, 272
Crawford, David (outfielder) 16
Crawford, Ian 224, 257, 308
Crawford, Robbie 48, 137, 177, 284
Crawford, Stevie 269
Creaney, Gerry 315
Creaney, James 48
Creighton, John 30
Crichton, Jimmy 257
Crichton (Third Lanark 1915/16) 37
Crilly, Mark 267, 318
Cringan, Robert 144
Cringan, Willie 37, 144
Croall, James 127
Crockett, Bert 278

Cromar, Bert 76, 130
Crombie (Berwick Rangers 1928/29) 44
Crombie, George 31
Cropley, Alex 191
Crosbie, Billy 257, 301
Crosbie, J 207
Crosbie, Johnny 39, 73, 144, 154, 274, 285, 301, 324
Crosshill Thistle 142
Cruickshank, George 308
Crump, Leslie 305
Crusaders 163
Cryle, George 308, 310
Culley, Willie 73
Cumming (League Select 1920/21) 301
Cumming, R viii
Cumming, W viii
Cumnock Juniors 301
Cunningham, Bobby 300
Cunningham, Harry 39, 40, 84, 85, 154, 218, 237, 255, 302, 303, 305
Cunningham, Kenny 82, 255, 259
Cunningham (St.Mirren 1935/36) 276
Cunningham, Willie 315
Curlett, Dave 131, 132, 134, 162
Curran, Harry 34
Currie, Davy 37, 74, 128, 207, 220, 275, 276, 307, 308
Currie, G 40
Currie, Willie 279
Cuthbert, Kevin 163

D

Daily Record vii, 33
Dainty, Herbert 39, 229
Dale, Billy 307
Dalziel, Gordon 65, 66, 89, 118, 230, 263, 282, 325
Dalziel, Jimmy 322

Davidson, Iain 86
Davidson, George 156
Davidson, Vic 208
Davie, Sandy 107
Davies, Darren 34
Davies, John 212, 263, 267
Dean, James 128, 305
Dempsey, Jim 210
Dempsie, Allan 86
Dempster (Bo'ness 1927/28) 257
Dempster, John 279
Dempster, Martin 130
Denham, Greig 267
Dens Park 2, 13, 18, 168, 214
Derry City 18
Deutsches Stadion 285
Devanney, Alec 277
Development Club 250
Deveronvale 45, 158, 193
Devine, James 127
Devine, John 130
Devlin (Arbroath 1937/38) 75
Devlin, Nicky 20, 56, 232, 298, 320
Devlin, Tom 302
Dick (Armadale 1919/20) 274
Dick, Ian 311
Dick, Jim 256, 257, 259, 263
Dick, Wattie 107
Dickie (Kilmarnock 1915/16) 73
Dickins, Matt 318
Dickoh, Francis 272
Dickson, George 279
Dickson, Joe 134
Dickson, John (1911/12) 49, 300
Dickson, John (1974–1976) 49, 172, 176, 279, 311
Dickson, Peter 279, 281
Dickson (St.Bernard's 1927/28) 128
Dimas, Pedro 318
Dimmer, Hyam 74, 75, 207, 255, 307
Dinamo Bucharest 178
Diver, Danny 99, 101

Divers, John 76
D'jaffo, Laurent 167, 212, 214, 259, 263
Djurgarden 173
Dobson, Tony 318
Docherty, Mark 137
Docherty, Ross 48, 56, 72, 137, 188, 190, 234, 257, 284, 320
Dodds, John 45, 269, 318
Doesburg, Michel 267
Doherty, Jim 210
Doherty, Michael 320
Dolan, Steven 45,
Dolan, Jamie 110
Dominion of Canada Football Association 174
Donald, Jim 279
Donald, Michael 137, 257, 320
Donaldson, Bobby 75
Donegal, 167
Donegan, Tom 45, 75
Donowa, Lou 212
Doohan, Ross 284, 294, 295
Donnelly, J 74
Donnelly, Ryan 257
Donnelly, Tommy 279
Doran, Aaron 163
Dossing, Finn 107
Dougal (Stenhousemuir 1945/46) 30
Douglas, D 49
Douglas, W 49
Dougray, Tom 94, 123
Dow, Robert 282
Dowie, Andy 199
Doyle, Jamie 119
Doyle, John 49, 77, 162, 171, 172, 255, 279, 281, 288, 311, 314
Drammen 171
Drogheda United 173
Drummond (St.Bernard's 1927/28) 128
Drury, Jimmy 129
Dublin 165, 173

Duffy, Mark 323
Duffy, Neil 34, 45, 168, 255, 267, 269, 272
Duke (St.Bernard's 1927/28) 128
Dumbarton 7, 13, 21, 24, 45, 57, 68, 75, 82, 89, 91, 92, 99, 114, 129, 137, 155, 191, 193, 194, 198, 199, 200, 203, 209, 210, 211, 212, 224, 238, 243, 244, 296
Dunbar Parish Church 78
Duncan, Cammy 83, 110, 115, 282, 315
Duncan, Graham 115
Duncan, John 75, 234, 245, 308, 310
Duncan, Lee 318
Duncan, Russell 108
Duncan (Stenhousemuir 1945/46) 30
Dundee 2, 13, 18, 37, 40, 78, 84, 96, 105, 111, 144, 168, 190, 207, 208, 210, 214, 238, 239, 245, 267, 278
Dundee United 16, 40, 50, 92, 107, 111, 190, 198, 199, 208, 210, 240, 243, 272
Dunfermline Athletic 28, 69, 72, 82, 83, 84, 86, 91, 122, 131, 193, 198, 199, 200, 205, 210, 224, 240, 243, 255, 269, 292
Dunlop, Frank 108
Dunlop, John 305
Dunn, David 257
Dunn (Dumbarton 1939/40) 129
Dunn, Sam 75
Dunne (Rangers 1911/12) 300
Durrant, Ian 263
Duthie, Mark 212, 234, 235
Dyer, Jimmy 74, 129, 207, 276, 307
Dykstra, Sieb 110
Dyson, Keith 162
Dziekanowski, Dariusz 315

E

Eagle, Robert 108
Easson, Dave 155
East End Park 83
East Fife 68, 87, 89, 130, 148, 198, 206, 239, 243
East Stirling 18, 26, 34, 81, 122, 134, 190, 193, 197, 198, 202, 205, 219, 227, 243, 251, 296
Easter Road 39
Easton, Craig 272
Easton, William 86, 108, 119, 272
Ecrepont, Finn 16
Edgar, Derek 122
Edinburgh University 296
Efrem, Giorgos 320
Egan, John 131
Eire 167
El Alagui, Farid 167
Elder, Graeme 122
Elgin City 45, 278
Elland Road 179
Elliot, David 191
Elliot (Rangers 1955/56) 310
Elliott, Dave 162
Elliott, John 129, 130
Elliott, Paul 315
Ellis, Laurie 86
Emslie, Paul 320
England 44, 179, 285, 311
Enugu Rangers 172
Erwin, Harry 34
Esson, Ryan 108, 163
Evans, Allan 34
Evans, Gareth 214
Evans, Stevie (ex-Albion Rovers) 134, 210, 212, 282
Evans, Stevie (ex-Clyde) 31, 35, 210, 314, 315
Evening Times 2
Everest, Jack 307
Ewing, Winnie 305

F

Faber, M viii
Fabiani, Roland 315
FA Cup 73, 88, 159, 307
Fagan (Bo'ness 1930/31) 274
Falconer, Garth 320
Falconer, Willie 267
Falkirk 24, 50, 56, 69, 79, 87, 95, 96, 97, 118, 127, 128, 131, 133, 134, 190, 191, 193, 195, 198, 199, 200, 207, 214, 216, 232, 240, 241, 253, 292, 296
Fallon, Jim 134
Fallon, John 76
Farmer (Inverness Caledonian) 277
Farquhar, John 75
Farquharson, Paul 118
Fasan, Leo 200
FC Stationary 172
Fearns, Willie 134
Ferguson, Alex 44, 251, 257, 296, 297
Ferguson (Alloa Athletic 1938/39) 276
Ferguson, Andrew 18, 102, 119, 255
Ferguson, Bert 44, 147
Ferguson, Billy 115
Ferguson, David 48, 284
Ferguson, George 75
Ferguson, Harry 275
Ferguson, Hugh 73
Ferguson, Iain 110
Ferguson, Ian 44, 191, 197, 212, 214, 255, 259, 263
Ferguson, Ian (Dunfermline Athletic 2001/02) 269
Ferguson, Jacky 147
Ferguson, Martin 282
Ferguson, Pearson 40, 105, 206, 255
Ferguson (Third Lanark 1915/16) 37
Ferreira, Fabio 119
Ferrier, Bob 73, 229
Ferries, Billy 282
Ferry, Mark 86
Filippi, Joe 44, 77, 162, 208, 279, 311, 314
Findlay, Bill 84
Findlay, Billy 173, 212, 214
Findlay, Willie 75
Finlay (Coleraine 2015/16) 320
Finlayson, Duncan 73
Finnbogason, Kristjan 167, 259, 263
Finnie, Gordon 107, 190, 255, 277
Finnie, Jim 45
Firhill 32, 129, 214, 275
Fir Park 48
Firs Park 81
First Division 2, 3, 9, 11, 16, 18, 22, 24, 26, 28, 34, 37, 39, 57, 68, 69, 73, 74, 76, 77, 84, 86, 92, 93, 95, 97, 108, 123, 127, 130, 134, 144, 154, 156, 188, 190, 191, 193, 194, 195, 197, 198, 199, 202, 206, 207, 210, 212, 218, 220, 232, 238, 240, 243, 247, 259, 274, 275, 276, 278, 281, 291, 303, 326
Fisher, Bud 257, 275, 307
Fitzgerald, Leslie 128, 206, 255
Flavell, Bobby 229
Fleck, John 320
Fleeting, Jim 218, 220, 225, 234, 281
Fleming, Garry 137
Fleming, Greg 72, 137, 240, 320
Fleming, Jim 86
Fleming, Jimmy 97, 105, 128, 206, 207, 255, 276
Fleming, Rikki 44, 162, 172, 176, 193, 208, 226, 255, 279, 311, 314
Fleming, Willie 37, 40, 74, 101, 105, 128, 206, 257, 275, 305, 306
Fletcher (1912/13) 300
Flexney, Paul 210
Florence, Jim 322
Flynn, Jim 42, 44
Foggan, Alan 162
Folkestone 289

Foran, Richie 108, 163
Forbes, Neil 122
Forbes (Rangers 2008/09) 320
Ford, David 162
Fordyce (Arbroath 1937/38) 75
Forfar Athletic 3, 28, 69, 92, 101, 118, 197, 198, 239, 240, 243
Forrest, Alan 18, 102, 137, 227, 257
Forrest, Eddie 118, 320
Forsyth, Adam 107
Forsyth, Alex 77
Forsyth, Billy 134
Forsyth (Clackmannan 1930/31) 40
Forsyth (Queen's Park 1912/13) 300
Fortes, Jose 167, 168
Fowler (King's Park 1934/35 128
Frame (Third Lanark 1924/25) 84
Fraser (Aberdeen 1933/34) 220
Fraser, Ally 254, 257
Fraser (Bo'ness 1930/31) 274
Fraser (Inverness Caledonian 1954/55) 278
Fraser, J 127
Fraser, Jim 45, 48, 193
Fraser, Ronnie 129, 130
Fraser, Tony 278
Fraser, Willie 45, 257, 277, 308
Fraserburgh 40, 278
France 28, 171
Frew, Billy 131, 134, 259
Frew, Jimmy 39
Frew, Willie 130
Frye, Derek 210, 218, 219, 220, 225, 234, 280, 281
Fullarton, Adam 156
Fullarton, Ned 156
Fulton, Billy 31, 131, 257
Fulton (Kilmarnock 1915/16) 73
Fulton, Steve 315
Furphy, Willie vii, 31, 33, 122, 282, 283, 314, 315
Fyfe, Andy 40, 218

G

Gahagan, John 220
Gaiety Theatre 187
Galabank 119
Galbraith, Curly 303
Galbraith, Daniel 272
Gall, Tommy 276
Gall, Willie 220
Gallacher (Alloa Athletic 1938/39) 276
Gallacher (Celtic 1931/32) 306
Gallacher, Gerry 44
Gallacher, Hughie 155
Gallacher, John 6, 131, 134, 259
Gallacher, Kevin 318
Gallacher, Nicholas 320
Gallacher, Paul 272
Gallagher, Brian 7
Galloway, Mike 315
Galston 126
Galway United 173
Garden (Queen's Park 1923/24) 303
Gardiner (1911/12) 49, 300
Gardner (Armadale 1919/20) 274
Gardner, Pat 208
Garick, W 49
Gavilan, Diego 318
Gayfield Park 18
Geddes (Stenhousemuir 1945/46) 30
Gefle 2, 173
Geggan, Andy 48, 163, 257, 284
Gemmell (1931/32) 306
Gemmell, David 74, 207, 257, 276, 307
Gemson, Lawrence 229, 247
George, Duncan 110, 122, 257, 282, 315
Gerrard, D 3
Gerrard, Jim 278
Getgood, George 39
Gibson, Alex 229

337

Gibson, Billy 108
Gibson, Brian 282
Gibson, Johnny 311
Gibson (Kilmarnock 1924/25) 304
Gibson (Rangers 1911/12) 300
Gibson, Willie 39, 73, 218, 302
Gilbert, George 278
Gilchrist, John 301, 302
Gilchrist (Third Lanark 1924/25) 84
Gill, Thomas 167
Gillan, George 30
Gillen, John 34
Gillespie, Alan 315
Gillespie, Alex 73, 127, 274, 301, 302, 303, 322
Gillespie (Alloa Athletic 1938/39) 276, 277
Gillespie, Bob 40, 74, 218
Gillespie, Dennis 107
Gillies, Ricky 9
Gillon, Felix 74
Gilmour, Brian 48, 137, 205, 320
Gilmour, Jim 161, 162
Gilmour, Jock 238
Gilroy, Jack 86
Gilzean, Ian 173
Girdwood, Neil 39
Girvan Amateurs 26, 27, 28, 205
Given, Jim 134, 137
Gjøa, Crana 171
Glasgow 1, 43, 78, 310
Glasgow Herald 208
Glasgow, Jamie, 284
Glasgow, Sam 302
Glasgow University 160
Glass, Stephen 318
Glavin, Ronnie 77, 314
Glebe Park 16, 26
Glen, Alex 64, 76, 130, 131
Glenbuck 144
Glenbuck Cherrypickers 144
Glendinning, George 94
Golabek, Stuart 282

Goldie, Hugh 75, 308
Goldie (Third Lanark 1915/16) 37
Golobart, Roman 163
Good, Hugh 322
Goodison Park 285
Goodman, Don 267, 269
Goodwin, Alex Hill 39, 49, 144, 190, 234, 300
Goodwin, Jacky 102, 127, 144, 300
Goram, Andy 267
Gordon (Armadale 1919/20) 274
Gordon (Clackmannan 1930/31) 40
Gordon, Lewis 130
Gorgues, Regis 167, 168
Gormley, David 86, 257, 320
Gossman, J 40, 218
Gould, Willie 301, 306
Gourlay, Jimmy 301
Gourlay, William, 305
Govan, Jock 107, 167, 277, 278, 308
Grady, James 34, 45, 173, 193, 255, 267, 269, 272, 318
Graham, Ally 110, 112, 122, 190, 227, 257, 315
Graham, Billy 259
Graham, Bobby 208
Graham, David 39
Graham, Gerry 278
Graham, Harry 39
Graham, Johnny 44, 49, 77, 171, 172, 176, 226, 255, 279, 281, 311
Graham, Sam 56, 102, 127
Graham, Tom 86
Grand Bank Select 172
Grand Slam 28
Grant, Arthur 281
Grant, Brian 282
Grant, Dicky, 103, 259
Grant, Dougal 278
Grant, Frank 282
Grant, Johnny 63, 86, 107, 109, 311
Grant, Lewis 157, 158
Grant, Lex 134

Grant, Peter (Celtic) 315
Grant, Peter (Dumbarton) 75
Grant, R 74
Grant, Roddy, 262, 267
Grant, Willie 45, 278
Gray, Alec 37, 39, 73, 257, 274
Gray, Bobby 282
Gray, Denis 44
Gray, Dougie 105
Gray, John 172
Gray (Kilmarnock 1924/25) 304
Gray (Kilmarnock (1928/29) 306
Gray, W 39
Green, Sandra 326
Green's Cinema 154, 156
Grierson, George 83, 110
Griffin, Danny 272
Grimes, John 1
Grindlay, Stephen 86, 108, 237
Gunning, Jimmy 308
Guthrie, Jimmy 37
Gwardia, Warsaw 176

H

Haggart, Larry 281
Hainey, Billy 107
Hair (Rangers 1926/27) 305
Hall, James 129, 207, 234, 276, 307
Hamilton Accies 65, 101, 102, 134, 147, 190, 191, 194, 198, 202, 244, 254, 291
Hamilton (Alloa Athletic 1938/39) 276
Hamilton, George 108, 110, 129
Hamilton, Gladstone 303, 304
Hamilton, Ian 131, 138
Hamilton, J 305
Hamilton, James 44
Hamilton, Lindsay 214
Hamilton Park 27, 28
Hamilton, R 305
Hamilton, Robert 105
Hamilton, Tom 105

Hampden Park 13, 18, 22, 24, 40, 90, 129, 275, 276, 285, 288, 311
Hampshire, Steven 269
Hanlon, Paul 272
Hannah (1924/25) 304
Hannah, David 272
Hannah, Jim 82, 199, 200
Hannah, John 75
Hansen, Jens 83, 167
Hansen, John 77
Hardy, Lee 190
Hare-Reid, Ellis 284
Hargidan, Bernard 1
Harkin, Ruairi 320
Harkins, Gary 137
Harkness, Colin 122
Harkness, David 320
Harkness, Jack 105
Harnett, I 130
Harnett, LG 76
Harper, Bernard 307
Harper, Bert 30, 31, 224
Harris, Tony 108, 110
Harrower, Ross 269
Hart, Archie 130
Hart, John 322
Hart, Jordan 48, 137
Hart, Michael 272
Hart, Robert 257
Hartlepool United 142, 314
Harvey, Joe 31
Harvey, Ross 320
Harvie, Daniel 104, 137, 284
Harvie, John 127
Hastie, WM 76, 130
Hastings, Sam 134
Haugh, Adam 31, 76, 160, 310
Hawkshaw, Ian 63, 76, 86, 107, 250, 278, 311
Hawthorn, William 207
Hay, Hugh 44
Hay, Jimmy 20, 37, 73, 94, 97, 229, 234
Hayes, Davie 200

339

Hayes, Jonny 108, 163
Hayes, Martin 315
Heale, Jimmy 307
Heap, John 44
Hearghty see Hargidan, Bernard 1
Hearton, George 51
Hearts 7, 39, 40, 105, 163, 165, 179, 194, 198, 199, 210, 224, 292, 301
Heathfield 69
Heathfield Hospital 50
Hegarty, Carolanne 326
Henderson, Darren 16, 17, 115, 147, 193, 212, 255, 257
Henderson, David 30
Henderson, David (Deveronvale) 45
Henderson, Murray 86
Henderson, Nicky 214
Henderson (Rangers 2008/09) 320
Henderson, Ross 308
Henderson, Roy 310
Hendren, James 39
Hendry, Billy 218, 219, 225, 257, 281
Hendry, Willie 237
Henry, Billy 303
Henry, John 263
Hepburn, Bob 37, 38, 40, 44, 74, 105, 128, 206, 220, 234, 238, 257, 274, 275, 276, 288, 305, 306, 307
Hepburn, Tony 75, 257
Herd, Alec 307
Herd, Andrew 105
Herd, Billy 282
Herd G 130
Herron, Des 134, 139
Hewitt, Brian 284
Hewitt, John 315
Hibernian 24, 39, 63, 78, 127, 147, 165, 191, 198, 206, 239, 241, 271, 272, 307, 308
Hickie (Falkirk 1918/19) 127
Higginbotham, Kallum 240
Higgins, Chris 48, 56, 284
Higgins, Ruaidhri 320
Highland League 278, 282

Hill (Dumbarton 1939/40) 129
Hill, George 162
Hill (Queen's Park 1912/13) 300
Hillan (King's Park 1934/35) 128, 275
Hillcoat, John 118
Hilton, James 284
Hindson, Gordon 162
Hodge, Lindsay 75
Hogg, Bobby 306
Hogg, Chris 163
Hogg, Jimmy 39, 73, 127, 218, 274, 277, 285, 286, 301, 302, 303
Hogg, Jimmy (Aberdeen) 259
Hogg, Jimmy (Berwick Rangers) 31
Hogg, Keith 263
Hogg, Robert 207
Holland 176, 285
Holland, Johnny 206, 275, 276, 307
Holt, Alan 281
Holt, Gary 263
Holt, John 122
Hood, Gregg 99
Hood J 304, 305
Hood, Jimmy 129
Hood, W viii
Hooper, Scott 48
Hope, Kenny 9
Hope, Tommy 307
Hopkins, Jim 44
Horace, Alain 92, 167
Horrower (Stenhousemuir 1945/46) 30
Houston (Third Lanark 1923/24) 302
Howard, Nigel 315, 319
Howe, Charlie 102, 127
Howie, Hugh 308
Howie (Kilmarnock 1910/11) 127
Hubbard, Johnny 134, 168, 170, 259, 297
Hughes, Jim 31, 115, 117, 314, 315
Hughes, John 16, 34, 45, 237, 269, 272
Hughes, John (1924/25) 84, 85

Hume, Bobby 259
Hume (Bo'ness 1927/28) 257
Hume, Colin 212, 281
Hunter (1920/21) 301
Hunter, Alex 129, 130
Hunter, Archie 159
Hunter (Clackmannan 1930/31) 40
Hunter, Donald 281
Hunter, Hugh 322
Hunter, Ian 86
Hunter, John 131
Hurlford 56
Hurst, Glynn 34, 36, 83, 115, 173, 188, 197, 263, 267
Hutchison, Steve 282
Hutton, Jacky 134
Hutton, Joe 45, 308
Hutton (Queen of the South 1975/76) 279
Huxtable, J 49
Hyslop, Dwayne 284
Hyslop, John 208,

I

Ibrox Park 97, 105, 207, 208, 210, 220, 288, 310
I.K. Sirius 173
Imrie, Adam 131, 162
Inglis, Jimmy 308
Inglis (Kilmarnock 1928/29) 306
Ingram, Alex 44, 77, 86, 107, 159, 171, 172, 176, 188, 190, 193, 195, 208, 226, 234, 251, 255, 278, 279, 311
Ingram, Cammy 73
Inverness Caledonian 277, 278
Inverness Caledonian Thistle 18, 82, 87, 108, 114, 156, 162, 163, 190, 245, 253
Ireland (2008/09) 320
Ireland 167, 172, 173, 285, 288
Ireland, Robert 303, 305

Ireland (St.Johnstone 1931/32) 275
Irn Bru Cup 26, 90, 199, 227, 294, 295
Irons, Davy 134, 137
Irvine Meadow 21, 102, 147, 311
Irvine, Willie 220, 257

J

Jack, Ross 122
Jackson (Celtic 1922/23) 302
Jackson, Colin 314
Jackson (Third Lanark 1923/24) 302
Jackson, John 37, 73
Jackson, Justin 173
James, Kevin 299
Jamieson, Mike 34
Jamieson (Third Lanark 1923/24) 302
Jamieson, Willie 282
Japp, Willie 45, 48, 76, 134, 255, 277, 308
Jarvie (Third Lanark 1924/25) 84
Jarvis (Stoke City 1923/24) 304
Jefferson (Berwick Rangers 1928/29) 44
Jeffrey (Berwick Rangers 1953/54) 277
Jenkins (Clackmannan 1930/31) 40
Johnson (1939/40) 129
Johnson (Berwick Rangers 1928/29) 44
Johnston and Graham 53
Johnston, Charlie 53
Johnston, John 105
Johnston, Sammy 315
Johnstone, Bobby 308
Johnstone Burgh 102
Johnstone, George 108
Johnstone, Lauren 54
Jones, Sandy 191, 257
Jordan, Jacky 130

K

Karelse, John 318
Kavanagh, Peter 306
Kay, R viii
Kean, Stewart 11, 12, 18, 102, 118, 203, 272, 318
Keenan, Dean 86, 108, 119, 257
Keith (Queen's Park 1912/13) 300
Kelly, Archie 277
Kelly (Celtic 1919/20) 301
Kelly, Charlie 205
Kelly, Douglas 326
Kelly, Jerry 74
Kelly, Jimmy 30, 108, 130
Kelly, Shaun 272
Kelly, Willie 208
Kelt (Ayr FC 1899/00) 83
Kemp, Calvin 284
Kendrick, Joe 318
Kennedy (1919/20) 301
Kennedy, Bobby 107
Kennedy, David 53, 54, 55, 110, 314, 315
Kennedy, Ian 208
Kerr, Billy 102, 103
Kerr, Gordon 37, 39, 73, 274, 300, 301
Kerr, John 147, 323
Kerr, Peter 39
Kerrigan, Don 259
Kidd, Albert 220
Kiernan (Armadale 1919/20) 274
Kiernan, Felix 75
Kilbowie Park 312
Kilgannon, Johnny 81, 134, 255, 259
Kilgannon, Sean 269
Kilmarnock 8, 9, 22, 23, 24, 73, 123, 127, 129, 130, 131, 154, 156, 160, 165, 190, 194, 198, 200, 205, 206, 212, 224, 247, 258, 259, 263, 264, 265, 301, 304, 305, 306, 311, 314, 315

Kilmarnock, Willie 3
Kilpatrick, James 303
Kilpatrick, Tommy 84, 85, 257, 302, 303, 305
Kilwinning 13
Kilwinning Rangers 102
King, Andy 311
King George V 276
King, Johnny 134
King (Third Lanark 1915/16) 37
King, W.S. 74
King's Park 126, 128, 129, 194, 275, 276
King, Wallace 131
Kinghorn, Matthew 45
Kingsmore, Brian 78, 277
Kinnaird, Lloyd 320
Kinnaird, Paul 92, 99, 282
Kinning Park 159
Kirkbride (Armadale 1919/20) 274
Kirkland, Mungo 30
Kirk of Shotts 156
Kirkwood, Alex 303
Kirkwood (Falkirk lawyer 1934/35) 96
Kisuka, Cristiana 320, 321
Knox, Jimmy 276
Knudsen, Jens 167
Krissian, Raffi 48
Kristensen, Brian 166, 167
Krivokapic, Miodrag 110

L

Lafferty, Daniel 108
Laing, Gordon 278
Laing, Martin 163
Laird, Davy 130
Laird (Falkirk 1918/19) 127
Laird (King's Park 1934/35) 128, 275
Lamb, John 39
Lamb, Peter 130
Lambert, Paul 122

Lamont, Joe 129
Lamont, Michael 51, 53
Lanark 167
Landsborough (1934/35) 275
Lanemark 165
Lang (King's Park 1934/35) 128, 275
Langfield, Jamie 267
Lannon, Brian 162
Larnach, Mike 134, 137, 220, 225, 257, 281, 282
Latimer, John 276
Latta, Brian 148
Latta, James 148
Lauchlan, Douglas 323
Lauchlan, Jim 263, 272
Lauchlan, Martin 214
Lavety, Barry 122
Law, John 207
Lawrence, Alan 214
Lawrence, Tommy 251
Lawrie, Bobby 77
Lawrie (Dundee 1937/38) 2
Lawrie (Rangers 1955/56) 310
League Cup 7, 21, 22, 24, 26, 45, 48, 50, 77, 79, 81, 82, 84, 87, 91, 102, 104, 110, 131, 134, 156, 163, 188, 190, 191, 193, 194, 195, 196, 197, 198, 199, 201, 202, 203, 224, 225, 238, 239, 244, 291, 292, 293, 294, 295, 296, 297, 298, 310
League One 16, 28, 65, 69, 72, 190, 195, 201, 253, 290
League Select 301
Leckie, Sam 75, 107, 162, 237, 277, 310
Lee (Berwick Rangers 1928/29) 44
Leeds City 73
Leeds United 179, 181
Leigh Sports Village 178
Leishman, Andy 284
Leishman, Willie 282
Leitch, James 30

Leith Athletic 101, 194, 198, 200, 206
Lennie (Motherwell 1920/21) 73
Lennon, Steven 320
Lennox, Bobby 76, 77
Lennox, Guy 3
Le Saux, Graeme 318
Leslie, James 206, 306
Lilley, Derek 272
Lindau, Peter 167
Linden, Craig 326
Lindie, James 173
Lindsay (Ayr FC) 83, 303
Lindsay, Jacky 75, 107, 277
Lindsay, Jim 259
Lindsay, John 301
Lindsay, Thomas 304
Little, J 49
Liverpool 219, 251, 297, 324
Livingston 18, 65, 69, 84, 102, 104, 115, 203, 292
Livingstone, Alec 282
Livingstone, Allan 105, 257
Lochend 102, 296
Lockhart, George 94
Lockhart, William 96
Logan, Davie 322
Logan, Hugh 49, 300
London & North Eastern Railway Company 43
Longworth, Jamie 87
Lossiemouth 158
Love, Ally 193, 218, 225
Love, Joe 121, 315
Love Street 9
Lovering, Paul 45, 269, 272, 273, 318
Low, John 39, 218
Lowe, John 75
Lowing, Alan 320
Loy, Rory 320
Lualua, Lomana 318
Lugar Boswell 79
Lumsden (Bo'ness 1930/31) 274
Lunn, John 86

Luton Town 250
Lyall, Jack 39
Lyle, Willie 20, 118, 257, 284
Lynas (Bo'ness 1927/28) 257
Lynch, John 207
Lynch, Matt 75
Lyons, Andy 214, 257, 263, 264
Lyons, Brad 320

Mac/Mc

McAdam (1923/24) 302
McAdam, Colin 208
McAllister, Darren 45
McAllister, Ian 7, 29, 31, 84, 198, 210, 212, 218, 234, 257, 281, 314, 315, 316
McAllister, James 207
McAllister, Rory 240
McAlpine, Hamish 240
McAlpine, JB 74
McAlpine, JM 40, 218
McAlpine (Kilmarnock 1915/16) 73
McAnespie, Alex 44, 76, 77, 147, 150, 162, 237, 257, 278, 279, 311, 314
McAtee, Andy 301
McAuley, John 44
McAvoy (Ayr FC) 83
McAusland, Kyle 87
McBain, John 105
McBain, Lawrence 275
McBain, Neil 20, 39, 73, 127, 154, 218, 229, 248, 249, 250, 274, 301
McBain, Roy 108
McBride, Kevin 272
McCabe, Gerry 134, 137
McCabe, Mike 122
McCafferty, Tom 34
McCaig (St.Bernard's 1927/28) 128
McCall, Alex 239
McCall, Andy 37, 40, 44, 74, 95, 96, 105, 128, 206, 220, 255, 274, 275, 306, 307

McCall, Ian 11, 230, 253, 281
McCall, Walker 226
McCall, Willie 108
McCallum, Donald 137
McCandless, Billy 303
McCann, Austin 272
McCann, Jim 122, 125, 314
McCarron, Frank 76, 276
McCart, Chris 110
McCarthy (Dundee 1932/33) 37
McCathie, Norrie 200
McCauley, Darren 320
McChesney, Iain 199, 255, 279
McClen, Jamie 318
McCloy, Henry 147, 276
McCloy, Peter 147, 314
McCloy, Phil 39, 73, 84, 85, 127, 218, 274, 285, 301, 302, 303
McCloy, Stephen 147
McCoist, Ally 263
McColgan, Dan 257
McColl (Berwick Rangers 1953/54) 277
McColl, Billy 225
McColl, Mark 18
McColl, Ronnie 44
McColl, RS 303
McColl, TN 304
McComb, Lenny 281
McConnell, Hugh 276, 277
McCormack (Third Lanark 1924/25) 84
McCosh, John 128, 305
McCowan, Luke 48, 284
McCoy, Gerry 191
McCracken, Craig 284, 320
McCracken, David 272
McCracken, Dougie 31, 257
McCracken, Jimmy 75
McCreath, Tom 63, 229
McCubbin, Bert 134, 142
McCulloch, Davy 44, 162, 171, 197, 208, 210, 226, 255, 279, 311, 314

McCulloch (Falkirk 1918/19) 127
McCulloch, Iain 314
McCulloch, Lee 267, 269
McCulloch, Willie 308
McCunnie, Jamie 272
McCurry, Michael 118
McCutcheon, Alex 44
McDaid, Declan 48, 255, 284
McDicken, Derrick 314
McDonald (Alloa Athletic 1938/39) 276
McDonald (Bo'ness 1930/31) 274
McDonald, Danny 208, 279
McDonald, Hugh 91
MacDonald, James 229
Macdonald, Murdoch 303
McDonald, Paul 34
McDonald, Robert 105
MacDonald, Roddie 214
MacDonald, Stuart 34
McDougall (Airdrie 1926/27) 198, 255
McDougall (Motherwell 1920/21) 73
McDougall, Robert 39, 40, 218, 257
McEwan, A 76, 130
McEwan, Craig 45, 269, 272
McEwan, Jock 206, 304, 305
McFadzean, Jim 77, 162, 239, 311
McFarlane, D 276
McFarlane, H 276
MacFarlane (Inverness Caledonian 1954/55) 278
McFarlane, Jean 302
McFaul, Willie 162
McGarry, Danny 307
McGee, Lawrie 210, 212, 213
McGhee, Jim 64, 93, 131, 155, 237, 257
McGhee, Joe 306
McGhie, Billy 134
McGibbons, Terry 63, 74, 128, 129, 188, 195, 198, 206, 207, 220, 255, 275, 276, 307
McGiffen, Ian 234, 279

McGill, Charlie 220
McGill, Hugh 279
McGillivray, Charlie 40, 74, 105, 197, 255, 274, 306
McGinlay, Pat 34, 45, 47, 173, 257, 269, 272, 318
McGinn, H 49
McGivern, Sam 9, 110, 173, 227
McGlashan, Colin 9
McGoldrick (Third Lanark 1923/24) 302
McGonigle, Jamie 320
McGovern (Berwick Rangers 1953/54) 277
McGovern, Phil 162
McGowan, Jamie
McGowan, John 279
McGowan, Martin 322
McGowan, Martin (Dumbarton) 212
McGowan, Michael 163, 257
McGowan, Neil 86, 257, 320
McGowan, Pat 212
McGowan, Ryan 108, 167
McGowne, Kevin 263
McGrath, William 220
McGregor, Alex 77, 162
McGregor, David 34
MacGregor, Jimmy 276
McGregor (Third Lanark 1923/24) 302
McGrillen, Paul 110
McGuffie, Craig 48, 137, 257, 284
McGuffie, Ryan 318
McGugan, Jacky 19, 20, 56
McGuigan, Tommy 30, 108, 129, 130, 257
McGurn, David 86
McHarg, Keith 51
McIlroy, Brian 311
McIlroy, Sean 284
McIlwain, Matt 75
McInally, Alan 190, 210, 212, 281, 315, 318

McInally (Arbroath 1937/38) 75
McInally, Jacky 311
McInally, Tommy 84
McInnes (Rangers 2008/09) 320
McIntosh, Gerry 34
McIntosh (Inverness Caledonian 1954/55) 278
McIntosh, Stuart 83, 115
McIntyre, Alastair 31, 130, 131, 146, 147, 155, 257
McIntyre, Jim 263
McIntyre, Stevie 31, 122, 134, 312, 314, 315
McIntyre, Tommy 119
McIntyre, Willie 131, 134, 146, 147, 193
McKay, Danny 108
Mackay, John 301
MacKay (Kilmarnock 1955/56) 162
McKay (Queen's Park 1974/75) 279
MacKay, Scott 281, 282
McKechnie, Robin 131, 134
McKeever, John 220
McKenna, J viii
McKenna, Mike 2, 16, 45, 75, 107
McKenna, Pat 108
McKenna, Scott 137
McKenzie, Alex (Alloa Athletic 1981/82) 281
McKenzie, Alex (Kilmarnock 1915/16) 37, 39, 73
McKenzie, Alistair 210
Mackenzie (Deveronvale 2001/02) 45
McKenzie, Hugh 49, 102, 127
Mackenzie (Inverness Caledonian 1954/55) 278
McKenzie, Jamie 214
McKenzie, John 276
McKenzie, John (Reverend) 78
McKenzie, Mrs 70
McKenzie, Murdoch 73, 84, 85, 255, 301, 302, 303

MacKenzie, Scott 108
McKenzie, Sean 320
McKeown, Joe 45
McKeown, Kevin 205, 212
McKernon, Jamie 26, 163
McKilligan, Neil 173
McKinnon, Rob 110
McKnight, Jim 131
McKnight (St.Bernard's 1927/28) 128
McLachlan (Rangers 2008/09) 320
McLaren, Billy 279
McLaren (Bo'ness 1930/31) 274
McLaren, Hugh 129
McLaren, Sandy 275
McLaren, Stewart 208
McLaughlan, Switcher 13, 37, 39, 49, 73, 102, 127, 237, 238, 257, 274, 300, 301, 302, 303
McLaughlin, Brian 45
McLaughlin, Brian (Ayr United/ Motherwell) 220, 255
McLaughlin, James 320
McLaughlin, Joe 108
McLaughlin, Scott 272
McLean, Adam 301
McLean, Ally 44, 77
McLean, Donald 76, 130
McLean (Dumbarton 1939/40) 129
McLean, George 44, 77, 162, 163, 171, 172, 197, 234, 255, 311
McLean, George (1930 – 1932) 105, 275
McLean, Graham 279
McLean, James 302, 304
McLean, Jim 86, 131, 234
McLean, John 257, 304
McLean, John (Stranraer 1958/59) 131
McLean, Scott 119
McLean, Stuart 122
McLean (Third Lanark 1915/16) 37
McLean, Tommy 311, 314

McLean, Willie vii, 220, 225, 229, 281
McLeish, Kevin 118
MacLellan, Kevin 323
McLelland, D 74
McLelland, Steve 27, 220, 257, 314
McLennan, Roy 31
MacLeod, Ally vii, 7, 63, 65, 102, 103, 148, 220, 229, 250, 296, 315, 318
MacLeod, Andrew 323
MacLeod, Andy 282
McLeod (Falkirk 1918/19) 127
McLeod, Jimmy 40, 44, 84, 85, 105, 206, 239, 274, 275, 302, 303, 305
McLuckie, Jimmy 307
McManus, Allan 115
McManus, Tam 108, 257
McMaster, John 302
McMenamin, Colin 318
McMenemy, Harry 207, 304
McMenemy, Jimmy 304
McMenemy, John 304
McMillan, Andy 168, 267
McMillan, Ian 3
McMillan, Jordan 320
McMillan, Sam 6, 7, 13, 21, 31, 68, 76, 86, 102, 103, 107, 109, 130, 131, 134, 162, 188, 193, 255, 259, 310, 311
McMurtrie (1928/29) 306
McNab, Neil 110
McNally, Mark 315
McNaughton, Sandy 210, 281
McNee, Chris 75
McNee, Jack 45, 75
McNeil, Donald 212
McNeil, Norrie 30, 45, 75, 108, 127, 129, 130, 205, 257, 277, 308
McNeill, Billy 76, 77
McNiven, John 134, 140
McNulty, Charlie 75

McPake (Third Lanark 1915/16) 37
McPartlin, James (Father Giles) 78
McPhail, John 75, 76
McPhail, Malcolm 73, 301
McPhee, Ian 191
Macpherson, Archie 156
MacPherson, Gus 199, 255, 263, 269
MacPherson, Jamie 282
McPherson, Neil 284
McQuade, Denis 77
McQueen, Colin 282
McQueen, Jacky 134
McQueen, Tommy 130
McQuilter, Ronnie 315
McSherry, Jim 49, 172, 208, 218, 225, 279, 314
McSkimming, Shaun 267
McStay, Jimmy 302
McStay, Jock 148
McStay, Paul 315
McStay, Willie 20, 37, 39, 56, 73, 148, 326
McVake, Alex 279
McVeigh, John 210
McVey, W viii
McVie, Willie 208
McWilliams, Ian 279
McWilliams, Ryan 163, 272

M

Maguire, Steven 323
Mackie (Kilmarnock 1915/16) 73
Mackie, Peter 314
Mackie, Tom 130
Mackin, Joe 239
Mahood, Alan 263
Main, Alan 13
Main, Davie 127, 128
Main (Inverness Caledonian 1954/55) 278
Mainge, Willie 167
Mair, A 307

Mair, Gordon 99, 122, 257
Maisano, John 167
Makel, Lee 318
Malcolm, Craig 178
Malcolm, John 30, 257
Malcolm, Karen 54
Maley, Willie 61
Malloch, Jacky 45
Malone, David 44
Malone, Dick 76, 86, 107, 109, 197, 257, 278, 311, 314
Malone, Eddie 87, 163, 272
Manchester 95, 178
Manchester City 303, 307
Manchester United 22, 296, 297, 307, 318, 324
Marenghi, Anthony 257
Marinello, Peter 208
Marker, Nicky 318
Marsh, Bill 37
Marshall, Bobby (Manchester City) 307
Marshall, Bobby (Stenhousemuir) 30
Marshall, Gordon, 263
Marshall, James 105, 305
Marshall, Jimmy 129
Martin, Alan 137
Martin, Alex 214
Martin, Bent 86
Martin (Bo'ness 1927/28) 257
Martin, Brian 110
Martin, Falkirk (1918/19) 127
Martin, Iain 53, 54
Martin, J 49
Martin, James 39
Martin, Jim 322
Martin, Janette 70
Martin, Lee 326
Mason, Gary 269
Mason, Willie 131
Massey, Lee 49, 102, 127, 300, 303
Massie, Alex 105, 305
Massie, Willie 303

Masterton, Danny 210, 257
Mather (Dumbarton 1939/40) 129
Matheson, Ross 34
Mathieson (1923/24) 302
Mathieson (Kilmarnock 1928/29) 306
Matthews, Stanley 310
Mauchline 16
Maxwell, Ally 34
Maxwell, Bud 206
Maxwell, Eddie 259
Maxwell, Hugh (Ayr United Media) 54
Maxwell, Hugh (Dunfermline Athletic) 86
Maxwell, Jim 45
Maxwell, Ken 75, 129
Maxwell, Paul 200
Maybole 164
Maybole Juniors 147
Mays, Gerry 148, 162, 229
Mays, Jock 74, 148, 207, 276
Meadowbank Thistle 26, 28, 212
Meiklejohn, David 105
Melville (1926–1928) 128, 305
Mercer, Bob 39
Melvin, James 30
Mendes, Junior 108
Mennie, Frank 129, 130, 205
Merrie, Alex 37, 95, 194, 206, 220, 255, 275, 306
Mid Annandale 79
Middlemass, Jimmy 162
Middleton, Billy 39, 127
Middleton (Bo'ness 1927/28) 257
Middleton, George 278
Midton Road 160
Mighty Jets of Kaduna, The 172
Mikkelson, Torben 176, 311
Miles, HJ 300
Milla, Roger 254
Millar, Ian 86, 107, 109, 278, 311
Millar, Peter 208
Millar, Tommy 107

Millen, Andy 212, 259, 263
Miller, Ally 107
Miller, Bobby 75
Miller (Celtic 1931/32) 306
Miller, Charlie 272
Miller, Colin 167, 169, 212
Miller, George 39
Miller, Graeme 157
Miller, Jimmy 279
Miller, Liam 272
Miller (Parkhouse) 303
Miller (Rangers 1955/56) 310
Miller (St.Mirren 1935/36) 276
Mills, Willie 220
Milne, Colin 282
Milne, Jimmy 131
Milton, John 142
Milton (King's Park 1934/35) 128, 275
Mimms, Bobby 318
Mitchell, Alex 48
Mitchell, Ally 263
Mitchell, Chris 108
Mitchell, Dougie 44, 86, 107, 162, 257, 278, 298
Mitchell, Ian 107
Mitchell (Kilmarnock 1915/16) 73
Mitchell, Ron 277
Mitchell (St.Bernard's 1927/28) 128
Moffat, Michael 48, 72, 87, 163, 188, 232, 237, 240, 255, 284
Monan, Eddie 76, 86, 102, 103, 107, 108, 311
Moncur, Bobby 162
Money, Campbell 230, 231, 234, 251, 252
Montford, Arthur 156
Montgomerie, Ray 212, 263
Montgomery, Eddie 303, 304
Montgomery, Nigel 45
Montgomery, Willie 199
Montrose 63, 122, 179, 190, 193, 194, 195, 198, 227, 244, 291
Mooney, Tom 207

Moore, Allan 212
Moore (Alloa Athletic 1938/39) 276, 277
Moore, Craig 48, 255, 284
Moore, Dale 272
Moore, Eddie 76, 84, 102, 109, 196, 197, 198, 255
Moore, Neil 131
More (Deveronvale 2001/02) 45
Morgan (Dundee 1937/38) 207
Morgan, Lewis 37
Morgan, Mattha 40, 74, 257
Morris, Chris 315
Morris, Eric 9, 134, 135, 137, 210, 217, 218, 225, 234, 257, 281
Morrison, A 102, 127
Morrison, Gavin 108, 163
Morrison, Jock 306
Morrison, Malky 30, 31, 129, 130, 176, 188, 190, 195, 257
Morrison, Steve 24
Morrow, Sammy 320
Morton 17, 21, 34, 90, 104, 188, 191, 197, 198, 200, 202, 207, 212, 238, 240, 291, 301
Morton, Alan 303
Morton, Hugh 206, 305
Morton (Kilmarnock 1924/25) 304
Motherwell 48, 68, 73, 77, 110, 154, 159, 188, 198, 199, 208, 210, 215, 218, 220, 244, 267, 291
Moyes (Rangers 1926/27) 305
Muir (1910/11) 127
Muir, Andrew 320
Muir, Archie L 197, 255
Muir (Berwick Rangers 1953/54) 277
Muir, Billy 103
Muir, Jim 206
Muir, Joe 107
Muir, Louden 299
Muir (Third Lanark 1923/24) 302
Muirkirk Juniors 24
Muirton Park 97, 275

Mulhall, George 191
Mullan, Adam 320
Munro, Bert 277
Mullen, Boyd 18
Munro (Dundee 1932/33) 37
Munro, Frank 107
Munro, Grant 108
Munro, Iain 118
Murdoch, Andy 284
Murdoch, Andy (Celtic) 315
Murphy (Celtic 1922/23) 302
Murphy, James 84, 85, 303
Murphy, Jim 302
Murphy, Jimmy 134, 137, 212, 257
Murphy, John 21, 44, 76, 77, 86, 102, 103, 107, 109, 162, 176, 208, 237, 259, 278, 279, 311, 314, 315,
Murphy, Leon 48
Murphy, Lloyd 320
Murphy, Peter 48, 137, 167, 168
Murray, Bruce 167, 168
Murray (Deveronvale 2001/02) 45
Murray, Donald 234
Murray, Eric 311
Murray, Gary 122
Murray, Hugh 115
Murray, Ian 272
Murray, Jimmy 131, 134
Murray (Kilmarnock 1915/16) 73
Murray, Mary 70
Murray, Max 310
Murray, Scott 281
Murray, Willie 105

N

Nanninga, Dick 176
Napier (Kilmarnock 1930/31) 206
National Library of Scotland 154
National Service 7
Nattrass, Irving 162
Naylor, Martin 34
Neil, Willie 44, 257, 306

Neilson, Tommy 107
Nellies, Peter 39
Nelson, Craig 34, 45, 118, 267, 269, 272
Nelson, Drew 102, 103
Nelson, Helen v, vii
Nelson, Hugh v, vii
Nesbit. Andy 45, 75, 108, 129, 130, 277, 308
Nevin, Jack 39, 73
Nevin, Pat 210, 267, 269
Newall, Jock 147
Newall, Tom 101, 147
Newcastle United 22, 37, 162, 179, 182, 310, 318, 324
New Cumnock 165
Newell, Mike 318
Newfoundland 49, 171
Newman, Shaun 320
News of The World 97, 99
Newton (Clyde 1920/21) 301
Newton, J 40, 218
Nibloe, Joe 206, 305, 306
Nichol (2008/09 320
Nicholas, Charlie 315
Nicholas, Steve 267
Nicholls, Davie 269
Nicholson, Barry 269
Nicholson, Jock 303
Nicholson (St.Johnstone 1931/32) 275
Nicol, Stevie 218, 219, 220, 225, 324
Nicol (St.Johnstone 1931/32) 275
Nigeria 172
Ninian Park 285
Nisbet, George 39, 73, 218, 302
Nisbet, Jim 44, 105, 128, 144, 171, 255, 257, 274, 285, 287, 305
Nisbet, Kevin 137
Nisbet, Ryan 320
Nish, Colin 272
Nithsdale Wanderers 40
Norway 171, 285

Nourredine, Maamria 167
Nuneaton Borough 289
Nylen, Niclas 167, 168

O

Oakes, Jacky 308
Ochilview Park 16, 18, 26, 87
O'Connell, Andy 137, 167
O'Connor (Dundee 1932/33) 37
O'Connor, Gary 86
O'Connor, Pat 311
Odhiambo, Eric 108
O'Donnell, Frank 306
O'Donnell, George 75, 107
O'Donnell, Phil 110
Ogilby, David 320
Ogilvie, John 308
Ogston, John 259
O'Hare, Jim 115
Okorie, Kelechi 167
Old Firm Select 314
Oliphant, Charlie 76, 102, 107, 109, 278, 311
Oliver, Andy 281
Oliver, Jim 131
Olympiakos 311
Olympisch Stadion 285
Omand, Willie 130
Omar, Rabin 48
O'Neill, Tommy 210
Ontario – Quebec Select 172
Ooestfold 171
Ormond, Willie 30, 31, 131, 308
O'Rourke, Jimmy 220
Orr, Bobby 11
Orr (Third Lanark (1915/16) 37
Orr, William 96, 97
Orsi, Daniel 48
Osborne, J 305
O'Sullivan, Pat 130
Oswald (Bo'ness 1927/28) 257
Otelul Galati 178
Ouchterlonie, Kinnaird 108

P

Paavola, Tommi 99, 167
Page (1912/13) 300
Palmerston Park 90, 143
Panda Pals 51
Panopoulas, Michael 269
Parkhead Station 1
Parkhill, Ian 320
Parkhouse 88, 102, 300, 303, 307
Partick Thistle 36, 40, 48, 77, 102, 162, 190, 191, 193, 195, 205, 212, 214, 244, 251, 292
Paterson, Alex 3
Paterson, Arthur 76, 84, 102, 103, 107, 109, 237, 255, 278, 311
Paterson, Davy 76, 109
Paterson, Drew 281
Paterson, Garry 119, 131,
Paterson, Jimmy 300
Paterson, John 308
Paterson, John (Berwick Rangers) 31
Paterson (Motherwell 1914/15) 73
Paterson, Roddy 26
Paton, Alastair 76, 102, 103
Paton, Bert 86
Paton, George 45, 75
Paton, Jimmy 279
Paton, Johnny 305
Paton, Willie 3, 6, 31, 130, 131, 155, 310
Patterson, Jim 308
Pattison, Kenny 129
Pearson (1926/27) 74
Pearson, Ellis 48
Peddie, Sarah 54
Peden, RG 74
Peebles Rovers 198, 255
Pender, Bob 322
Percival, Jack 307
Peron, Jean Francois 167
Perrie, Alec 308
Persson, Orjan 107

Perthshire Advertiser 190
Peterhead 28, 72, 110, 118, 126, 202, 216, 240, 292
Petrescu, Dan 177
Petrie, Stewart 269
Phillips, Charlie 1, 39, 49, 102, 190, 300, 303, 304
Phillips, Eric 18
Phillips, Gerry 49, 172, 176, 208, 226, 257, 279, 314
Piermayr, Thomas 163
Pierson, Jim 131
Pirie, T 40, 218
Pogba, Paul 176
Polish Army XI 176
Poole (Armadale 1919/20) 274
Pope, Fred 276
Pope, Gordon 177, 284
Porter, Willie 301
Port Glasgow Athletic 56, 79, 102
Port Glasgow Juniors 147
Portsmouth 37
Power, Lee 168
Pratt (Bo'ness 1930/31) 274
Pratt, David 301
Premier Division 159, 208, 212
Premier League 21, 69, 97, 99, 163, 227, 240, 251, 281, 315
Prenderville, Barry 115, 116, 167
Pressley, Ryan 45
Preston, Jordan 190
Preston North End 88, 300
Prestwick 297
Price, Norman 44, 306
Price, Peter 7, 21, 34, 62, 63, 76, 84, 86, 87, 130, 131, 155, 162, 188, 193, 194, 197, 198, 200, 224, 232, 255, 310
Prior, Ken 31
Proctor, David 108
Professional Footballers' Association 157
Provan, Davie 314

Prunty, Bryan 86, 257
Pryde, Jim 310
Pullar, John 109
Purdie Bryan 281
Purdie, David 309, 312, 314, 315
Purdon, J 257, 305

Q

Quaite, James 94, 322
Quebec – Ontario select 172
Queen of the South 68, 78, 84, 90, 92, 111, 142, 198, 199, 207, 208, 227, 251, 255, 279, 281, 305, 308
Queen's Park 13, 18, 39, 40, 68, 74, 76, 90, 102, 122, 130, 131, 197, 198, 203, 210, 218, 224, 227, 241, 243, 279, 298, 300, 301, 303, 304
Quinn, Jimmy 76
Quinn, John 39, 40, 190, 218, 257, 302
Quinn, Paul 34
Quinn, Stan 147, 162, 237, 278, 298

R

Rae, Alex 77
Rae, Davie 210
Rae, Gavin 267
Rae, Harry 322
Rae, Ian 131, 199
Rae, Tommy 77
Raeburn (St.Bernard's 1927/28) 128
Raeside, Robbie 267
Raith Rovers 26, 65, 66, 68, 69, 86, 87, 93, 100, 126, 195, 198, 202, 212, 245, 253, 304, 318
Raitt, William 304
Ramsay (Bo'ness 1927/28) 257
Ramsay, G.S. 39
Ramsay (Kilmarnock 1928/29) 306

Ramsay, Tommy 75, 129, 130, 257
Ramsdens Cup 18, 26, 102, 227
Rangers, Glasgow 22, 24, 31, 37, 39, 105, 114, 144, 147, 154, 176, 186, 193, 199, 207, 208, 220, 250, 251, 278, 297, 300, 303, 305, 310, 314, 320
Rankin, John 272
Rankin, Willie 73
Rattray, Alan 118
Recreation Park (Alloa) 13
Recreation Park (Perth) 190
Redmond, Gavin 34
Regional League 129, 216, 218
Reid, Bobby 322
Reid, Brian 69, 230
Reid (Clackmannan 1930/31) 40
Reid, Craig 48
Reid, David 220, 221
Reid, Ian 279
Reid (Motherwell 1920/21) 73
Reid, Robert 39
Reid, Sammy 131
Reid (Third Lanark 1924/25) 84
Reid, Thomas 257
Reid, Thomas (Rangers) 303
Reilly, Lawrie 308
Reilly, Mark 263
Reilly, Robert 210
Rennie (Dundee 1937/38) 207
Rennie, John 101
Rennie (Queen's Park 1974/75) 279
Rennie, Stewart 208, 210, 218, 220, 223, 281
Renwick, Michael 15, 16, 34, 318
Republic of Ireland 167, 173
Reserve League 195, 239
Reynolds, Mickey 34, 263, 267, 269, 318
Reynolds, Stephen 18
Reynolds, Tommy 162
Richards, Len 207
Richardson, Jimmy 37, 39, 73, 188, 229, 257, 274, 285, 301, 302, 303
Richardson (Leith Athletic) 200
Richmond (Rangers 1911/12) 300
Riordan, Derek 272
Ripley, Stuart 318
Ritchie, Billy 310
Ritchie, Harry 275
Robb (Armadale 1919/20) 274
Robb, Iain 51, 54
Robb, JF 76
Robb, Jim 282
Robb, Ross 34
Robb, Willie 303
Roberts (Dundee 1937/38) 207
Roberts, Mark 16, 72, 108, 163, 177, 230, 237, 239, 251, 255, 263, 271, 272, 274
Robertson (Arbroath 1937/38) 75
Robertson, Cammy 282
Robertson (Clackmannan 1930/31) 40
Robertson, David 77
Robertson, Derek 97
Robertson, Graeme 110, 315
Robertson, Hugh 34, 267
Robertson, Hugh (Dunfermline Athletic) 86
Robertson, Jacky 234, 277, 278
Robertson, Jimmy 37
Robertson, John 45, 148, 163, 239, 257, 259, 263, 267, 269, 272
Robertson, John (Inverness Caledonian Thistle) 253
Robertson, Malky 97, 208, 210, 226, 279
Robertson, Ross 26, 163
Robertson, Stuart 34
Robertson (Third Lanark 1923/24) 302
Robertson, Tommy 37, 105, 206, 238, 275
Robertson, Willie 44, 123, 128, 306

Robinson, Bobby 199
Robinson, Lee 320
Robson, Bryan 162
Roda JC 176
Rodger, Alan 162
Rodger, Fally 37, 97, 98, 128, 129, 190, 206, 220, 234, 239, 275, 306
Rodgers, Andy 239, 257, 272
Rogers, Dave 118
Rolling, Franck 167, 168
Ronald, Gerry 134
Rooney, Adam 108
Rose, Michael 137, 284, 298
Ross (1938/39) 276
Ross (Airdrie 1934/35) 207
Ross, Bobby 199
Ross County 16, 198, 227, 282
Ross, Nick 163
Rough, Alan 77
Rough, Bobby 77, 162, 237, 257
Round, Len 45, 75, 76, 79, 107, 162, 277, 308, 310
Rovde, Marius 34, 167, 318
Rowan, Jim 130
Rowe, Tom 129
Roy, Ludovic 118, 120, 167
Royal Albert 40
R.S. McColl's XI 303, 304
Rubescu, Raul 177
Rugby Park vii, 24, 29, 33, 73, 122, 156, 160
Rundell, Jock 73
Russell (1926/27) 305
Russell (Queen's Park 1912/13) 300
Russell, Robert 95, 96, 97
Rutherglen Glencairn 147

S

Sa, Orlando 177
Saint Pierre 49, 172
Samson, Craig 108
Samson, Keir 284

Sanchez, Danni 108
Sanderson, Tommy 278
Sandvikens I.F. 173
San Marino 26
Savage, Garry 53
Scally, Neil 34, 267, 269
Scarff, Peter 306
Scobbie, George 95, 128, 306
Scobie, W 76
Scotland 26, 28, 31, 37, 54, 78, 144, 147, 154, 157, 176, 250, 259, 274, 285, 286, 287, 288, 303, 308, 311
Scotsport 155, 250
Scott (1920/21) 79, 301
Scott, Barry 102, 110
Scott, E 40, 218
Scott (Falkirk 1918/19) 127
Scott, Jimmy 18
Scott, Jimmy (Dumbarton) 45
Scott, Ross 29, 31, 121, 122, 124, 237
Scottish Consolation Cup 79
Scottish Cup 16, 18, 21, 22, 23, 24, 26, 31, 36, 40, 43, 44, 45, 78, 79, 81, 89, 97, 108, 110, 111, 114, 122, 126, 128, 129, 131, 142, 143, 154, 156, 159, 179, 188, 190, 193, 195, 197, 198, 201, 202, 226, 231, 238, 239, 241, 243, 244, 245, 247, 254, 255, 257, 258, 263, 264, 265, 271, 272, 274, 277, 278, 290, 291, 292, 293, 294, 295, 296, 297, 298
Scottish Football Association 20, 94, 95, 96, 287, 310
Scottish Football League 57, 96, 97, 100, 227
Scottish Professional Football League 157
Scottish Qualifying Cup 49, 91, 126, 165, 193, 238
Scoullar (Armadale 1919/20) 274
Second Division 1, 3, 7, 21, 28, 31, 34, 56, 57, 63, 65, 68, 69, 74, 79,

82, 86, 92, 128, 131, 155, 190,
191, 193, 194, 195, 198, 199, 201,
202, 207, 212, 216, 238, 239,
240, 243, 247, 259, 274, 275,
276, 279, 282, 290, 293
Semple, John 39, 127, 274
Shankland, Lawrence 190, 193,
198, 200, 240, 255
Shankland, Mark 16, 18, 284
Shankly, Alex 144
Shankly, Bill 144
Shankly, Bob 144, 145
Shanks, Davie 134
Shanks, Mark 134, 210, 212, 218,
220, 225, 230, 233, 281
Shannon, Rab 110
Sharp, Alex 44, 197, 255, 306
Sharp, Doug 308
Sharp, Lee 34, 45, 267, 269, 272
Sharples, John 119, 173, 282
Shaw (Airdrie 1934/35) 207
Shaw, Charlie 301
Shaw, Hugh 45
Shea, Daniel 301
Shearer, Dan 127
Sheerin, Paul 45, 237, 257, 269, 272
Shepherd (Clackmannan 1930/31) 40
Shepherd, Paul 212, 267, 268
Sherry, James 165
Sherwood, Tim 318
Shettleston Juniors 147
Shewan, Ally 259
Shields (Dumbarton 1939/40) 129
Shields, Willie 51
Shinnie, Andrew 163, 320
Shinnie, Graeme 163
Shotton, Malky 110, 113
Silesian XI 176
Silvestro, Chris 86
Simpson, Bobby 131
Simpson, Harry 49, 300
Simpson, Jocky 171, 306
Simpson, Jocky (Falkirk) 127

Sinclair, David 257
Sinclair, George 39
Sinclair, Jimmy 210
Sinnamon, Ryan 48
Skerla, Andrius 269
Skinner, Bobby 84
Skinner, Justin 269
Skol Cup 156
SKY 157
Slade, Donald 39, 40, 73, 154, 218,
255, 301, 302
Sloan, Robert 86
Sloan, Tommy 212, 237, 246, 284
Sludden, John 31, 34, 65, 255, 314,
315, 317, 318
Small, John 131
Smith, Aidan 48
Smith, Albert 193, 257
Smith (Alloa Athletic 1938/39) 276
Smith (Armadale 1919/1920) 274
Smith, Barry 267
Smith, Bob 74
Smith, Chris 163, 272
Smith, Dave 259
Smith, David 137
Smith, Doug 107
Smith (Dundee 1932/33) 37
Smith (Dundee 1937/38) 207
Smith, Gordon 314
Smith, Graeme 272
Smith, Henry 13, 14
Smith (Hibs 1913/14) 39
Smith, Hugh 306
Smith, Ian 281
Smith, Jimmy 44, 60, 61, 63, 101,
128, 129, 171, 188, 193, 195, 198,
200, 220, 255, 257, 259, 305
Smith, Jimmy (Newcastle United)
162
Smith, Jock 39, 73, 84, 85, 151,
218, 234, 274, 285, 301, 302,
303, 304, 305
Smith, Joe 310

Smith, Kevin 86
Smith, Liam 284
Smith, Mark 282
Smith, Mattha 37, 206, 275, 304, 305
Smith, Mike 227
Smith, Paul 92
Smith, Peter 30, 108, 307
Smith, Peter (Elgin City) 278
Smith (Rangers 1955/56) 310
Smith (Stenhousemuir 1945/46) 30
Smith, Steve 220
Smith, Tom 104
Smith, William 39
Smyth, David 315, 316
Smyth, Marc 11, 20
Sneddon T 40, 218
Soden (1923/24) 302
Solis, Jerome 306
Somerset Park vii, 1, 9, 13, 18, 22, 24, 26, 28, 73, 79, 82, 83, 84, 89, 91, 96, 101, 129, 137, 148, 154, 156, 159, 161, 162, 163, 176, 178, 179, 207, 227, 243, 244, 250, 251, 267, 292, 293, 307, 311, 320, 324, 326
Sonkur, Ayrton 48
Sonor, Luc 167
Soutar (Dumbarton 1939/40) 129
Soutar (King's Park 1934/35) 128, 275
Southampton 73
Speedie (Dumbarton 1911/12) 238
Speedie (Dumbarton 1939/40) 129
Speir, Billy 210
Speirs (Armadale 1919/20) 274
Speirs, Fraser 45
Spence (Berwick Rangers 1928/29) 44
Spence, Willie 315
Spennymoor United 289
Sporting Lisbon 119
Sportscene 155
Springvale Park 160, 300
Sproat, Hugh 134, 204, 205, 208, 215, 220, 240, 279, 311
Stack, Graham 272
Stainrod, Simon vii, 168, 230, 325
Stair Park 81
Stampworks 107
Stanley, Arthur 51
Stark's Park 65
Station Park 3
St.Bernard's 101, 128, 301
Steel, Tommy 151, 282
Steele, John 74, 257, 276, 307
Steen, Tom 94, 95, 97
Stenhousemuir 16, 28, 30, 31, 34, 40, 63, 82, 87, 91, 191, 194, 195, 197, 198, 202, 240, 245, 292
Stevens, Gregor 208
Stevenson, Andrew 51
Stevenson, Bobby 7, 40, 160, 190, 197, 255, 310
Stevenson, Craig 318
Stevenson, John 301
Stevenson, Ryan 48, 69, 86, 87, 137, 158, 177, 251, 257, 320
Stewart, Bobby 84, 85, 303, 304, 305
Stewart, Davy 162, 234, 294
Stewart (Dumbarton 1939/40) 129
Stewart, Fraser 86, 320
Stewart, Greg 191
Stewart (Hamilton Accies 1962/63) 134
Stewart, Jim (Alloa Athletic) 281
Stewart, Jim (Kilmarnock) 314
Stewart, Jimmy 108
Stewart (Kilmarnock 1928/29) 306
Stewart (Motherwell 1920/21) 73
Stewart, Sandy 119
Stirling 129, 275
Stirling Albion 48, 65, 68, 119, 126, 134, 193, 198, 205, 214
Stirling, Alex (Director) 94
Stirling, Alex (Dumbarton) 75
Stirling, Andy 137
Stirling, Ian 199

Stirling, Jered 214
Stirling (Rangers 2008/09) 320
Stirrat, Jack viii
St.James Gate 173
St.James Park 179
St.John's All Stars 172, 176
St.Johnstone 63, 81, 91, 95, 97, 99, 105, 190, 191, 194, 198, 199, 202, 208, 210, 227, 238, 275, 299, 301, 315
St.Lawrence Select 172
St.Lorient 171
St.Mirren 9, 11, 16, 57, 69, 95, 97, 102, 115, 122, 163, 165, 167, 168, 191, 193, 194, 195, 198, 199, 207, 231, 240, 251, 276, 296, 326
St.Mirren Park 9
Stockholm 171
Stoke City 60, 106, 304
Strachan, Hugh 77
Stranraer 16, 26, 42, 44, 72, 81, 82, 86, 92, 115, 122, 126, 131, 147, 148, 195, 197, 198, 199, 200, 202, 205, 240, 241, 243
Strasbourg 168
Strathclyde Homes Stadium 82
Strathclyde University 296
Strickland, Johnny 130, 134
Struthers (Queen's Park 1920/21) 301
Stuart, Alex vii 228, 229
STV 155
Suggett, Ernie 74
Summers, Eddie 322
Sunday Mail 99, 100
Sutherland, Shane 163
Swanson (St.Bernard's 1927/28) 128
Sweden 171, 173
Sweeney (1993/94) 315
Swift, Frank 307
Swindon Town 106
Swinglehurst, Steven 48
Sylla, Mohammed 167
Syme, David 9

Syme, John 30
Symon, Scot 37
Szymckac, Ryszard 176

T

Tade, Gregory 163
Taggart, Bobby 277
Taggart, George 162
Tait, Andy 45
Tait, Bobby 208, 279
Tait (Hamilton Accies 1962/63) 134
Tannadice Park 16
Targino, Tiago 177
Tarrant, Neil 83, 188, 189, 255, 267, 269
Taylor (Bo'ness 1930/31) 274
Taylor, FP 74
Taylor, George 108
Taylor, Jock 37, 74, 128, 206, 207, 255, 275, 307
Taylor, John 311
Taylor, Lyndsey 326
Taylor, Stuart 122
Taylor, Tam 326
Teale, Gary 34, 255, 263, 266, 267, 269, 324
Teale, Shaun 199
Telfer, John 31, 131
Telford Street 278
Temple (King's Park 1934/35) 128, 275
Templeton, Bobby 39
Templeton, Dan 84, 85
Templeton, Henry 31, 34, 65, 66, 200, 255, 314, 315
Texaco Cup 21, 226, 296, 311
Third Division 282, 307
Third Lanark 37, 81, 84, 94, 102, 107, 193, 195, 247, 302, 304
Thompson (Airdrie 1934/35) 207
Thompson (Deveronvale 2001/02) 45
Thompson, Frank 229

357

Thompson, Steven 272
Thomson (1924/25) 304
Thomson, Adam 76, 86, 102, 107, 109, 311
Thomson, Alec 302
Thomson, Billy 199
Thomson, Bobby 31, 75, 76, 130, 308, 310
Thomson (Bo'ness 1927/28) 257
Thomson, David (1912/13) 300
Thomson, David (2008/09) 320
Thomson, Fraser 279
Thomson, George 220
Thomson, Ian 34
Thomson, Jim 86
Thomson, Joe 137
Thomson (Motherwell 1993/94) 110
Thomson, Robert 75
Thomson, Robert (Dumbarton) 137
Thomson, Scott M 269
Thomson, Scott Y 269
Thorburn, Mrs 70
Thow, Lewis 101, 129, 207, 276, 307
Thow, Louis 122
Thyne, Bob 129, 130, 308
Tickle, Bert 49, 56, 79, 102, 300, 301
Tiffoney, Jonathan 163, 271, 272
Timmons, Joe 122
Tokely, Ross 108, 163
Tolland, Danny 40, 44, 74, 105, 128, 171, 191, 197, 206, 255, 257, 274, 275, 305, 306
Toner, Willie 82, 200, 259
Toonira (Roda JC) 176
Torbet, John 276
Torrance, Andy 101, 197
Toseland, Ernie 307
Tottenham Hotspur 58, 59
Townsley, Derek 267
Tracy, Gerry 107, 277, 310
Train, Les 311
Trainer (Berwick Rangers 1928/29) 44
Travers, Willie 23, 31, 130, 131, 238

Traynor, Jim 44
Traynor, John 71, 110, 212, 237, 259, 263, 282, 315, 318
Traynor, Johnny 68, 107, 162, 277, 310
Treanor, Mark 134
Troup, Alex 37
Trouten, Alan 239, 255
Tryfield Place 50
Tuffey, Jonny 163
Tulloch, George 131
Turf Moor 179
Turnbull, David 44, 74, 105, 257, 274, 304
Turnbull, Eddie 308
Turnbull, John 129
Twaddle, Kevin 267
Twain, Mark xv
Tweed, Steven 267
Tweedie, Garry 34
Tynecastle Park 26, 292
Tyson, John 108, 110, 237, 257

U

Umbro 89
Unirea Urziceni 177
United States 173, 179
United States Football Association 173, 175
University College Dublin 173
University of the West of Scotland 54
Ure, William 37, 128, 220, 237, 257, 275, 307
Urquhart (Arbroath 1937/38) 75
Urquhart, Paul 45

V

Valakari, Simo 267
Valentine, J.C. 76
Vale of Leven 1, 159
Valetta, Claudio 167, 168

Vance, J viii
Vareille, Jerome 167, 257, 263
Vasalunds 173
Venetis, Anastasios 272
Vienna Rapide 78
Visconte, Rocky 167

W

Wacker Burghausen 173
Waddell (Rangers 1911/12) 300
Waddell, Willie 310
Waite, David 284
Waldie, Simon 308
Walker, Allan 86
Walker, Andy 255, 263, 267, 315
Walker (Bo'ness 1927/28) 257
Walker, Colin 34
Walker, H 49
Walker, James 84
Walker (Kilmarnock 1924/25) 304
Walker, P 84
Walker (Queen's Park 1912/13) 300
Walker, Scott 86
Walker (St.Bernard's 1927/28) 128
Walker, Tommy 31, 32, 34, 65, 67, 110, 122, 227, 257, 315
Walker, WG 50, 324
Walker, WO 74
Wallace, Jock 108, 129, 130, 190, 257
Wallace, Jock (Berwick Rangers) 31
Wallace, Willie 322
Walls (Celtic 1922/23) 302
Walls, James 303
Walsh, Martin 212
Walters, Jacky 74, 128, 257, 305
Ward, Joe 210, 281
Ward, John 122
Wardlaw, Gareth 163, 255
Wardrope (1928/29) 306
Wardrope, Michael 257, 320
Warholm, Rune 167
Wark, Joe 208

Watson (Airdrie 1934/35) 207
Watson, Bobby 208
Watson, George 29, 31
Watson, Gregg 214
Watson, John 306
Watson, Lynne 70
Watson, Matt 162
Watson, Peter 48
Watson, Richard 167
Watt (Deveronvale 2001/02) 45
Watt, Neil 157, 168, 230
Wdowczyk, Dariusz 315
Weaver, Paul 86, 320
Webb (1917/18) 165
Wedderburn, Craig 86
Weir, Graham 86
Weir, James 305, 306
Weir, Peter 257, 261
Weir (Rangers 1926/27) 305
Weir (Third Lanark 1915/16) 37
Welfare Home 50
Wells, Davy 121, 162, 171, 199, 314
Wells (Peebles Rovers 1959/60) 198, 255
Welsh Football Association 174
Welsh, Jimmy 3
Welsh, Kevin 167
Welsh, Steve 263
Welsh (St.Johnstone 1931/32) 275
Wembley Stadium 285, 303
West Sound 253
Whigham, Willie 131
White, Archie 303
White, Jock 105
White, Sprigger 87, 237, 294
White, Steven 284
Whiteford, Derek 147, 149
Whiteford, Jock 147
Whitehead, Ian 162
Whithorn 49, 193
Whittington, Bert 103, 191, 296
Whittle, Jimmy 31, 76, 130, 239, 257
Whyte, Derek 315

359

Whyte, Jimmy 45
Whyte (Stenhousemuir 1945/46) 30
Wilcox, Jason 318
Wilkie, Lee 267
Wilkie (Stenhousemuir 1945/46) 30
Williams, Alex 86, 227, 255
Williams, Emlyn 307
Williams, Richie 167
Williams, Stan 108, 110
Williamson, Jimmy 306
Williamson, Robbie 282
Williamson (Third Lanark 1924/25) 84
Willis, David 40, 74, 105, 274, 306
Wills, Tom 91
Wilson (Berwick Rangers 1928/29) 44
Wilson, Craig 86
Wilson (Dumbarton 1939/40) 129
Wilson, Garry 122
Wilson, George 275
Wilson, Graham 284
Wilson, Kenny 31, 257, 260, 314
Wilson (Kilmarnock 1924/25) 304
Wilson, Marvyn 34, 45, 83, 257, 267, 269, 270, 272
Wilson, Paul 314
Wilson (Queen's Park 1912/13) 300
Wilson, Robert 39
Wilson, Stephen 284
Wilson (St.Johnstone 1931/32) 275
Wilson (St.Mirren 1935/36) 276
Wilson (Third Lanark 1923/24) 302
Wilson, Willie 191, 282
Winchester, Ernie 259
Windsor Park 285
Wing, Lennart 107
Winnie, David 263, 265
Winters, David 148, 272
Winters, Robbie 148
Wood, John 39
Woodburn, Ally 108, 272
Woodburn, John 74, 128, 301, 303, 304, 305
Woodlesford 178
Woods, George 79
Woods, Kieran 320
Woods, Tom 115
Workington 179, 183, 184, 185
World Cup 26, 167, 176, 311
Wotherspoon, David 272
Wright, Andrew 250
Wright (Clackmannan 1930/31) 40
Wright, Frazer 137
Wright, Paul 263
Wyles, Willie 131
Wyrich, Sunny 54

Y

Yardley, Jimmy 207, 255, 276
Yeudal (Queen's Park 1912/13) 300
YMCA Hall 94
Yorke, Bobby 40, 41, 74, 105, 206, 274, 306
Young (Clackmannan 1930/31) 40
Young, Cutty 162, 163, 199,
Young, Greig 210, 234
Young, Ian 76
Young, James 74, 274
Young (King's Park 1934/35) 128, 275
Young (Queen's Park 1912/13) 300
Younger (Berwick Rangers 1953/54) 277
Younger, Tommy 308
Young's Tea Rooms 88
YouTube 157

Z

Zemmama, Merouane 272

www.ingramcontent.com/pod-product-compliance
Lightning Source LLC
Chambersburg PA
CBHW070958160426
43193CB00012B/1830